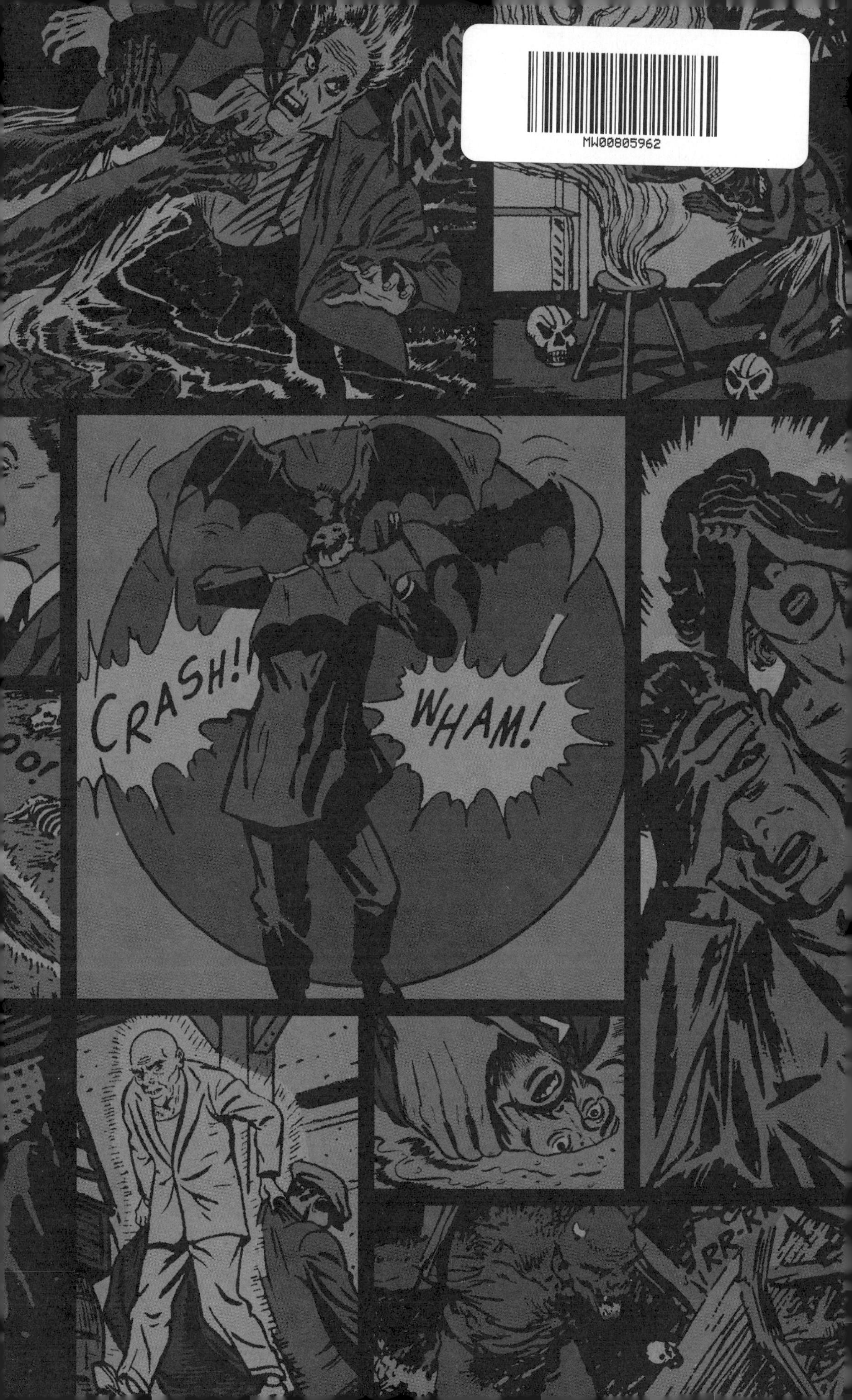
CRASH!!
WHAM!

FORBIDDEN WORLDS

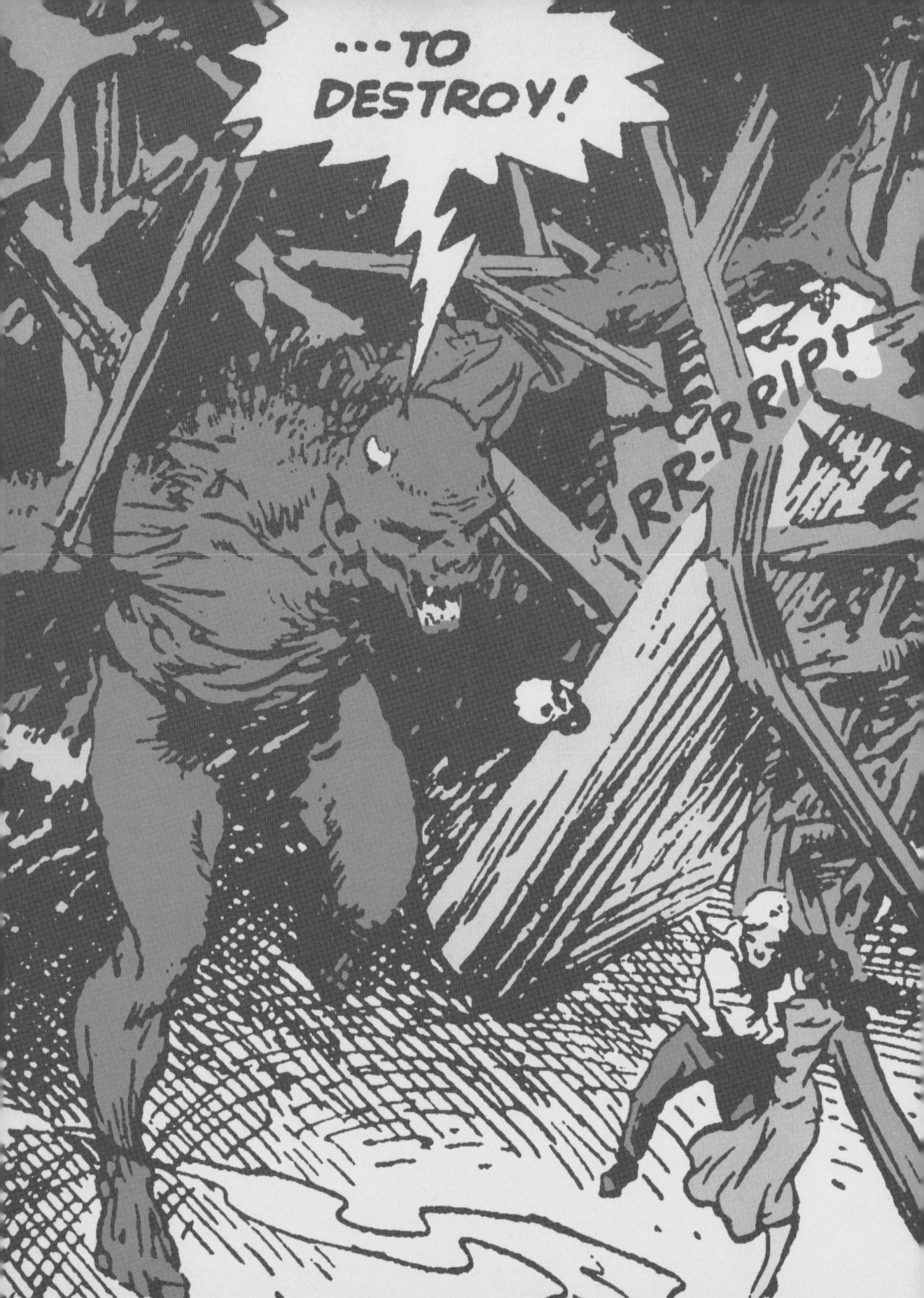
...TO DESTROY!
RR-R-RRIP!

VENTURE INTO FORBIDDEN, UNKNOWN WORLDS!

REPRINTING *FORBIDDEN WORLDS* ISSUES #1–#4

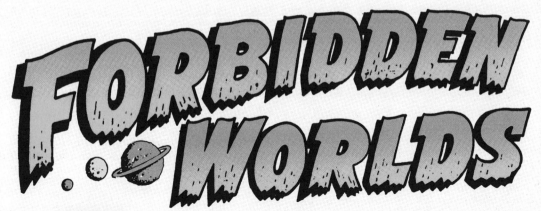

**DARK HORSE
ARCHIVES**

VOL.
1

FEATURING THE WORK OF

*AL WILLIAMSON, FRANK FRAZETTA,
OGDEN WHITNEY,
WALLY WOOD,* AND *OTHERS!*

FOREWORD BY
DAN NADEL

DARK HORSE BOOKS

President and Publisher
MIKE RICHARDSON

Collection Editor
PHILIP R. SIMON

Assistant Editor
EVERETT PATTERSON

Collection Designer
TINA ALESSI

Digital Production and Retouch
RYAN JORGENSEN

Special thanks to Annie Gullion and Jemiah Jefferson.

Published by Dark Horse Books
A division of Dark Horse Comics, Inc.
10956 SE Main Street, Milwaukie, Oregon 97222
DarkHorse.com

To find a comic shop in your area, call the Comic Shop Locator Service: (888) 266-4226

First edition: December 2012
ISBN 978-1-61655-000-4
10 9 8 7 6 5 4 3 2 1

Printed at 1010 Printing International, Ltd., Guangdong Province, China

This volume collects *Forbidden Worlds* issues #1–#4, originally published in 1951 and 1952 by
Preferred Publications, Inc., an imprint of American Comics Group (ACG).

NEIL HANKERSON Executive Vice President TOM WEDDLE Chief Financial Officer RANDY STRADLEY Vice President
of Publishing MICHAEL MARTENS Vice President of Book Trade Sales ANITA NELSON Vice President of Business
Affairs DAVID SCROGGY Vice President of Product Development DALE LAFOUNTAIN Vice President of Information
Technology DARLENE VOGEL Senior Director of Print, Design, and Production KEN LIZZI General Counsel MATT
PARKINSON Senior Director of Marketing DAVEY ESTRADA Editorial Director SCOTT ALLIE Senior Managing
Editor CHRIS WARNER Senior Books Editor DIANA SCHUTZ Executive Editor CARY GRAZZINI Director of Print and
Development LIA RIBACCHI Art Director CARA NIECE Director of Scheduling

CONTENTS

While all attempts have been made to restore proper attribution to the creators who worked on these comic books, we regret if errors or omissions have been made. Please contact the publisher at help@darkhorse.com with any new information. These stories are a product of their time, and therefore certain elements may be out of step with present-day sensibilities. The material presented here is unedited to maintain historical accuracy.

FOREWORD By Dan Nadel

Forbidden Worlds, like much of what American Comics Group (ACG) released, is an understated title that has quiet gems sprinkled throughout its run. This title was the follow-up to *Adventures into the Unknown*, which began in 1948 and was the first ongoing horror title in comics, beating EC by nearly two years. With sales booming and, indeed, EC nipping at its heels, ACG launched *Forbidden Worlds* in 1951. Skewing towards the supernatural over the straight-up horrific, ACG was a relatively clean house, so gore and excessive nastiness were out—instead there were well-executed short tales of the fantastic employing the usual tropes of vampires, apocalypses, spooky towns, and strange creatures.

Partly this was owing to ACG's perennial light touch, thanks to editor Richard Hughes, who introduced the new series as the answer to readers' requests: "So here it is—your own special magazine—chock-full of the very thrilling fare we've learned you want! We *dare* you to read each and every issue of this startling new publication—to venture into forbidden, *Unknown* worlds!" This is followed by a solicitation for more letters—all very jovial and yet quite serious. Hughes did indeed respond to and discuss readers' letters over the years, which helped build ACG a devoted, if small, audience.

It takes a certain sense of the absurd to launch a new comic book with a lead story called "Demon of Destruction." But then, Hughes had Al Williamson and Frank Frazetta working on it, so maybe it wasn't too much of a risk. This is Williamson's first of a handful of appearances in *Forbidden Worlds*—inked by Frazetta. Williamson was just twenty years old at the time and Frazetta only twenty-three, both breaking into the business simultaneously and on the cusp of work for EC that would make them both famous in fandom circles. "Demon of Destruction" shows both artists at their best. Williamson, obviously enthralled with Alex Raymond (whose *Flash Gordon* and *Rip Kirby* strips he would later draw), penciled the piece as a classic hero-and-dame adventure, complete with swirling lines for atmosphere and stoic poses for nobility. Frazetta brought his vibrant rendering skills to the titular demon, whose scale and strength are evident in Frazetta's swooping, dynamic marks as cities and landmarks are crushed. Everything here is high drama and the tale even ends with a passionate embrace, heads posed just so and rendered with fleshy passion—playing to all of Frazetta's strengths. Williamson's other contribution to this volume, "Skull of the Sorcerer," brings in another special guest: Wally Wood. The young cartoonist's lines are all over this story, accentuating the knotty patterns of the trees, and adding shadows and worry lines to the stressed faces of our hero. After Frazetta's graceful, easygoing flow, coming upon Wood's more neurotic work is bracing.

The proceedings were all guided by Richard Hughes, about whom we know very little, but what we do know has been unearthed by Michael Vance and published first in his book, *Forbidden Adventures*, and then in *Alter Ego* #113 and #114. Hughes was born Leo Rosenbaum and lived from 1909 to 1974. According to Vance, "At ACG's peak, in 1952, Hughes edited and wrote for at least sixteen titles." He'd arrived at ACG in 1943 and stayed until it closed around him in 1967—a particularly long and extremely strong run for any editor. He was at his best writing romance comics and, later, *Herbie*, which utilized his hip sense of humor and love of wordplay.

Hughes helped make ACG known as a particularly artist-friendly house and attracted a number of unique talents who stuck around, apparently, for the quality of Hughes's treatment and his scripts. In an interview for Vance's *Forbidden Adventures*, Williamson remembered Hughes: "He was a very sweet man. I think he was a very honest man. The editor that I think I like best—this is not putting down EC guys at all—the one that I think I feel I should have done more work for, should have been the better artist for, is Richard Hughes." And while the artists of these stories have mostly been identified, the writers remain unknown—the records are mostly empty. It's possible that some were written by Hughes's assistant editor, Norman Fruman, or by any number of freelancers passing through the office.

The issues in this volume are also graced with art by Emil Gershwin ("The Way of the Werewolf" and "Lair of the Vampire"), a distant relative of George and Ira's and a stunningly talented unknown artist. His thick, expressive brush strokes bring to mind Harvey Kurtzman's drawings for EC, as well as work by Alex Toth, but the imagery is so assured that it begs to be taken on its own terms. George Wilhelms ("The Fiend in Fur" and "The Doom of the Moonlings") is another pleasant surprise in these pages. Wilhelms was a journeyman artist who had a lush and pulpy style somewhere between Virgil Finlay and Matt Fox. His labored-over imagery was all too rare in comic books at the time. He worked in comics from the 1940s through the sixties, and appears to have peaked with his work for ACG.

Finally, as is the case with ACG in general, there is Ogden Whitney. One of the last mysteries in comics, Whitney began his comic-book career in 1939, joined ACG in 1950, and stayed until the bitter end. Little is known about the man himself aside from a stint in World War II and rumors of a drinking problem. Norman Fruman remarked that "Whitney was very correct. He seems to me to have been kind of withdrawn. Not a socially amiable, but not unamiable, person. Someone who might be coming in like an accountant." Whoever he was, Whitney meshed perfectly with Hughes's sensibility and became the emblematic visual force behind the company—the man responsible for giving the romance and fantasy comics an unnervingly bland look, as well as, of course, the cocreator of *Herbie*. Whitney has just one story here, "The Vengeful Spirit," and it finds him still entrenched in a "good girl" mode of art, with beautiful women front and center and hapless men all around.

In these four issues, *Forbidden Worlds* gets off to a strong start and also indicates the direction of ACG itself. These are strong stories that, unlike those of EC, are not highly eccentric, but nonetheless feature solid and, at times, stunning story-telling marked by the high standard of craft that Richard Hughes cultivated throughout his run.

DAN NADEL
June 2012

SPECIAL THANKS TO MICHAEL VANCE, ROY THOMAS, AND JIM VADEBONCOEUR.

DAN NADEL is the owner of PictureBox, Inc. (PictureBoxInc.com), a Grammy Award–winning publishing company. Dan has authored books including *Art Out of Time: Unknown Comics Visionaries, 1900–1969*, *Gary Panter*, *Art in Time: Unknown Comic Book Adventures, 1940–1980*, and, most recently, coauthored *Electrical Banana: Masters of Psychedelic Art*. He is the coeditor of *The Comics Journal*, and has published essays and criticism in the *Washington Post*, *Frieze*, and *Bookforum*. As a curator, he has mounted exhibitions including *Return of the Repressed: Destroy All Monsters 1973–1977* in Los Angeles; *Karl Wirsum: Drawings 1967–1970* in New York; the first major Jack Kirby retrospective, *The House That Jack Built*, in Lucerne, Switzerland; and *Macronauts* for the 1st Athens Biennale 2007 in Greece. Dan lives in Brooklyn.

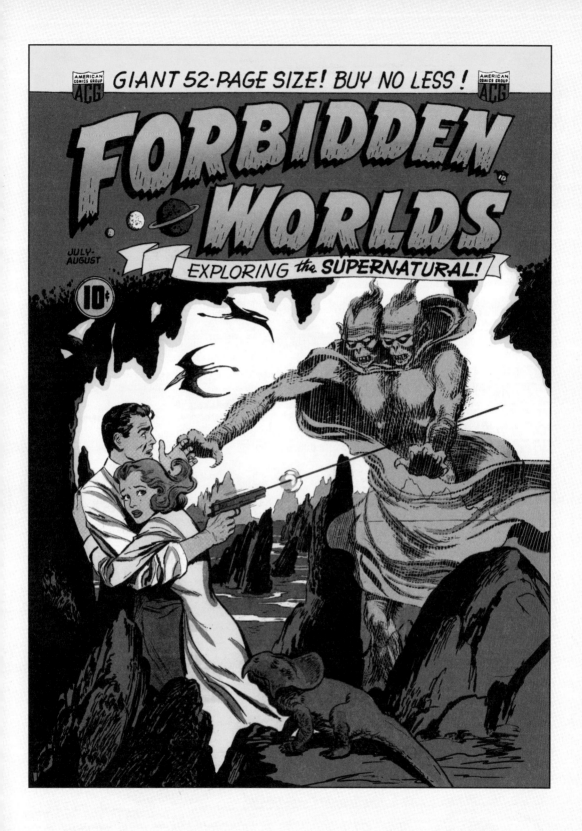

FORBIDDEN WORLDS #1 | July–August 1951

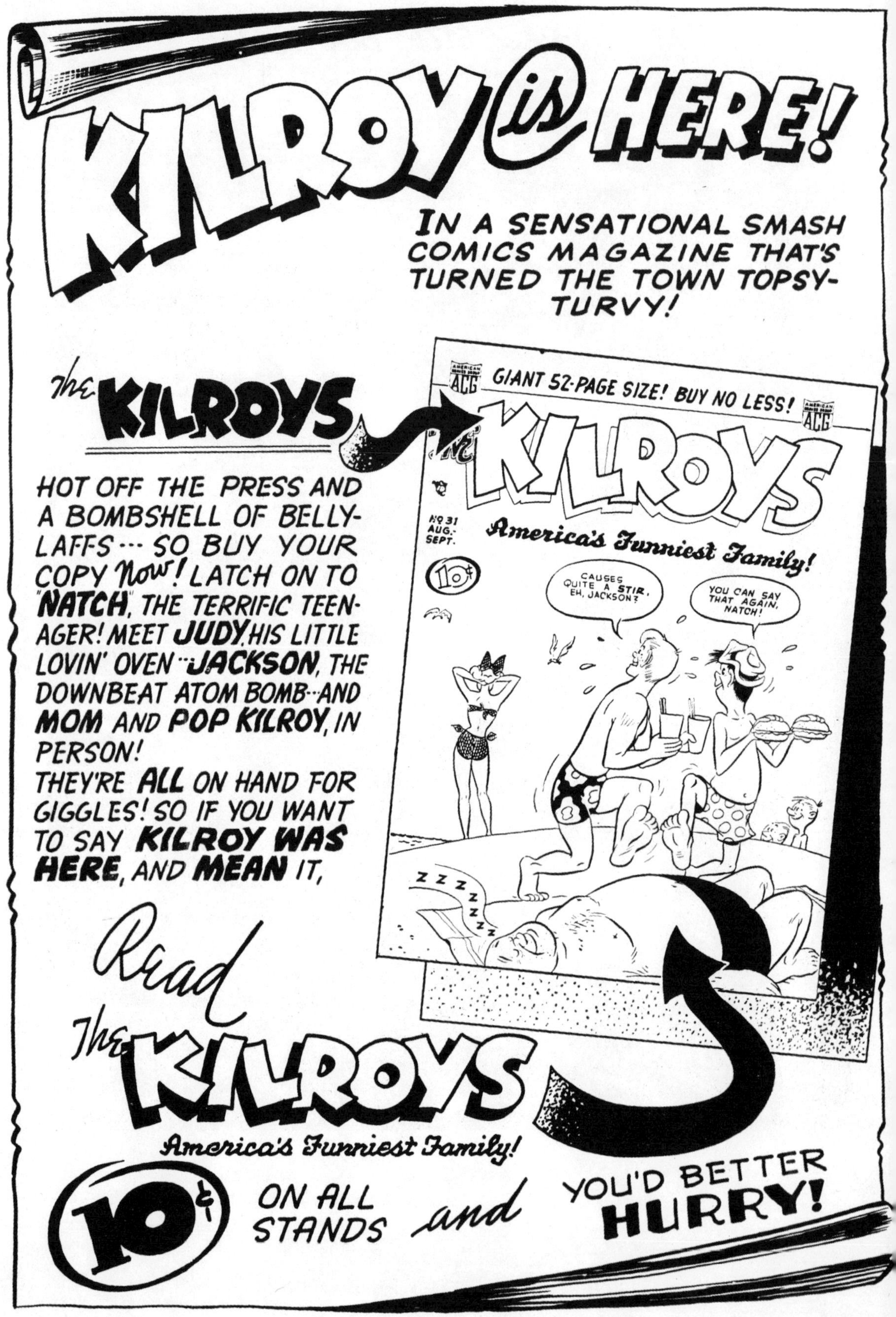
KILROY is HERE!
IN A SENSATIONAL SMASH COMICS MAGAZINE THAT'S TURNED THE TOWN TOPSY-TURVY!
The KILROYS
HOT OFF THE PRESS AND A BOMBSHELL OF BELLY-LAFFS --- SO BUY YOUR COPY Now! LATCH ON TO "NATCH", THE TERRIFIC TEEN-AGER! MEET JUDY, HIS LITTLE LOVIN' OVEN --- JACKSON, THE DOWNBEAT ATOM BOMB --- AND MOM AND POP KILROY, IN PERSON!
THEY'RE ALL ON HAND FOR GIGGLES! SO IF YOU WANT TO SAY KILROY WAS HERE, AND MEAN IT,
AMERICAN COMICS GROUP ACG
GIANT 52-PAGE SIZE! BUY NO LESS!
The KILROYS
No 31 AUG.-SEPT.
America's Funniest Family!
10¢
CAUSES QUITE A STIR, EH, JACKSON?
YOU CAN SAY THAT AGAIN, NATCH!
Z Z Z Z Z Z Z
Read The KILROYS
America's Funniest Family!
10¢
ON ALL STANDS
and
YOU'D BETTER HURRY!

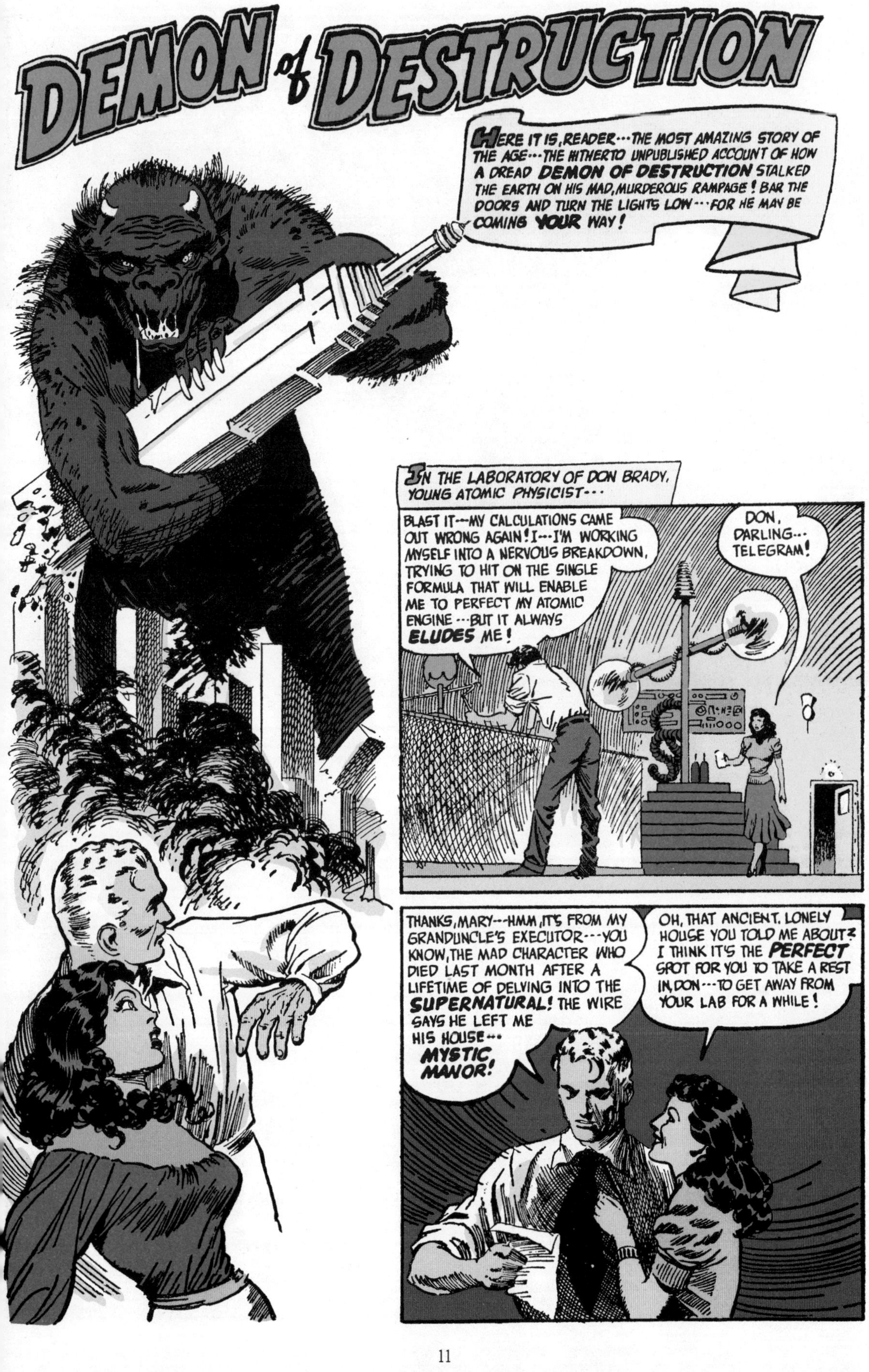
DEMON of DESTRUCTION
HERE IT IS, READER··· THE MOST AMAZING STORY OF THE AGE··· THE HITHERTO UNPUBLISHED ACCOUNT OF HOW A DREAD DEMON OF DESTRUCTION STALKED THE EARTH ON HIS MAD, MURDEROUS RAMPAGE! BAR THE DOORS AND TURN THE LIGHTS LOW··· FOR HE MAY BE COMING YOUR WAY!
IN THE LABORATORY OF DON BRADY, YOUNG ATOMIC PHYSICIST···
BLAST IT---MY CALCULATIONS CAME OUT WRONG AGAIN! I---I'M WORKING MYSELF INTO A NERVOUS BREAKDOWN, TRYING TO HIT ON THE SINGLE FORMULA THAT WILL ENABLE ME TO PERFECT MY ATOMIC ENGINE ---BUT IT ALWAYS ELUDES ME!
DON, DARLING... TELEGRAM!
THANKS, MARY---HMM, IT'S FROM MY GRANDUNCLE'S EXECUTOR---YOU KNOW, THE MAD CHARACTER WHO DIED LAST MONTH AFTER A LIFETIME OF DELVING INTO THE SUPERNATURAL! THE WIRE SAYS HE LEFT ME HIS HOUSE--- MYSTIC MANOR!
OH, THAT ANCIENT, LONELY HOUSE YOU TOLD ME ABOUT? I THINK IT'S THE PERFECT SPOT FOR YOU TO TAKE A REST IN, DON---TO GET AWAY FROM YOUR LAB FOR A WHILE!

RIDICULOUS...WHAT SANE MAN WOULD WANT TO STAY IN THAT SPOOKY, BROKEN-DOWN PILE OF BRICKS?

BUT YOU'RE WORKING YOURSELF TO DEATH ON THAT INVENTION OF YOURS! YOU NEED A CHANGE, A REST...AND AFTER YOU COME BACK FROM YOUR VACATION AT MYSTIC MANOR, YOU'LL BE ABLE TO ATTACK YOUR WORK WITH REDOUBLED VIGOR!

ALL RIGHT, DEAREST...YOU'RE RIGHT, AS USUAL! I'LL HEAD UP THERE AND TRY TO FORGET MY ATOMIC ENGINE! BUT YOU'VE GOT TO COME ALONG AND HELP LOOK AFTER ME!

SWEETHEART...!

MYSTIC MANOR? MISTER...I WOULDN'T DARE SEND ANYONE OUT TO THAT DEVIL-RIDDEN PLACE!

YOU MUST BE CRAZY! BUT IF YOU WON'T HELP ME, I'LL FIND SOMEONE WHO WILL IF I HAVE TO GO TO EVERY HOUSE IN TOWN!

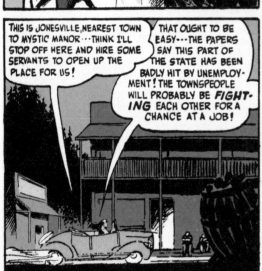

THIS IS JONESVILLE, NEAREST TOWN TO MYSTIC MANOR...THINK I'LL STOP OFF HERE AND HIRE SOME SERVANTS TO OPEN UP THE PLACE FOR US!

THAT OUGHT TO BE EASY...THE PAPERS SAY THIS PART OF THE STATE HAS BEEN BADLY HIT BY UNEMPLOYMENT! THE TOWNSPEOPLE WILL PROBABLY BE FIGHTING EACH OTHER FOR A CHANCE AT A JOB!

S...LE EMERGEN...LOYMENT SERVICE
DOMESTIC WORKERS

MYSTIC MANOR? WELL, SIR, AS A PHYSICIAN I HATE TO ADMIT IT...BUT THE TOWNSPEOPLE HAVE GOOD REASON TO BE TERRIFIED OF THAT PLACE! AN AURA OF FIENDISH EVIL HOVERS OVER THE HOUSE, ALMOST LIKE SOME PRESENCE FROM OUT OF THE VAST UNKNOWN...A GRISLY SOMETHING IN THE AIR THAT WORKS ITS EVIL WAY INTO YOUR VERY SOUL AND FILLS YOU WITH ANCIENT, CLAMMY DREAD!

THAT'S RIDICULOUS, DOCTOR...HOW CAN YOU BELIEVE SUCH SUPERSTITIOUS NONSENSE?

BUT EVERYWHERE IN TOWN, THE SAME STRANGE TERROR!

I'D STARVE BEFORE I'D WORK IN THAT HOUSE OF DEMONS! SATAN HIMSELF IS MASTER THERE!

HAS THE WHOLE TOWN GONE MAD?...COME ON, MARY...LET'S LOOK UP THE LOCAL DOCTOR! MAYBE A MAN OF SCIENCE WILL TELL US WHAT THIS SUPERNATURAL POPPY-COCK IS ALL ABOUT!

AL WILLIAMSON

2

I'LL TELL YOU···AND THEN MAYBE **YOU'LL** BELIEVE! YOUR GRANDUNCLE'S HOUSEKEEPER WAS BROUGHT TO MY OFFICE SOME TIME AGO···SHE WAS DELIRIOUS, SCREAMING INCOHERENTLY ABOUT SOMETHING SHE CALLED **MARZO!** I WENT TO MYSTIC MANOR MYSELF TO FIND OUT WHAT HAD FRIGHTENED HER···BUT I DIDN'T STAY THERE LONG··· I **COULDN'T!** SOMETHING HORRIBLY EVIL SEEMED TO REACH INTO THE DEPTHS OF MY BEING THE MOMENT I NEARED THAT ACCURSED HOME··· SOMETHING COLD AND MALIGNANT···SOMETHING THAT WANTED MY **SOUL!**

ARE YOU TRYING TO TELL ME THAT MY UNCLE'S **GHOST** IS HAUNTING THAT HOUSE?

NO···IT ALL STARTED **BEFORE** HE DIED···WHEN A HUGE, COFFIN-LIKE CARTON ARRIVED FROM SOMEWHERE IN THE ORIENT! YOUR UNCLE BEGAN DYING BY INCHES SOON AFTER THAT ···EACH TIME I SAW HIM, HIS EYES WERE MORE HAUNTED! WHEN HE FINALLY DIED, I ISSUED A DEATH CERTIFICATE FOR HEART FAILURE ···BUT I NEVER DARED ASK MYSELF **WHAT** STOPPED HIS HEART! FOR IF EVER I SAW STARK TERROR ON A DEAD MAN'S FACE, IT WAS ON **HIS!** BE WARNED··· STAY AWAY FROM **MYSTIC MANOR!**

I···I'M BEGINNING TO BE SORRY I EVER SUGGESTED COMING HERE, DON! LET'S GO BACK··· **PLEASE!**

SO THIS MASS HYSTERIA IS BEGINNING TO AFFECT YOU, TOO, EH? WELL, IT'S NOT GOING TO GET **ME** DOWN···I'M GOING TO TAKE YOU TO MYSTIC MANOR AND **PROVE** THAT THERE'S NO SUCH THING AS THE SUPERNATURAL!

UP --UP THE LONELY, WINDING MOUNTAIN ROAD, UP TO WHERE THE CLAMMY MISTS HANG LOW AND A STRANGE AURA OF SOME UNKNOWN MENACE HOVERS OVER THE FORBIDDING GABLES OF A HOUSE CRUMBLING WITH THE WEIGHT OF THE AGES···

THAT···THAT CREEPY OLD PLACE MUST BE MYSTIC MANOR, DON···AND **LOOK**···IT IT SEEMS AS IF A GIGANTIC PHANTOM HAND IS CLUTCHING THE HOUSE!

STRANGE, I SEEM TO SEE IT TOO ··BUT IT'S PROBABLY JUST THE FINGERS OF MIST CURLING AROUND THE HOUSE! THERE'S **NOTHING** TO BE AFRAID OF!

Then, PAST THE CREAKING DOOR AND INTO THE MUSTY INTERIOR, WHERE FLICKERING SHADOWS WRITHE ON FURNITURE SHROUDED LIKE WHITE, CROUCHING CORPSES···

DON, I · I'M AFRAID ·· **TERRIFIED!**

DON'T BE SILLY, DARLING! THIS CANDELABRA I FOUND OUGHT TO GIVE US ENOUGH LIGHT TO EXPLORE THE OLD JOINT··· AND YOU'LL SEE HOW CHILDISH YOUR FEARS ARE!

THIS MUST HAVE BEEN YOUR UNCLE'S ROOM --HIS DEATH CHAMBER! AND IT··· IT LOOKS AS IF SOME DEMONIACAL POWER HAD BEEN LET LOOSE IN HERE···TO RAVAGE AND DESTROY!

NONSENSE ···UNCLE PHINEAS ALWAYS WAS UNTIDY! HMM, HERE'S AN ANCIENT-LOOKING BOOK ···PROBABLY PART OF HIS STUDIES INTO THAT OCCULT POPPYCOCK! LET'S SEE WHAT IT SAYS ···IT OUGHT TO GIVE US A **LAUGH!**

3

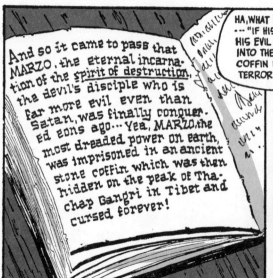

And so it came to pass that MARZO, the eternal incarnation of the spirit of destruction, the devil's disciple who is far more evil even than Satan, was finally conquered eons ago... Yea, MARZO, the most dreaded power on earth, was imprisoned in an ancient stone coffin which was then hidden on the peak of Thachap Gangri in Tibet and cursed forever!

HA, WHAT BOSH...LISTEN, IT GETS EVEN FUNNIER! ..."IF HIS COFFIN IS REMOVED FROM THAT PLACE, HIS EVIL AURA WILL SEEP OUT AND STRIKE DREAD INTO THE HEARTS OF MEN! BUT IF EVER HIS COFFIN IS OPENED AND HE ESCAPES, THEN TERROR AND DESTRUCTION WILL STALK FOREVER AMID THE FLAMES AND RUINS OF A RAVAGED WORLD!"

DON, IT *ISN'T* BOSH--- THAT HUGE COFFIN-LIKE CARTON WHICH CAME TO YOUR UNCLE FROM THE ORIENT MUST HAVE BEEN *MARZO'S* COFFIN--- BECAUSE THE AURA OF EVIL AND DREAD AROUND THIS HOUSE ARRIVED TOGETHER WITH THAT CARTON!

MARZO IS SOMEWHERE IN THIS HOUSE ---I ---I CAN ALMOST *FEEL* HIS CLAMMY SPIRIT GROPING FOR MY SOUL!

THE ONLY WAY TO RESTORE YOUR SANITY, MARY, IS TO TURN THIS HOUSE UPSIDE DOWN UNTIL YOU'RE *CONVINCED* THE MYTHICAL MARZO ISN'T HERE ---OR ANYWHERE! *COME ON!*

ROOM AFTER SHROUDED ROOM IS SEARCHED IN VAIN--- BUT FINALLY, IN THE DIM RECESSES OF THE SUBTERRANEAN CELLAR...

THE ATMOSPHERE OF HOVERING EVIL SEEMS TO BE MORE INTENSE DOWN HERE ---AS ---AS IF WE'RE GETTING *WARM!* OH, LOOK---THAT HEAVY IRON DOOR! IT'S BOLTED ON *THIS* SIDE ---AS IF TO KEEP SOMETHING IN THERE FROM GETTING OUT!

WELL, THAT JUST MAKES IT EASY TO OPEN---AND *DON'T* TRY TO STOP ME!

AS THE UNBOLTED DOOR IS FLUNG OPEN, AN OVERWHELMING AURA OF ALMOST TANGIBLE, DEMONIACAL EVIL SURGES OUT--- LIKE A STAGGERING BLAST FROM THE DEPTHS!

MARZO'S COFFIN ---HE'S IN THERE!

OH, *YEAH?* I'LL SHOW YOU THERE'S NOTHING SUPERNATURAL IN THAT BOX---I'LL BREAK IT OPEN AND *PROVE* IT!

NO, DON, *DON'T*...!

THERE---THAT DID IT! NOW TO SEE WHAT'S *INSIDE!*

CLANK!

NOW LET'S SEE, I'LL NEED A CROWBAR OR LEVER OF SOME KIND TO GET THAT HEAVY LID OPEN...

YOU...YOU WON'T NEED IT, DON...IT ...IT'S OPENING BY ITSELF!

CR-REAK

DON...THAT...THAT HAND UNDER THE LID...!

GREAT SCOTT... SOMEONE IS IN THERE ...BUT WHO...OR WHAT?

SUDDENLY...

OHHH!

STAND BACK... WHATEVER YOU ARE!

FEAR NOT! ALTHOUGH I AM MARZO, THE SPIRIT OF DESTRUCTION, SWORN TO KILL AND DESTROY, I SHALL SPARE YOU...BECAUSE YOU HAVE DELIVERED ME FROM AGE-OLD CAPTIVITY AND FREED ME TO STALK AND RAVAGE THE EARTH ONCE MORE!

AS A REWARD TO YOU WHO SHATTERED MY PRISON, I WILL CONFER UPON YOU THE PRICE-LESS GIFT OF THREE WISHES! NO MATTER WHAT THREE WISHES YOU MAKE, THEY SHALL BE GRANTED...AND NO POWER IN THE UNIVERSE, NOT EVEN I MYSELF, WILL BE ABLE TO DENY THEM TO YOU! BUT NOW, AFTER ALL THESE CENTURIES, I AM READY TO GO FORTH ONCE MORE...

CRASH!

...TO DESTROY!

RR-RRIP!

5.

15

STUNNED BY THE FALLING WRECKAGE... DON REVIVES!

OH, MY...MY HEAD! THE WHOLE HOUSE COLLAPSED AROUND OUR EARS...BUT WE WERE MIRACULOUSLY SPARED SOMEHOW! MARY'S BEGINNING TO STIR...I'VE GOT TO GET HER OUT OF HERE!

I DON'T KNOW HOW IT HAPPENED, DARLING...I GUESS THE PLACE WAS SO OLD AND UNSAFE THAT IT WAS READY TO COLLAPSE THE MOMENT ANYONE STEPPED FOOT IN IT! I MUST'VE BEEN REALLY KNOCKED OUT COLD, THOUGH...BECAUSE I SEEM TO REMEMBER SOME AWFUL DREAM ABOUT HOW I UNWITTINGLY RELEASED A DREAD SPIRIT NAMED MARZO, WHO SAID HE WOULD GRANT ME THREE WISHES! CRAZY DREAM FOR A SCIENTIST, EH?

BUT...BUT THAT'S WHAT I THOUGHT I'D DREAMED! AND IF WE BOTH EXPERIENCED IT, IT MUST HAVE BEEN REALITY!

WE'VE GOT TO GET A GRIP ON OURSELVES, MARY...IT COULDN'T HAVE REALLY HAPPENED! THE MASS HYPNOSIS THAT GRIPPED THE PEOPLE OF SMITHVILLE MUST HAVE STARTED WORKING ON US, TOO!

THINK SO? LOOK... DOWN THERE!

SEE, DON?...ALL OF SMITHVILLE IS IN FLAMES! AND MARZO SAID HE WAS GOING OUT TO WREAK DESTRUCTION ON THE WORLD!

LET...LET'S GET OUT OF HERE AND HEAD FOR HOME, MARY! WE'RE BOTH OVERWROUGHT...THAT FIRE IS JUST A COINCIDENCE, AND NOTHING MORE!

COINCIDENCE? WELL, IN THE DAYS THAT FOLLOW...

NO... NO... HELP!

THIS IS THE TWENTY-NINTH GHASTLY MURDER LIKE THIS IN THESE PARTS ...BUT WE CAN'T SEEM TO LAND THE KILLER! HE SLIPS THROUGH THE HEAVIEST POLICE CORDON ...ALMOST AS IF HE'S A SPIRIT!

YEAH, AND THE TRAIL OF MURDERS SEEMS TO BE HEADING TOWARDS NEW YORK...WE'D BETTER WARN THE POLICE THERE TO EXPECT HIM... OR IT!

6.

BUT THE POLICE OF NEW YORK HAVE NOT BEEN WARNED TO EXPECT A SPIRIT OF DESTRUCTION THAT CAN BECOME IN-VISIBLE····MONSTROUS····THAT CAN STALK THROUGH A CITY AND LEAVE A TRAGIC TRAIL OF DEATH AND HORROR BEHIND!

MEANWHILE, IN DON BRADY'S LAB···

YOU'VE JUST WITNESSED THE MOST HORRIFYING AND UNBELIEVABLE SIGHT IN HISTORY, LADIES AND GENTLEMEN OF THE TELEVISION AUDIENCE···A MASSIVE BRIDGE OF STEEL AND CONCRETE, RIPPED APART BY SOME INVISIBLE FORCE, PINIONING HUNDREDS OF PEOPLE IN THE WRECKAGE···!

DON····THAT··· THAT MUST BE **MARZO'S** TERRIBLE WORK!

HA HA HA!

RR RIP!

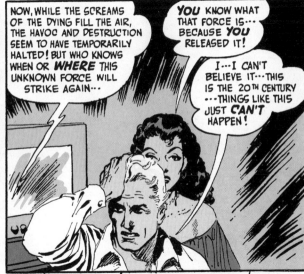

NOW, WHILE THE SCREAMS OF THE DYING FILL THE AIR, THE HAVOC AND DESTRUCTION SEEM TO HAVE TEMPORARILY HALTED! BUT WHO KNOWS WHEN OR WHERE THIS UNKNOWN FORCE WILL STRIKE AGAIN···

YOU KNOW WHAT THAT FORCE IS··· BECAUSE **YOU** RELEASED IT!

I···I CAN'T BELIEVE IT···THIS IS THE 20TH CENTURY ···THINGS LIKE THIS JUST **CAN'T** HAPPEN!

AH, BUT THEY JUST **DID** HAPPEN!

CRASH!

YOU!

YES, I···THE **SPIRIT OF DESTRUCTION** WHO WILL GO ON AND ON···BURNING···KILLING··· DESTROYING! WHAT I'VE DONE SO FAR IS **NOTHING** COMPARED TO WHAT I'M ABOUT TO DO···· BUT I CAME TO REASSURE YOU THAT NO MATTER WHAT DESTRUCTION I WREAK, YOU WILL BOTH BE SPARED! AND YOU WHO RELEASED ME FROM MY COFFIN WILL BE ALL-POWERFUL···BECAUSE THE THREE WISHES I GRANTED YOU WILL ENABLE YOU TO ACCOM-PLISH **ANYTHING** YOUR HEART DESIRES··· **ANYTHING!**

7.

AND NOW··· FAREWELL··· FOREVER!

HE···HE VANISHED!

HE WAS REAL···ALL THIS ISN'T A DREAM! AND IF MARZO HAS SUCH POWER, MAYBE THE THREE WISHES I MAKE WILL COME TRUE!

YES, YOUR THREE WISHES ···THE REWARD YOU RECEIVED FOR BETRAYING HUMANITY! IS THAT ALL YOU CAN THINK ABOUT AT A TIME LIKE THIS ···WHEN MARZO IS ABOUT TO DESTROY THE WHOLE WORLD?

THAT'S ALL I WANT TO THINK ABOUT! I CAN USE MY FIRST WISH TO OBTAIN THE SECRET OF THE ATOMIC ENGINE THAT'S BEEN ELUDING ME SO LONG···THAT WILL GIVE ME POWER! ANOTHER WISH WILL MAKE ME THE RICHEST MAN IN HISTORY···

YOU···YOU MURDERER! ALL YOU CARE ABOUT IS RICHES AND POWER···WHEN YOU'RE THE ONE WHO FREED THAT MURDEROUS SPECTER FROM OUT OF THE UNKNOWN···TO PREY UPON A HELPLESS WORLD! YOU'RE RESPONSIBLE···YOU'RE AS MUCH A KILLER AS MARZO!

YES, YOU'RE FURIOUS AT ME···BLIND WITH RAGE, BECAUSE DEEP IN YOUR HEART YOU KNOW I'M RIGHT AND YOU'RE GUILTY···BUT YOU CAN'T ADMIT IT TO YOURSELF···

GET AWAY FROM ME! I'M GOING TO BE THE MOST POWERFUL MAN IN THE WORLD···WHY SHOULD I LET YOU AND YOUR CHILDISH RAVING STAND IN MY WAY? I ···I WISH YOU WERE DEAD!

INSTANTLY···

CRAK!

OHH··HH!

SHE···SHE'S DEAD···AND MY WISH KILLED HER! BUT···BUT I JUST BLURTED OUT THOSE WORDS WITHOUT MEANING THEM··· I NEVER WANTED HER TO DIE··· SHE'S ALL I EVER LOVED! AND NOW I'VE LOST HER···BECAUSE I UNWITTINGLY USED THE TERRIBLE POWER MARZO CONFERRED ON ME! SHE'S GONE··· FOREVER!

WAIT···NOT FOREVER! I'VE STILL GOT TWO MORE WISHES ···I CAN USE ONE OF THEM TO···

8

I...I WISH THAT MARY REVIVES...COMES BACK FROM THE DEAD INTO LIFE, EXACTLY AS SHE WAS!

DON...WHAT...WHAT HAPPENED? THE LAST THING I KNEW...

NEVER MIND, DARLING...YOU'RE BACK WITH ME, AND THAT'S ALL THAT MATTERS! YOU...YOU JUST FAINTED...YOU'LL FEEL BETTER AS SOON AS YOU GET SOME FRESH AIR AT THE WINDOW!

AT THAT MOMENT--THE SOUND OF DESTRUCTION!

HA HA HA!

THERE...THERE GOES THE EMPIRE STATE BUILDING!

CRRRAK!

DON...L...LOOK!

GREAT SCOTT ...NEW YORK... IT...IT'S BEING UTTERLY DESTROYED!

THIS IS WHAT MARZO MEANT WHEN HE SAID THAT WHAT HE'D DONE SO FAR WAS NOTHING COMPARED TO WHAT HE WAS GOING TO DO! HE...HE'S GOING ON A RAMPAGE OF DESTRUCTION SUCH AS THE WORLD NEVER DREAMED OF...AND ONLY YOU CAN STOP HIM, DON! YOU'VE GOT THE THREE WISHES HE AWARDED YOU...WISHES HE SAID NOT EVEN HE HIMSELF COULD DENY! YOU CAN USE ONE OF THOSE WISHES TO DESTROY HIM...YOU'VE GOT TO DO IT!

NO, NOT THREE WISHES ANYMORE ...JUST ONE...

9.

JUST ONE WISH LEFT··· AND WITH IT, I CAN ASK FOR THE SECRET I NEED TO PERFECT MY ATOMIC ENGINE··· THE SECRET I'VE HUNGERED FOR, THE ONE THAT WILL MAKE ME THE RICHEST AND MOST POWERFUL MAN IN THE WORLD!

I···I CAN SEE I WAS WRONG IN ASKING YOU TO STOP MARZO···YOUR GREED IS GREATER THAN YOUR CONCERN FOR HUMANITY! GO AHEAD, THEN···USE YOUR LAST WISH FOR WHATEVER YOU WANT! GAIN YOUR WEALTH AND POWER··· BUT LOSE ME···BECAUSE I···I'M GOING OUT THERE TO DIE WITH ALL THE OTHERS!

NO, MARY···WAIT! I···I REMEMBER WHAT IT MEANT TO HAVE LOST YOU ONCE···I COULDN'T GO ON LIVING WITHOUT YOU, WITHOUT YOUR LOVE! YOU···YOU'VE MADE ME REALIZE WHAT'S REALLY IMPORTANT IN LIFE···NOT WEALTH OR POWER··· BUT LOVE AND HUMANITY! I'LL USE MY LAST WISH TO STOP MARZO!

OH··· DON!

TURN BACK, TIME, TO BEFORE I RELEASED MARZO FROM HIS STONE COFFIN IN MYSTIC MANOR! LET HIM BE STILL A PRISONER··· SO THAT ALL THE DEATH AND DESTRUCTION HE CAUSED WILL BE UNDONE, AS IF IT HAD NEVER HAPPENED!

INSTANTLY···

YAAAGHH!

HE···HE VANISHED ···YOU DID IT, DON!

YES, AND THE CITY'S INTACT, AND ALL THE PEOPLE ARE ALL RIGHT··· EVERYTHING IS JUST THE WAY IT WAS, AS IF MARZO NEVER ACTUALLY WENT ON HIS RAMPAGE! AND SINCE THE DESTRUCTION HE CAUSED WAS ALL UNDONE, AS IF IT NEVER EVEN HAPPENED, THE MEMORY OF IT WILL BE WIPED OUT OF PEOPLE'S MINDS···NO ONE WILL REMEMBER MARZO, EXCEPT US!

YES, HE'S SECURELY IMPRISONED IN HIS STONE COFFIN AGAIN, BACK IN MYSTIC MANOR··· AND WE'LL MAKE SURE THAT HE STAYS THERE!

RIGHT, DARLING! I DON'T REALLY CARE ABOUT THOSE WASTED THREE WISHES NOW··· AS LONG AS I HAVE YOU!

The END! 10.

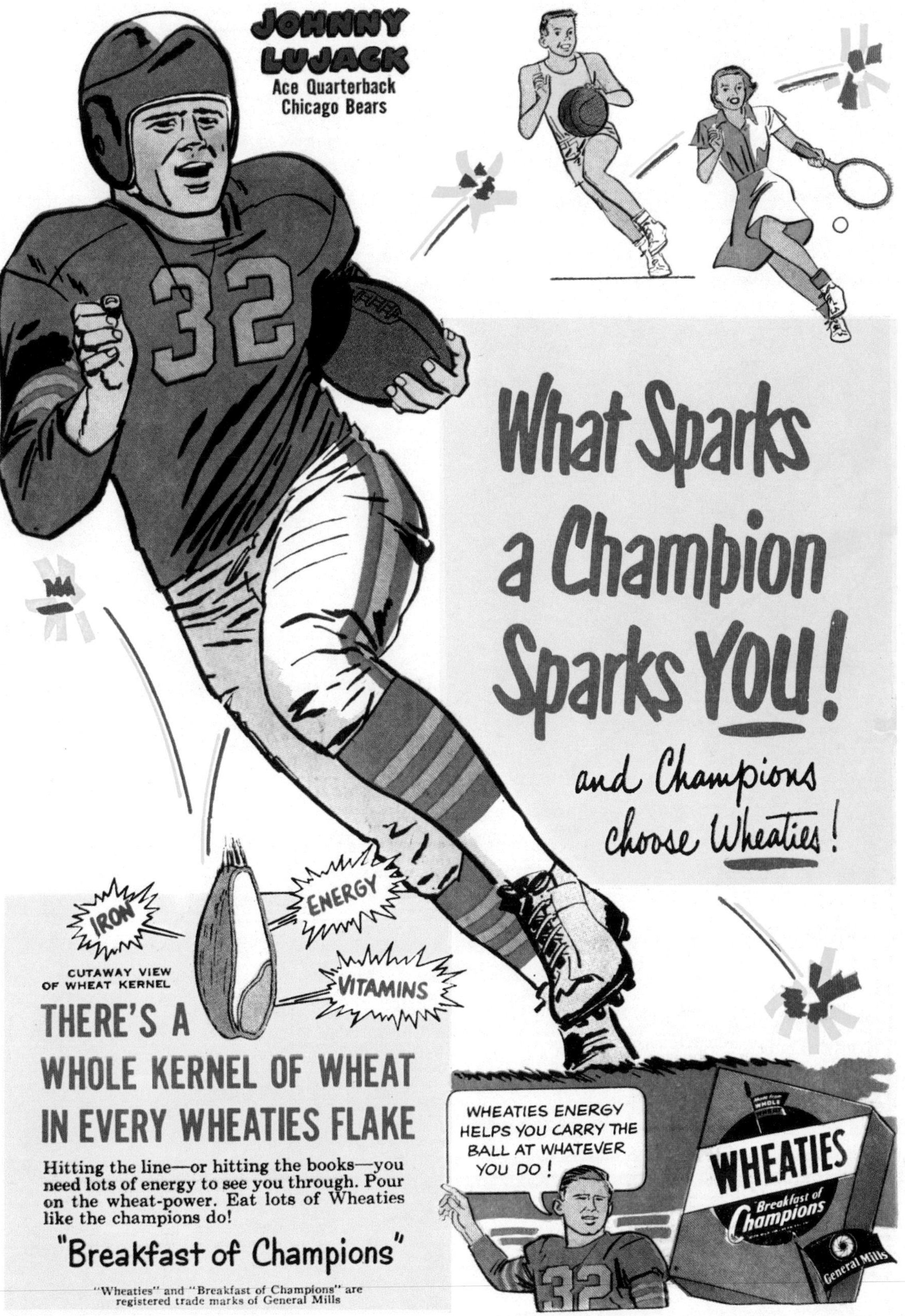
JOHNNY LUJACK
Ace Quarterback
Chicago Bears
What Sparks a Champion Sparks YOU!
and Champions choose Wheaties!
IRON
ENERGY
VITAMINS
CUTAWAY VIEW OF WHEAT KERNEL
THERE'S A WHOLE KERNEL OF WHEAT IN EVERY WHEATIES FLAKE
Hitting the line—or hitting the books—you need lots of energy to see you through. Pour on the wheat-power. Eat lots of Wheaties like the champions do!
"Breakfast of Champions"
"Wheaties" and "Breakfast of Champions" are registered trade marks of General Mills
WHEATIES ENERGY HELPS YOU CARRY THE BALL AT WHATEVER YOU DO!
WHEATIES
Breakfast of Champions
General Mills

Monsieur WEREWOLF

"AH, COME IN, come in," the old man said, peering out from under enormous eyebrows at the visitor at his door. "No one ever seems to come up this lonely mountain to visit me anymore, and strangers pass by only too infrequently. The last one passed by here more than three weeks ago...and ever since then, I've been rather hungry for...er, conversation and news of the village below."

The visitor took his hat off and followed the old man into the ancient-looking house. "I'm not really a stranger just passing idly by," he said. "I came here expressly to see you, sir. You see, I'm a student at Heidelberg University, studying for my doctorate in Occultology. In the course of writing my dissertation on lycanthropy, I came across your name as the author of some extraordinarily curious books on werewolves. So I decided to look you up and ask you where you got all the information and source material.

"But I must confess I had a devilishly hard time finding out where you live. As soon as I mentioned the name of Monsieur Jacques Turenne, all the villagers down below fled from me as if I'd asked for Satan himself. It was only when I cornered one little lad and promised to buy him all the sweets he could eat, that I learned you lived atop this mountain."

The old man smiled, revealing a perfect set of white, gleaming teeth that seemed incongruous in a face as old and sagging as his. "We explorers of the occult must expect such treatment from the masses, mustn't we?" he said. "But come into my study. I'll show you what the superstitious fools are so afraid of."

Inside the study, M. Turenne took out a strangely shaped bottle from a drawer and shook the vile green liquid it contained. "See...this is what they fear. They think it's a magical liquid that can turn anyone into a werewolf! Actually, it's merely a mixture of eleoselinum, aconitum, frondes populeae, sium, pentaphyllon, uespertilioris sanguis and solanum somniferum."

"Mnn," the visitor murmured. "That means it's composed of hemlock, aconite, poplar leaves, cowbane, cinquefoil, bat's blood and deadly nightshade. But how do the superstitious villagers think it's supposed to work?"

Jacques Turenne laughed this time, revealing incisor teeth that were strangely elongated and pointed, almost like a wolf's. Dipping his hands into the bottle, he said, "They believe that if anyone smears his hands with it, like this...and then rubs the concoction across his face, like this...then one in transformed into a werewolf, with an insatiable desire to kill!"

The visitor shuddered involuntarily. "Well, obviously it doesn't work...you're still Jacques Turenne. But it is an interesting belief. I think I'll just jot the details down in my notebook, in case I want to mention it in my thesis."

Bending low over his notebook, the student of occultology didn't notice the sudden change that overtook Turenne, and he didn't even bother to look up as the old man started to speak. "Oh, I neglected to tell you something else," the werewolf said. "It takes a few moments for the mixture to take effect! And now..."

The visitor turned at the hideous animal snarl behind him. For one horrified moment he stared at the awful half-man, half-wolf shape before him...and by the time he turned to flee, it was already too late, for the fangs were at his throat.

IT'S MIDNIGHT, READER, AND A BANSHEE WIND WAILS AMID THE TOSSING TREETOPS! ACROSS THE PALLID MOON DRIFTS THE EERIE SHADOW OF-- *A BAT!* HERE'S AS STRANGE AND GRIPPING A STORY AS YOU'VE EVER READ-- THE STORY OF A LOST SOUL-- THE TALE OF A *VAMPIRE LOVE* YOU'LL REMEMBER FOREVER!

LOVE OF A VAMPIRE

IT'S GETTING DARK, KEN-- AND THERE'S A SMALL ROADSIDE HOTEL RIGHT UP AHEAD! LET'S STOP OFF *THERE!*

VILLAGE OF KRAUSTON SLOW!

HOTEL

JUST MARRIED

YES, IT ALL STARTED INNOCENTLY ENOUGH! A HONEYMOON COUPLE, CONFIDENT OF A LIFE OF HAPPINESS BEFORE THEM! LITTLE DID THEY REALIZE THAT THIS WAS A FATEFUL MOMENT-- THAT BEFORE THEM LOOMED NIGHTMARE TRAGEDY!

WE'LL JUST BE HERE FOR ONE NIGHT, MR.-- ER--

BRUNT-- HANS *BRUNT!* I'M THE NIGHT MANAGER! WE WELCOME HONEYMOONERS HERE! AND YOUR WIFE IS VERY-- *BEAUTIFUL!*

HERE'S YOUR ROOM, AND I TRUST YOU'LL BE VERY COMFORTABLE! GOOD NIGHT-- *AND PLEASANT DREAMS, MRS. CUMMINGS!*

I-- I WISH WE HADN'T STOPPED HERE! THERE'S SOMETHING-- *EVIL* ABOUT THAT OLD MAN!

WHAT A VIEW! LOOK AT THE MOON, BETH!

BUT THERE WAS SOMETHING ABOUT THAT GHOSTLY MOON THAT TERRIFIED BETH! *SOMETHING--*

GREAT SCOTT, THAT BAT-- LOOK AT THE *SIZE* OF IT! BUT DON'T LET IT SCARE YOU, DARLING-- YOU'RE *TREMBLING!*

I-- I CAN'T HELP IT! I'VE GOT THE STRANGEST FEELING THAT SOMETHING *HORRIBLE* IS GOING TO HAPPEN!

SOMETHING HORRIBLE! PROPHETIC WORDS-- FOR IN THE WEIRD HUSH OF MIDNIGHT, A GREAT BAT WHEELED CLOSER-- *CLOSER--*

1

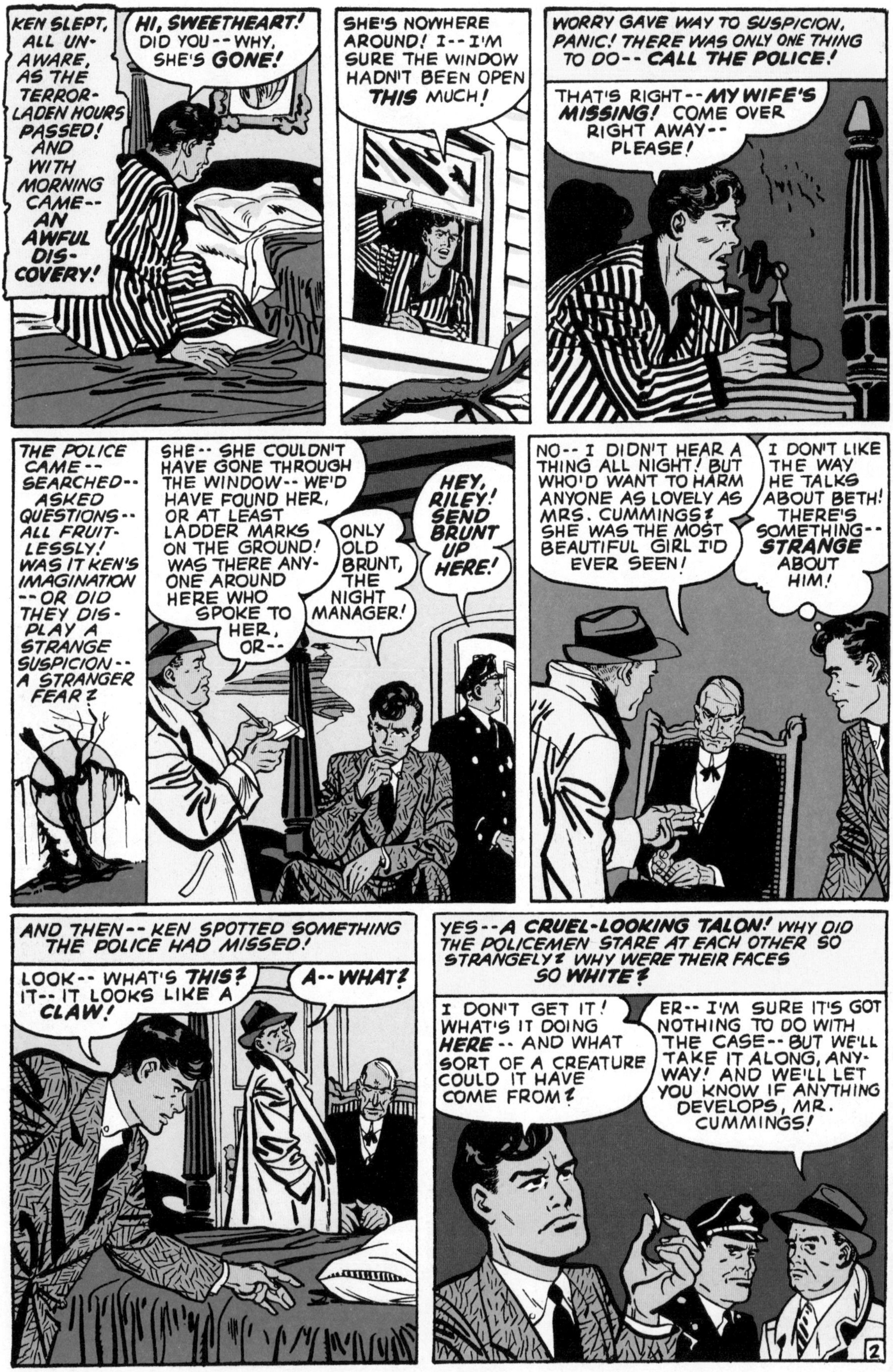
KEN SLEPT, ALL UN-AWARE, AS THE TERROR-LADEN HOURS PASSED! AND WITH MORNING CAME-- AN AWFUL DIS-COVERY!
HI, SWEETHEART! DID YOU--WHY, SHE'S GONE!
SHE'S NOWHERE AROUND! I--I'M SURE THE WINDOW HADN'T BEEN OPEN THIS MUCH!
WORRY GAVE WAY TO SUSPICION, PANIC! THERE WAS ONLY ONE THING TO DO-- CALL THE POLICE!
THAT'S RIGHT--MY WIFE'S MISSING! COME OVER RIGHT AWAY-- PLEASE!
THE POLICE CAME-- SEARCHED-- ASKED QUESTIONS-- ALL FRUIT-LESSLY! WAS IT KEN'S IMAGINATION --OR DID THEY DIS-PLAY A STRANGE SUSPICION-- A STRANGER FEAR?
SHE-- SHE COULDN'T HAVE GONE THROUGH THE WINDOW-- WE'D HAVE FOUND HER, OR AT LEAST LADDER MARKS ON THE GROUND! WAS THERE ANY-ONE AROUND HERE WHO SPOKE TO HER, OR--
ONLY OLD BRUNT, THE NIGHT MANAGER!
HEY, RILEY! SEND BRUNT UP HERE!
NO-- I DIDN'T HEAR A THING ALL NIGHT! BUT WHO'D WANT TO HARM ANYONE AS LOVELY AS MRS. CUMMINGS? SHE WAS THE MOST BEAUTIFUL GIRL I'D EVER SEEN!
I DON'T LIKE THE WAY HE TALKS ABOUT BETH! THERE'S SOMETHING-- STRANGE ABOUT HIM!
AND THEN-- KEN SPOTTED SOMETHING THE POLICE HAD MISSED!
LOOK-- WHAT'S THIS? IT-- IT LOOKS LIKE A CLAW!
A--WHAT?
YES--A CRUEL-LOOKING TALON! WHY DID THE POLICEMEN STARE AT EACH OTHER SO STRANGELY? WHY WERE THEIR FACES SO WHITE?
I DON'T GET IT! WHAT'S IT DOING HERE-- AND WHAT SORT OF A CREATURE COULD IT HAVE COME FROM?
ER-- I'M SURE IT'S GOT NOTHING TO DO WITH THE CASE-- BUT WE'LL TAKE IT ALONG, ANY-WAY! AND WE'LL LET YOU KNOW IF ANYTHING DEVELOPS, MR. CUMMINGS!
2

FOLLOWED DREARY, CAREWORN DAYS OF WAITING, AND STILL NO WORD! FINALLY, AT POLICE HEADQUARTERS...

WHERE CAN I FIND INSPECTOR JACKSON? HE WAS ASSIGNED TO THIS CASE THREE DAYS AGO -- AND I HAVEN'T HEARD FROM HIM SINCE!

HE'S BEEN SPENDING HIS TIME IN THE *LIBRARY* -- BUT DON'T ASK ME *WHY!*

KEN SOUGHT OUT THE DETECTIVE AT THE LIBRARY...

INSPECTOR JACKSON? THERE HE IS -- AT THAT TABLE OVER THERE!

GOOD GOSH -- HE MUSTN'T SEE ME READING THIS BOOK!

SILENCE

PUT THIS AWAY, MISS JONES -- I'M FINISHED WITH IT...

HI, MR. CUMMINGS -- SORRY TO RUSH OFF THIS WAY, BUT I'M LATE! I'LL NOTIFY YOU IF ANYTHING BREAKS!

HE DOESN'T WANT ME TO SEE THAT BOOK! *WHY?*

SILENCE Please!

AFTER INSPECTOR JACKSON LEFT...

MAY I SEE THE BOOK HE WAS READING? WE HAVE THE SAME SORT OF TASTE!

CERTAINLY! MY, I DON'T KNOW WHY *ANYONE'D* WANT TO READ *THIS!*

Folk Tales of Krauston VOL. I Vampires

VAMPIRES! WHAT NONSENSE! HMM -- JACKSON MARKED HIS PLACE WITH THIS CARD! MAYBE I'D BETTER READ IT!

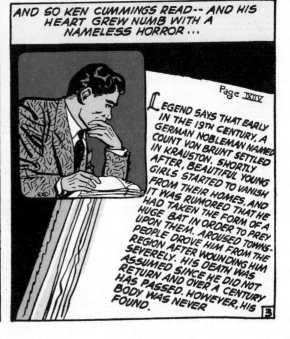

AND SO KEN CUMMINGS READ -- AND HIS HEART GREW NUMB WITH A NAMELESS HORROR...

Page LXIIV

LEGEND SAYS THAT EARLY IN THE 19TH CENTURY, A GERMAN NOBLEMAN NAMED COUNT VON BRUNT SETTLED IN KRAUSTON. SHORTLY AFTER, BEAUTIFUL YOUNG GIRLS STARTED TO VANISH FROM THEIR HOMES, AND IT WAS RUMORED THAT HE HAD TAKEN THE FORM OF A HUGE BAT IN ORDER TO PREY UPON THEM. AROUSED TOWNS-PEOPLE DROVE HIM FROM THE REGION AFTER WOUNDING HIM SEVERELY. HIS DEATH WAS ASSUMED SINCE HE DID NOT RETURN AND OVER A CENTURY HAS PASSED. HOWEVER, HIS BODY WAS NEVER FOUND.

3

WITHIN KEN'S MIND GREW THE MEMORY OF AN OLD MAN CAPTIVATED BY BETH'S BEAUTY-- OF A STRANGE CLAW! IT COULDN'T BE -- BUT--

IT'S --INCREDIBLE! HANS BRUNT--THE NIGHT MANAGER-- AND COUNT VON BRUNT--WHO VANISHED OVER A CENTURY AGO! A-- A VAMPIRE! BUT THAT WOULD EXPLAIN THE STRANGE FEAR THE POLICE SHOWED! WELL, IF THEY WON'T DO ANYTHING ABOUT IT, I WILL! I'LL FIND BETH IF IT'S THE LAST THING I DO!

SHH-H!

BACK AT THE HOTEL ∴

HOW DARE YOU BREAK INTO MY ROOM THIS WAY? GET OUT-- OR I'LL CALL THE POLICE!

THAT BANDAGE ON YOUR FINGER, BRUNT-- DOES IT CONCEAL A MISSING FINGERNAIL? GO AHEAD AND CALL THE POLICE-- MAYBE THEY'LL RETURN A CLAW THAT FITS!

AND THIS HANDKERCHIEF ON THE TABLE-- BETH'S! HOW DO YOU EXPLAIN THAT?

I-- I FOUND IT-- I WAS GOING TO TAKE IT TO HEADQUARTERS! WHAT ARE YOU ACCUSING ME OF, YOUNG MAN?

I'M ACCUSING YOU-- COUNT VON BRUNT-- OF THE ABDUCTION OF MY WIFE -- AND HER PROBABLE MURDER! MAYBE I HAVEN'T GOT ANY REAL EVIDENCE, BUT WHEN I GIVE THE POLICE THESE EXTRA FACTS IN THE MORNING, THEY MAY COME UP WITH ENOUGH TO HANG YOU!

THINK SO, EH? WE'LL SEE!

THAT NIGHT, KEN'S SLEEP WAS TROUBLED! ODD, NIGHTMARE VISIONS FLITTED THROUGH HIS TORTURED MIND! AND, FLITTING, CAME A VISION THAT WAS REAL -- THE AWFUL SHAPE OF A HUGE BAT!

A SIXTH SENSE WARNED THE SLEEPING MAN, BROUGHT HIM TO WAKEFULNESS--- IN THE NICK OF TIME!

HOLY HANNAH! THAT THING---IT---IT'S MONSTROUS!

4

ONLY A BOTTLE OF INK TO THROW AT IT-- AND I *MISSED*, DRAT IT! THERE IT GOES! NOW TO GET DOWNSTAIRS AND SEE IF OLD BRUNT IS AROUND! IF HE *ISN'T*, IT SPELLS *ANOTHER LINK* IN MY CASE!

OH, BRUNT-- BRUNT! WHERE ARE YOU?

GOOD-- HE'S NOT HERE! THAT *COULD* MEAN--

BUT THE NEXT MOMENT...

DID YOU CALL, MR. CUMMINGS? I WAS SITTING OUT ON THE PORCH-- WARM NIGHT FOR THIS TIME OF YEAR!

ER-- I HAD A NIGHTMARE, THAT'S ALL!

GUESS MY IMAGINATION MUST'VE BEEN RUNNING WILD! THERE'RE NO SUCH THINGS AS VAMPIRES-- I'LL HAVE TO SEARCH FOR A NEW CLUE TO BETH'S DISAPPEARANCE!

AND SO KEN RETURNED TO BED, CERTAIN HE'D MADE A FOOL OF HIMSELF! BUT NEXT MORNING, AS BRUNT WENT OFF DUTY...

OH, MR. BRUNT-- I WANT TO APOLOGIZE FOR --

WHAT! ON HIS COLLAR-- INK STAINS! THEN-- I *DIDN'T* MISS LAST NIGHT! BUT IF I'M GOING TO BE *SURE*-- THERE'S *ONE MORE TEST* TO MAKE!

CAUTIOUSLY, KEN MANEUVERED TO GET OLD BRUNT WITHIN RANGE OF A LARGE, FULL-LENGTH MIRROR! AND WITHIN IT HE SAW ONLY HIS OWN IMAGE! FOR A VAMPIRE HAS NO REFLECTION!

WE ALL MAKE MISTAKES, MR. CUMMINGS! NO HARD FEELINGS!

THERE'S-- NO DOUBT ABOUT IT NOW! I'M SHAKING HANDS WITH *COUNT VON BRUNT*-- A DEADLY VAMPIRE OUT OF THE PAST!

THERE WAS ONE THING HE HAD TO DO NOW-- *TRAIL THE EERIE KILLER TO HIS LAIR!*

PERHAPS IT ISN'T TOO LATE, AFTER ALL! MAYBE MY BETH IS *ALIVE*-- AND THIS FIEND WILL LEAD ME TO HER!

5

THROUGH A THICK AND GLOOMY FOREST THE TRAIL LED, THROUGH SWAMPLAND AND GLADE! FINALLY, KEN SAW OLD BRUNT DISAPPEAR INTO A RUINED, DESERTED OLD MANSION THAT SEEMED TO BREATHE FORTH THE AURA OF THE *UNKNOWN* -- OF DEATH ITSELF!

I'VE -- TRACKED THE BEAST TO ITS LAIR! OH, BETH -- BETH DARLING! IF ONLY --

INSIDE, A MAZE OF CRUMBLING CORRIDORS AND COBWEBBED CHAMBERS -- WITH A DARK MENACE BROODING OVERALL!

OLD BRUNT SEEMS TO HAVE DISAPPEARED -- WHICH SHOULD MAKE MY SEARCH EASIER!

ROOM AFTER ROOM -- *NOTHING!* AND FINALLY, IN A VAULTED CHAMBER DEEP WITHIN THE OLD PILE, KEN FOUND -- *TRAGEDY!*

GREAT HEAVENS -- IT'S *BETH!* AND SHE'S *BEYOND HUMAN HELP!*

BEHIND HIM, THERE ECHOED A CACKLING DEMONIAC LAUGH! IT WAS THE MAN HE HAD FOLLOWED -- BUT HOW CHANGED! THIS WAS A DEVIL OUT OF THE DEAD PAST! THIS WAS COUNT VON BRUNT -- VAMPIRE!

SO -- NOW YOU *KNOW!* AND BEFORE I KILL *YOU*, YOU'LL KNOW THE POWER OF A *VAMPIRE!* FOR YOU -- YOUR WIFE IS DEAD! BUT FOR *ME*, SHE'LL *RISE AT MY COMMAND!* WATCH!

YOU -- FIEND!

6

A CRISP ORDER-- A COMMANDING GESTURE-- AND A DREADFUL RESULT! FOR THE STILL, COLD FORM STIRS--*RISES!*

BETH-- BETH! YOU'RE NOT DEAD! TELL ME YOU'RE NOT!

YOU'RE TOO LATE, FOOL! SHE'S DEAD-- AND ALREADY A VAMPIRE LIKE MYSELF! TONIGHT SHE WILL ASSUME HER BAT'S SHAPE-- AND GO FORTH TO SEARCH FOR PREY! AND NOTHING YOU CAN DO CAN STOP HER!

IT WAS THEN THAT GRIEF, HATRED, MADE KEN THROW CAUTION TO THE WINDS! IN A HEADLONG, SUICIDAL RUSH--

I'LL STOP IT-- BY RIPPING YOU APART WITH MY BARE HANDS!

BUT OF WHAT USE RAW COURAGE--AGAINST THE *SUPERNATURAL*? WITH AN AWFUL STRENGTH OUT OF THE *UNKNOWN,* THE VAMPIRE STRUCK A MORTAL BLOW!

DIE, YOU FOOL!

OH-HH!

DOWN WENT THE FATALLY-WOUNDED MAN, CLUTCHING AT THE METAL CHAIN THAT EN-GIRDLED HIS WIFE'S WAIST! IT SNAPPED, CAME LOOSE IN HIS HAND--

THIS CHAIN-- MADE OF PURE SILVER-- THE ONLY METAL THAT CAN *KILL A VAMPIRE!* OH, GIVE ME STRENGTH-- GIVE ME STRENGTH!

7

IT WAS A STRENGTH BORN OF DESPERATION-- OF *LOVE!* DYING, KEN FLUNG HIMSELF ON THE SURPRISED VON BRUNT-- AND--

I-- CAN'T LIVE-- BUT I'LL-- *TAKE YOU WITH ME!*

ARGHH!

YES, THE SILVER CHAIN DID ITS WORK WELL-- AND TIME CLAIMED THE MOULDERING BODY OF VON BRUNT! AND AS THE VAMPIRE DREW HIS LAST BREATH--

KEN-- OH, KEN, MY HUSBAND--

HER-- HER VOICE-- AS IF SHE LIVED AGAIN--

OH, BETH, BETH, YOU HEAR-- YOU UNDERSTAND! TAKE ME-- IN YOUR ARMS! ONE LAST KISS BEFORE I--I--

IT'S-- *TOO LATE!* YOU'RE *DYING*-- AND I'M CONDEMNED TO A LIVING DEATH AS A *VAMPIRE-- FOREVER!* GOODBYE, DARLING-- *GOODBYE!*

HE'S-- *DEAD!* AND-- AND ALREADY I FEEL THE OVERPOWERING VAMPIRE URGE WITHIN ME! BUT I STILL HAVE A TRACE OF THE HUMAN-- I'VE NEVER CLAIMED A VICTIM-- I CAN STILL WEEP! PERHAPS I STILL HAVE ENOUGH MORTAL LOVE WITHIN ME TO SAVE US BOTH! I MUST TRY-- *TRY!*

THEN IT WAS THAT THE CURSE OF THE VAMPIRE TOOK EFFECT, AND WHAT HAD ONCE BEEN A LOVELY WOMAN BECAME-- A FLITTING *BAT!* WAS IT TOO LATE-- WAS BETH EMBARKED ON HER GRISLY MISSION? *NO!* THE REMNANTS OF A HUMAN HEART SURGING STRONGLY WITHIN HER, SHE SOARED TO THE VAULTED CEILING! THEN, IN A SINGLE, SWIFT, SUICIDAL PLUNGE, SHE CRASHED DOWNWARDS-- JOINING HER HUSBAND IN EVERLASTING DEATH!

CRASH!

AND THUS IT WAS THAT TRUE LOVE CONQUERED THE VAMPIRE'S EVIL, AND EMERGED TRIUMPHANT! NOW, FINALLY, THE SOULS OF BETH AND KEN WERE AT PEACE AND THEY FACED ETERNITY-- TOGETHER-- FOR ALWAYS!

THE END

8

30

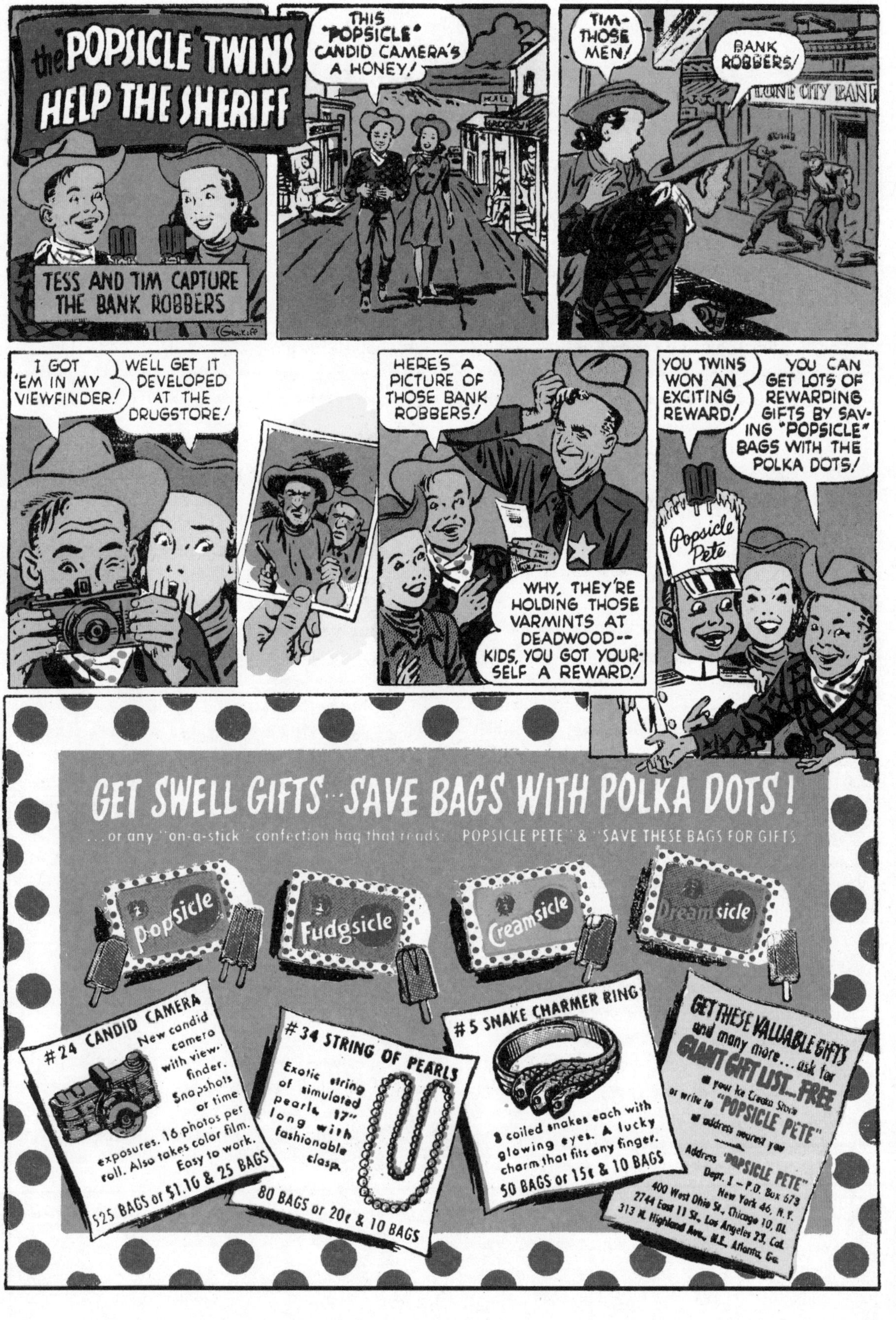
the "POPSICLE" TWINS HELP THE SHERIFF
TESS AND TIM CAPTURE THE BANK ROBBERS
THIS "POPSICLE" CANDID CAMERA'S A HONEY!
TIM– THOSE MEN!
BANK ROBBERS!
LONE CITY BANK
I GOT 'EM IN MY VIEWFINDER!
WE'LL GET IT DEVELOPED AT THE DRUGSTORE!
HERE'S A PICTURE OF THOSE BANK ROBBERS!
WHY, THEY'RE HOLDING THOSE VARMINTS AT DEADWOOD-- KIDS, YOU GOT YOURSELF A REWARD!
YOU TWINS WON AN EXCITING REWARD!
YOU CAN GET LOTS OF REWARDING GIFTS BY SAVING "POPSICLE" BAGS WITH THE POLKA DOTS!
Popsicle Pete
GET SWELL GIFTS...SAVE BAGS WITH POLKA DOTS!
...or any "on-a-stick" confection bag that reads: "POPSICLE PETE" & "SAVE THESE BAGS FOR GIFTS"
Popsicle
Fudgsicle
Creamsicle
Dreamsicle
#24 CANDID CAMERA
New candid camera with view-finder. Snapshots or time exposures. 16 photos per roll. Also takes color film. Easy to work.
525 BAGS or $1.10 & 25 BAGS
#34 STRING OF PEARLS
Exotic string of simulated pearls 17" long with fashionable clasp.
80 BAGS or 20¢ & 10 BAGS
#5 SNAKE CHARMER RING
3 coiled snakes each with glowing eyes. A lucky charm that fits any finger.
50 BAGS or 15¢ & 10 BAGS
GET THESE VALUABLE GIFTS and many more... ask for GIANT GIFT LIST...FREE
at your Ice Cream Store or write to "POPSICLE PETE" at address nearest you
Address "POPSICLE PETE"
Dept. I – P.O. Box 673
New York 46, N.Y.
400 West Ohio St., Chicago 10, Ill.
2744 East 11 St., Los Angeles 23, Cal.
313 N. Highland Ave., N.E. Atlanta, Ga.

From YOUR EDITOR—to YOU!

GREETINGS, ALL YOU fans of the great *Supernatural*—special greetings, since this is the first time that we're meeting in the pages of a brand-new, actionful and challenging magazine. Welcome to *"Forbidden Worlds"*—and may our friendship be both long and rewarding!

As friends-to-be, we can talk plainly. So let's start off by saying that this isn't just another magazine. It's a *special* kind of publication—for *special* people! For a long time, your editor has known that the dread realm of the *Unknown* exercised a magnetic fascination over thinking people—that the Supernatural thronged with thrills and chills that challenged the imagination as does no other subject. It was this thought that gave rise to the creation of our great companion magazine, *"Adventures Into The Unknown"*. And the astounding success of this original publication left no room for doubt. This was what the public wanted—and we gave it to them! We delved deeply into weird and eerie subjects—came up with strange, fascinating stories that packed an out-of-the-world punch—and fans flocked to our bandwagon! They demanded greater frequency of issue, and we gave it to them in the shape of a hard-hitting and thrilling monthly magazine. But this wasn't enough—they cried out for a companion publication to *"Adventures Into The Unknown"*—and now we're providing it in the form of *"Forbidden Worlds"*!

So here it is—your own special magazine—chockful of the very thrilling fare we've learned you want! We *dare* you to read each and every issue of this startling new publication—to venture into forbidden, *Unknown* worlds! And as you read, you'll watch the Supernatural come alive! You'll meet ghosts, zombies, werewolves, vam-

pires—you'll chill to black magic from beyond life itself—you'll gasp at stranger things than ever the mind of man conceived!

A tall order? Maybe—but we've got the know-how to deliver! Read the stories in this issue, and let them speak for themselves. There's *"Demon of Destruction"*, one of the most imaginative and spine-chilling stories in years, and a sample of the type of fare we'll try to bring you. There's *"Love of A Vampire"*, a thrilling adventure into old folk-lore guaranteed to keep you glued to the edge of your seat. There's *"The Way of the Werewolf"*, which plummets you into a gasp-laden epic of supernatural exploit. And let's not overlook *"The Monster Doll"*, an eerie and challenging effort you won't soon forget! These and others make up our first issue—from us—to you!

We hope that you'll like this initial attempt, as well as the others which will follow. But we'll have no way of knowing unless you tell us! Won't you please write us, informing us as to what stories you like, as well as those you don't go for? And let us know what you'd wish to see in future issues! Address your letters to:

The Editor
Forbidden Worlds
45 West 45th Street
New York 19, N. Y.

We'll reprint whatever letters space will allow in later issues. And until we meet again on this page, so long—from the magazine that *dares* to be different—that dares to *tell all!*

Don't miss our companion publication—*"Adventures Into The Unknown"*!

The WAY of the WEREWOLF

DO YOU CONSIDER THE UNKNOWN JUST A PASSING THRILL THAT CAN BE LEFT SAFELY IN THE SHADOWS AT MIDNIGHT...A GLIMPSE OF THE TERROR THAT HAS GRIPPED NAMELESS PEOPLE IN SOME TIMELESS AGE? THEN WAIT...WAIT FOR THE DARK HOUR THAT BRINGS ONDOK...HIS FANGED MUZZLE RAISED IN A BAYING SUMMONS...HIS RED-RIMMED EYES LURING YOU TO THE WAY OF THE WEREWOLF!

ONE AFTERNOON...AT THE DAILY HERALD...

THE LACK OF SENSATIONAL NEWS MAKES THIS A NICE TOWN TO LIVE IN, ROY...BUT IT'S MURDER FOR A REPORTER TRYING TO DIG UP SOMETHING THAT'LL MAKE THE HEADLINES!

I'M WONDERING...MAYBE WE CAN RING IN THAT WEIRD PLAGUE OF MAN-EATING WOLVES THAT ARE SWEEPING THROUGH THE VILLAGES OF CENTRAL INDIA!

YOU KNOW, ROY...THAT'S AN ANGLE LOADED WITH QUESTION MARKS! HORRIBLE AS THOSE WOLF RAIDS ARE, THERE'S SOMETHING EVEN MORE SIGNIFICANT THAN PEOPLE BEING DRAGGED FROM THEIR BEDS...NAMELY, WHY HASN'T IT HAPPENED BEFORE?

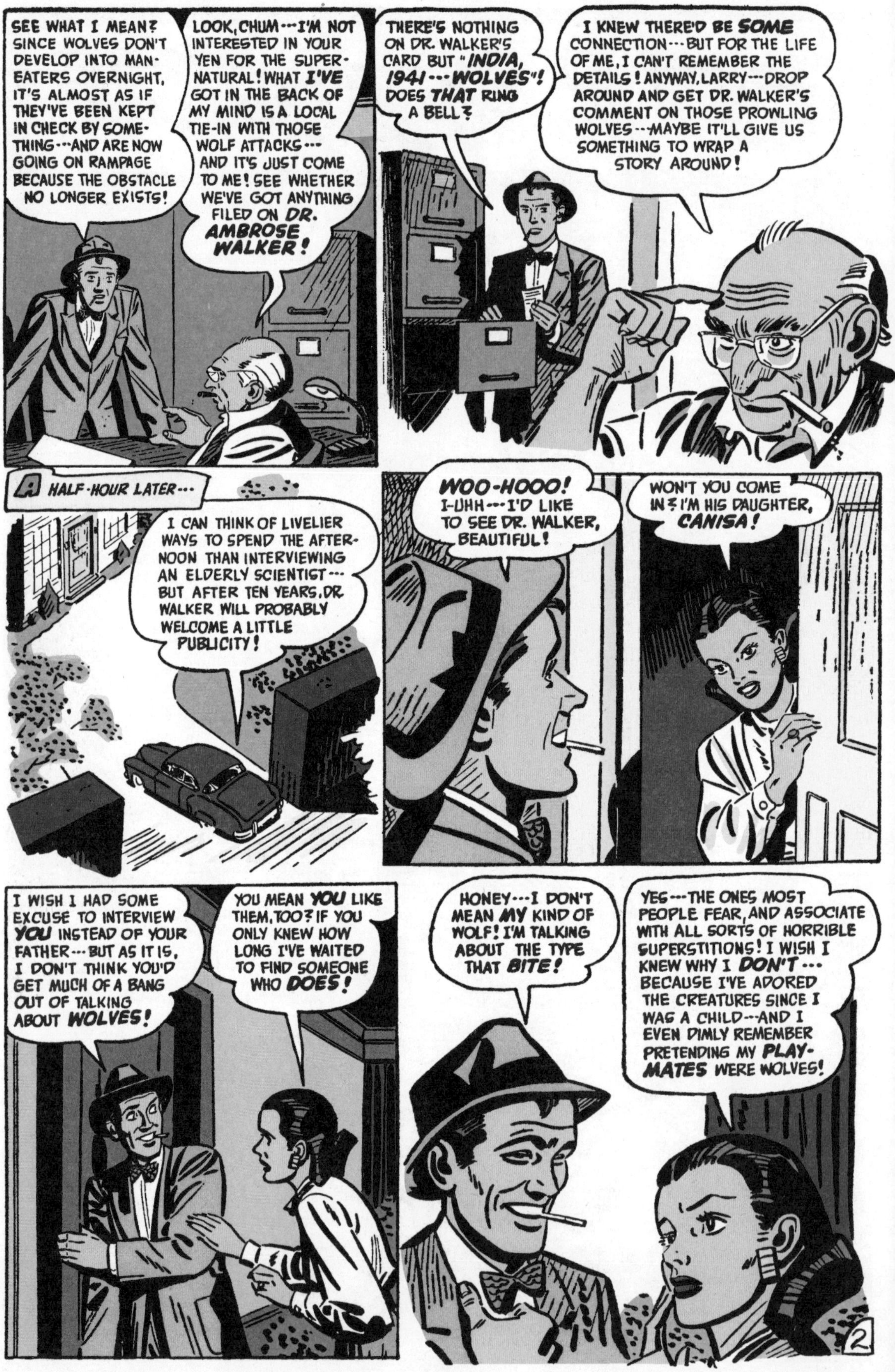
SEE WHAT I MEAN? SINCE WOLVES DON'T DEVELOP INTO MAN-EATERS OVERNIGHT, IT'S ALMOST AS IF THEY'VE BEEN KEPT IN CHECK BY SOMETHING---AND ARE NOW GOING ON RAMPAGE BECAUSE THE OBSTACLE NO LONGER EXISTS!
LOOK, CHUM---I'M NOT INTERESTED IN YOUR YEN FOR THE SUPERNATURAL! WHAT I'VE GOT IN THE BACK OF MY MIND IS A LOCAL TIE-IN WITH THOSE WOLF ATTACKS---AND IT'S JUST COME TO ME! SEE WHETHER WE'VE GOT ANYTHING FILED ON DR. AMBROSE WALKER!
THERE'S NOTHING ON DR. WALKER'S CARD BUT "INDIA, 1941---WOLVES"! DOES THAT RING A BELL?
I KNEW THERE'D BE SOME CONNECTION---BUT FOR THE LIFE OF ME, I CAN'T REMEMBER THE DETAILS! ANYWAY, LARRY---DROP AROUND AND GET DR. WALKER'S COMMENT ON THOSE PROWLING WOLVES---MAYBE IT'LL GIVE US SOMETHING TO WRAP A STORY AROUND!
A HALF-HOUR LATER---
I CAN THINK OF LIVELIER WAYS TO SPEND THE AFTERNOON THAN INTERVIEWING AN ELDERLY SCIENTIST---BUT AFTER TEN YEARS, DR. WALKER WILL PROBABLY WELCOME A LITTLE PUBLICITY!
WOO-HOOO! I-UHH---I'D LIKE TO SEE DR. WALKER, BEAUTIFUL!
WON'T YOU COME IN? I'M HIS DAUGHTER, CANISA!
I WISH I HAD SOME EXCUSE TO INTERVIEW YOU INSTEAD OF YOUR FATHER---BUT AS IT IS, I DON'T THINK YOU'D GET MUCH OF A BANG OUT OF TALKING ABOUT WOLVES!
YOU MEAN YOU LIKE THEM, TOO? IF YOU ONLY KNEW HOW LONG I'VE WAITED TO FIND SOMEONE WHO DOES!
HONEY---I DON'T MEAN MY KIND OF WOLF! I'M TALKING ABOUT THE TYPE THAT BITE!
YES---THE ONES MOST PEOPLE FEAR, AND ASSOCIATE WITH ALL SORTS OF HORRIBLE SUPERSTITIONS! I WISH I KNEW WHY I DON'T---BECAUSE I'VE ADORED THE CREATURES SINCE I WAS A CHILD---AND I EVEN DIMLY REMEMBER PRETENDING MY PLAYMATES WERE WOLVES!
2

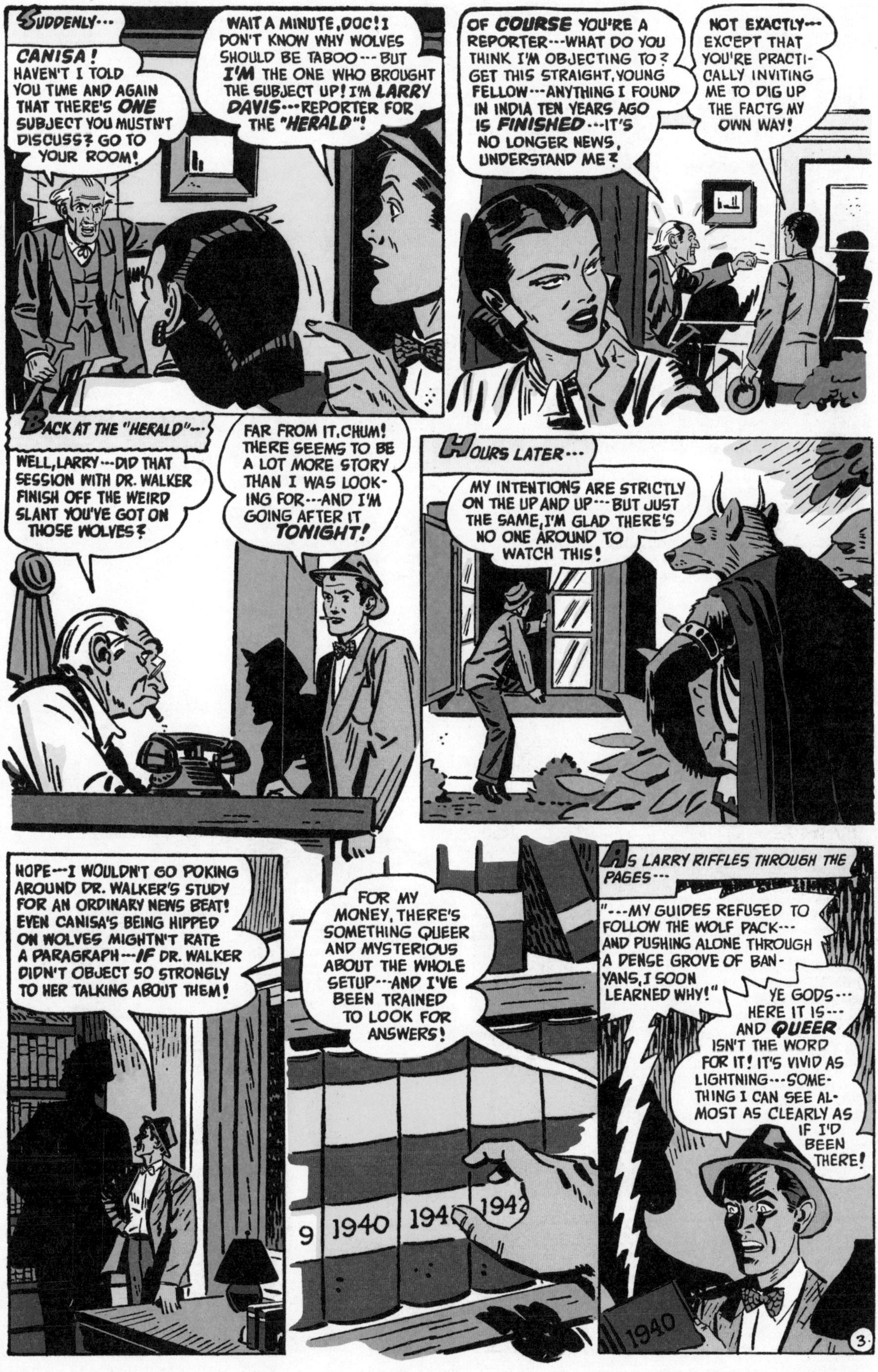
SUDDENLY---
CANISA! HAVEN'T I TOLD YOU TIME AND AGAIN THAT THERE'S ONE SUBJECT YOU MUSTN'T DISCUSS? GO TO YOUR ROOM!
WAIT A MINUTE, DOC! I DON'T KNOW WHY WOLVES SHOULD BE TABOO --- BUT I'M THE ONE WHO BROUGHT THE SUBJECT UP! I'M LARRY DAVIS --- REPORTER FOR THE "HERALD"!
OF COURSE YOU'RE A REPORTER --- WHAT DO YOU THINK I'M OBJECTING TO? GET THIS STRAIGHT, YOUNG FELLOW --- ANYTHING I FOUND IN INDIA TEN YEARS AGO IS FINISHED --- IT'S NO LONGER NEWS, UNDERSTAND ME?
NOT EXACTLY --- EXCEPT THAT YOU'RE PRACTICALLY INVITING ME TO DIG UP THE FACTS MY OWN WAY!
BACK AT THE "HERALD"---
WELL, LARRY --- DID THAT SESSION WITH DR. WALKER FINISH OFF THE WEIRD SLANT YOU'VE GOT ON THOSE WOLVES?
FAR FROM IT, CHUM! THERE SEEMS TO BE A LOT MORE STORY THAN I WAS LOOKING FOR --- AND I'M GOING AFTER IT TONIGHT!
HOURS LATER---
MY INTENTIONS ARE STRICTLY ON THE UP AND UP --- BUT JUST THE SAME, I'M GLAD THERE'S NO ONE AROUND TO WATCH THIS!
HOPE --- I WOULDN'T GO POKING AROUND DR. WALKER'S STUDY FOR AN ORDINARY NEWS BEAT! EVEN CANISA'S BEING HIPPED ON WOLVES MIGHTN'T RATE A PARAGRAPH --- IF DR. WALKER DIDN'T OBJECT SO STRONGLY TO HER TALKING ABOUT THEM!
FOR MY MONEY, THERE'S SOMETHING QUEER AND MYSTERIOUS ABOUT THE WHOLE SETUP --- AND I'VE BEEN TRAINED TO LOOK FOR ANSWERS!
9 1940 1941 1942
AS LARRY RIFFLES THROUGH THE PAGES---
"---MY GUIDES REFUSED TO FOLLOW THE WOLF PACK --- AND PUSHING ALONE THROUGH A DENSE GROVE OF BANYANS, I SOON LEARNED WHY!"
YE GODS --- HERE IT IS --- AND QUEER ISN'T THE WORD FOR IT! IT'S VIVID AS LIGHTNING --- SOMETHING I CAN SEE ALMOST AS CLEARLY AS IF I'D BEEN THERE!
1940
3.

"THERE WAS A BURROW UNDER THE TOWERING ROOTS...AND FROM IT CAME A SOUND...HIGH PITCHED AND UNMISTAKABLE!"

IT'S INCREDIBLE...BUT THAT WAS A HUMAN VOICE! *THERE'S A CHILD DOWN IN THAT HOLE!*

"A CHILD? YES, SHE SOUNDED LIKE *ONE*...SHE EVEN REMOTELY *LOOKED* LIKE ONE...BUT THE WRITHING CREATURE I DREW FROM THE DEN FOUGHT WITH THE SAVAGERY OF A SNAPPING BEAST!"

EASY...EASY...I CERTAINLY HOPE MY TONE QUIETS HER DOWN ...BECAUSE *LANGUAGE* DOESN'T MEAN A THING TO HER!

ARRRRGH!

"SOMETHING KEPT TELLING ME I HAD MADE A MISTAKE...AND THE FEELING MOUNTED WHEN I CARRIED HER, STRUGGLING, TO THE NEAREST VILLAGE!"

TAKE HER BACK, *SAHIB!* LET HER BE CLAIMED BY HIM WHOSE MARK IS UPON HER!

YOU MEAN YOU'RE WILLING TO SEE THE LITTLE WRETCH STAY WITH *WOLVES?* IF SHE BEARS A MARK, IT'S FROM HUNGER AND PRIVATION ...AND I'M GOING TO DO SOMETHING ABOUT IT! IT'S A DUTY ...A DUTY TO A FELLOW HUMAN!

"HOW MANY TIMES BEFORE HAD I LAUGHED AT SUPERSTITION...ONLY TO LISTEN NOW, IN THE PANTING DUSK, WITH A JAB OF TERROR?"

NO, SAHIB...NOT HUMAN! A GIRL REARED BY THE PACK WILL BE CLAIMED AS *BRIDE* BY THE LEADER OF THE WEREWOLVES! THE WOLVES HATE THESE WEREWOLF FIENDS, AND WILL NOT APPROACH A VILLAGE AROUND WHICH THEY LURK!

"I'VE THOUGHT IT OVER FOR A WEEK...KNOWING HOW DEEPLY ROOTED THE WEREWOLF LEGEND IS...AND YET THRUSTING IT OUT OF MY MIND WHENEVER I LOOK INTO THE CHILD'S QUESTIONING EYES! NOW THAT SHE HAS BEGUN TO TRUST ME, I HAVE NO CHOICE...SHE HAS BOTH A *CURSE* AND THE MEMORY OF A BRUTE EXISTENCE TO OUTGROW...BUT I WILL TAKE HER BACK TO THE STATES AS MY DAUGHTER...AND I WILL CALL HER *CANISA*..."

WOLVES...GOOD LORD... NO WONDER THE POOR OLD DEVIL DIDN'T WANT HER TALKING ABOUT THEM! AND AS FOR THAT *WEREWOLF* NONSENSE...

AS ONE SHAGGY SHADOW FOLLOWS ANOTHER ACROSS THE WALL--

FOR A MOMENT, I THOUGHT MY IMAGINATION'S HOPPED UP BY WHAT I READ---BUT THAT CREEP IN THE CAPE IS *OPENING THE FRONT DOOR!* THEY'RE AFTER SOMETHING---SOMETHING THEY'RE SURE THEY'LL FIND *HERE*--- CANISA!

A MOMENT LATER---

GOOD HEAVENS--- WHAT ARE *YOU* DOING HERE AT THIS HOUR?

HONEY---THIS IS NO TIME FOR EXPLANATIONS! WOLVES---DEMONS---*WHATEVER* THEY ARE, THEY'RE COMING!

WOLVES! YOU CAN'T BE SERIOUS ---BUT THERE'S NOTHING TO FEAR FROM *THEM!*

NO? WHAT'S *THAT* SOUND LIKE?

AAAAGH!

HAA HA HA! DID YOU THINK YOU COULD CHEAT *ONDOK*, DR. WALKER---AFTER HE WAITED TEN YEARS TO CLAIM WHAT IS HIS?

THAT VOICE! IT'S *SPEAKING*--- BUT IT'S ALMOST A GROWL---THE SOUND OF A *BEAST!*

OR A *WOLF?* CANISA, YOU'D BETTER NOT FACE THIS! GET BACK TO YOUR ROOM ---AND LOCK THE DOOR!

NO! SOMETHING *DREADFUL* HAS HAPPENED TO FATHER---AND I'VE *GOT TO FIND OUT!*

SOMETHING DREADFUL---DREADFUL BEYOND ANY WORDS---BEYOND ANY FORGETTING!

FOOL! TAKING HER FROM ME HAS COST YOU TEN YEARS OF NIGHTMARES ---AND TRYING TO KEEP HER HAS COST YOU YOUR LIFE!

FATHER!

FRONT DOOR--- FAST!

POW!

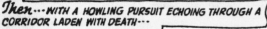

Then---WITH A HOWLING PURSUIT ECHOING THROUGH A CORRIDOR LADEN WITH DEATH---

AAOOO! AAOOO!

SECONDS LATER---

ARRRGH!

POW!

WITH HIS FURRY FACE A MASK OF LIVING VENOM---

TWELVE THOUSAND MILES FROM INDIA---AND STILL ONDOK FOUND HER! HOW FAR CAN YOU TAKE HER--- HOW LONG CAN YOU FLEE ---BEFORE ONDOK FINDS HER AGAIN?

FATHER---FATHER! WHAT DO THOSE HIDEOUS FIENDS WANT---WHY DID THEY KILL HIM?

THERE'S NO USE LOOKING FOR REASONS, CANISA ---IT HAPPENED! WHAT MATTERS NOW IS THAT YOU'VE GOT TO BEAR UP---SO THAT NOTHING ELSE HAPPENS!

6.

THEN IT *WASN'T* JUST A CHANCE OUTBURST OF EVIL? THOSE CREATURES REALLY *ARE* SEARCHING ···FOR *ME*?

HONEY···IT'S WILD, AND CRAZY, AND FANTASTIC···BUT THAT'S THE WAY IT STACKS UP! FINDING A WAY TO FORESTALL THOSE CREEPS IS GOING TO KEEP ME BUSY FOR THE REST OF THE NIGHT···AND MEANWHILE, I WANT YOU TO STAY PUT AT MY PLACE!

SOON AFTERWARD···

IF HE'S IN SUCH A PLACE AS THE SPIRIT WORLD··· DR. WALKER CAN BE HAPPY FOR HAVING DONE A GOOD JOB! SHE DOESN'T REMEMBER···SHE DOESN'T KNOW *WHY* ONDOK IS AFTER *HER*··· AND SHE'LL NEVER LEARN FROM *ME*!

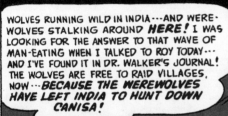

WOLVES RUNNING WILD IN INDIA····AND WEREWOLVES STALKING AROUND *HERE*! I WAS LOOKING FOR THE ANSWER TO THAT WAVE OF MAN-EATING WHEN I TALKED TO ROY TODAY···AND I'VE FOUND IT IN DR. WALKER'S JOURNAL! THE WOLVES ARE FREE TO RAID VILLAGES, NOW···*BECAUSE THE WEREWOLVES HAVE LEFT INDIA TO HUNT DOWN CANISA*!

HERALD BUILDING

CAN I PUT ANY STOCK IN WHAT THAT NATIVE SAID···THAT *WOLVES HATE THESE FIENDS*? IT'LL MEAN TAKING A HAIR-RAISING CHANCE···*BUT I'M GOING AHEAD WITH IT*!

YOU MUST BE CLEAN WORN OUT AFTER KEEPING ME HERE ALL NIGHT WAITING FOR A ROUTINE STORY, PAL! IS THERE ANY LITTLE FAVOR YOU'D LIKE TO ASK BEFORE YOU'RE *FIRED*?

YEP! I WANT YOU TO LEND ME AN ARTIST TO MAKE A SKETCH I CAN TAKE TO A COSTUME COMPANY···AND *THEN* I WANT YOU TO BOOK ME WITH THE CITY ENGINEER FIRST THING IN THE MORNING!

THE FOLLOWING NIGHT···

IT DOESN'T MATTER ANY LONGER *WHY* THEY'RE COMING ···IF I ONLY KNEW *WHEN*!

SUPPOSE YOU LET *ME* WORRY ABOUT THAT? TRY TO GET SOME REST, CANISA···AND REMEMBER ····YOU PROMISED TO COUNT ON ME NO MATTER *WHAT* HAPPENS!

7

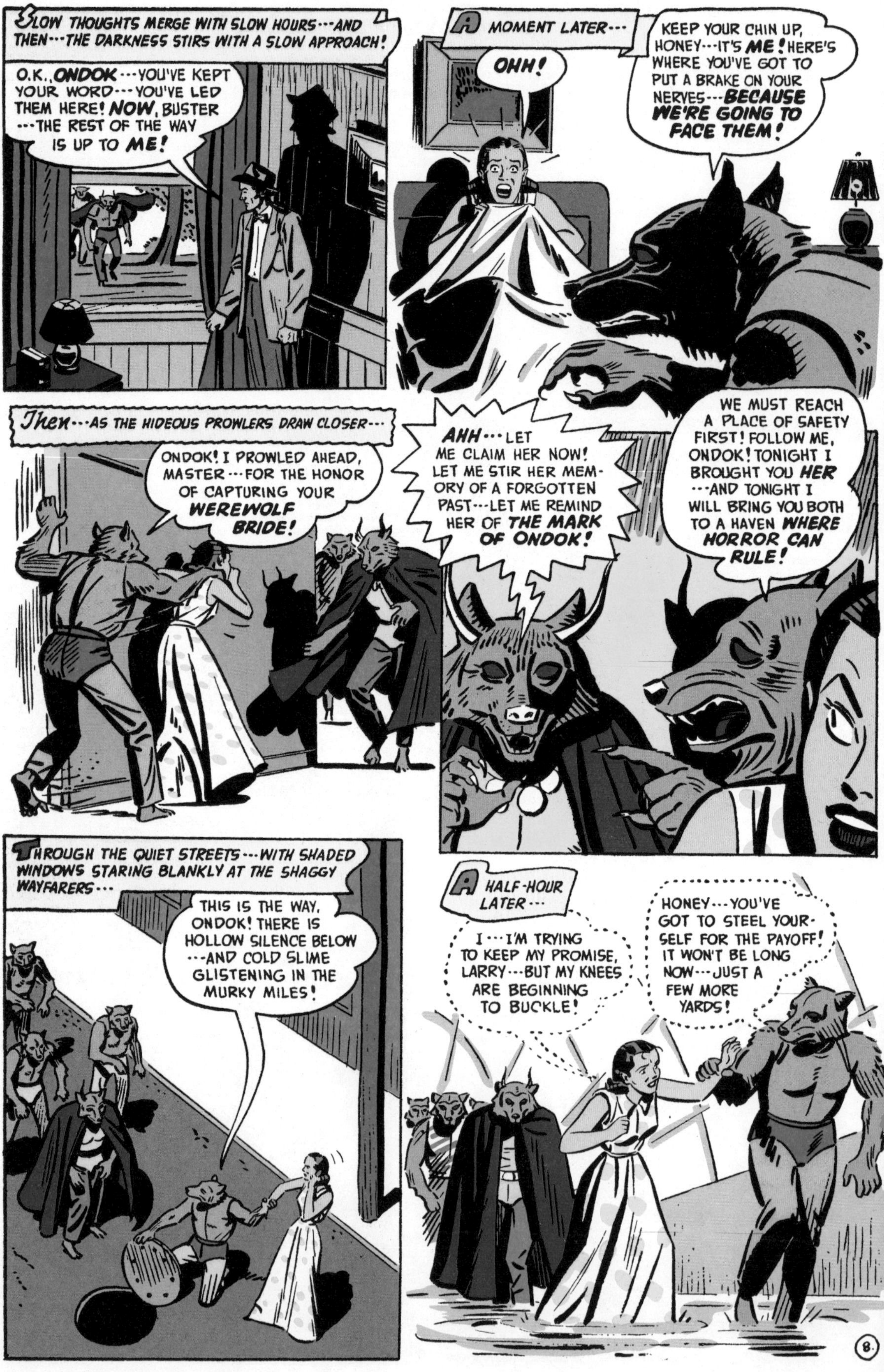
SLOW THOUGHTS MERGE WITH SLOW HOURS---AND THEN---THE DARKNESS STIRS WITH A SLOW APPROACH!
O.K., ONDOK---YOU'VE KEPT YOUR WORD---YOU'VE LED THEM HERE! NOW, BUSTER ---THE REST OF THE WAY IS UP TO ME!
A MOMENT LATER---
OHH!
KEEP YOUR CHIN UP, HONEY---IT'S ME! HERE'S WHERE YOU'VE GOT TO PUT A BRAKE ON YOUR NERVES---BECAUSE WE'RE GOING TO FACE THEM!
Then---AS THE HIDEOUS PROWLERS DRAW CLOSER---
ONDOK! I PROWLED AHEAD, MASTER---FOR THE HONOR OF CAPTURING YOUR WEREWOLF BRIDE!
AHH---LET ME CLAIM HER NOW! LET ME STIR HER MEMORY OF A FORGOTTEN PAST---LET ME REMIND HER OF THE MARK OF ONDOK!
WE MUST REACH A PLACE OF SAFETY FIRST! FOLLOW ME, ONDOK! TONIGHT I BROUGHT YOU HER ---AND TONIGHT I WILL BRING YOU BOTH TO A HAVEN WHERE HORROR CAN RULE!
THROUGH THE QUIET STREETS---WITH SHADED WINDOWS STARING BLANKLY AT THE SHAGGY WAYFARERS---
THIS IS THE WAY, ONDOK! THERE IS HOLLOW SILENCE BELOW ---AND COLD SLIME GLISTENING IN THE MURKY MILES!
A HALF-HOUR LATER---
I---I'M TRYING TO KEEP MY PROMISE, LARRY---BUT MY KNEES ARE BEGINNING TO BUCKLE!
HONEY---YOU'VE GOT TO STEEL YOURSELF FOR THE PAYOFF! IT WON'T BE LONG NOW---JUST A FEW MORE YARDS!
8

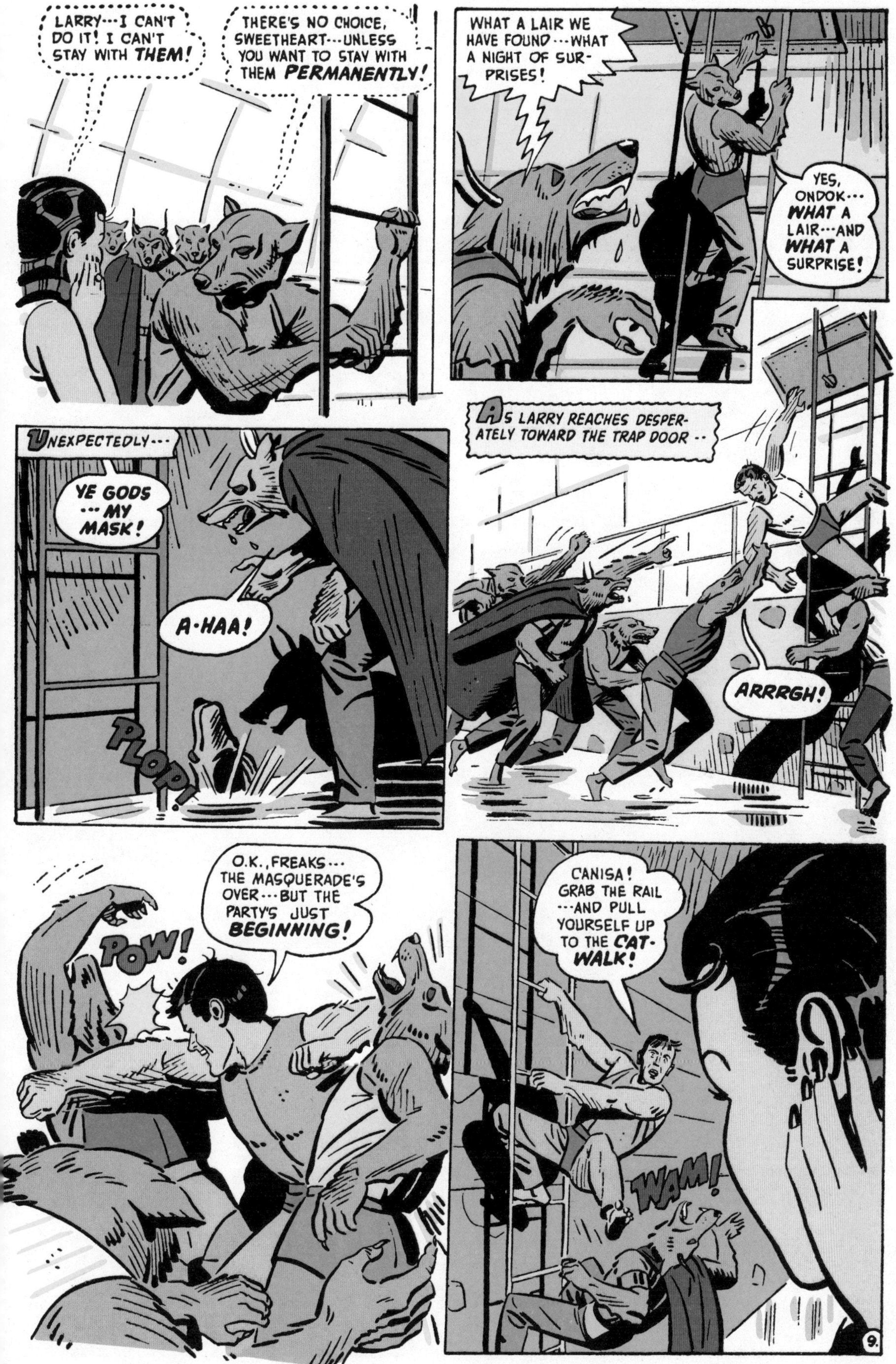
LARRY···I CAN'T DO IT! I CAN'T STAY WITH THEM!
THERE'S NO CHOICE, SWEETHEART···UNLESS YOU WANT TO STAY WITH THEM PERMANENTLY!
WHAT A LAIR WE HAVE FOUND···WHAT A NIGHT OF SUR-PRISES!
YES, ONDOK··· WHAT A LAIR···AND WHAT A SURPRISE!
UNEXPECTEDLY···
YE GODS ··· MY MASK!
A-HAA!
PLOP!
AS LARRY REACHES DESPER-ATELY TOWARD THE TRAP DOOR --
ARRRGH!
POW!
O.K., FREAKS··· THE MASQUERADE'S OVER···BUT THE PARTY'S JUST BEGINNING!
CANISA! GRAB THE RAIL ···AND PULL YOURSELF UP TO THE CAT-WALK!
WAM!
9.

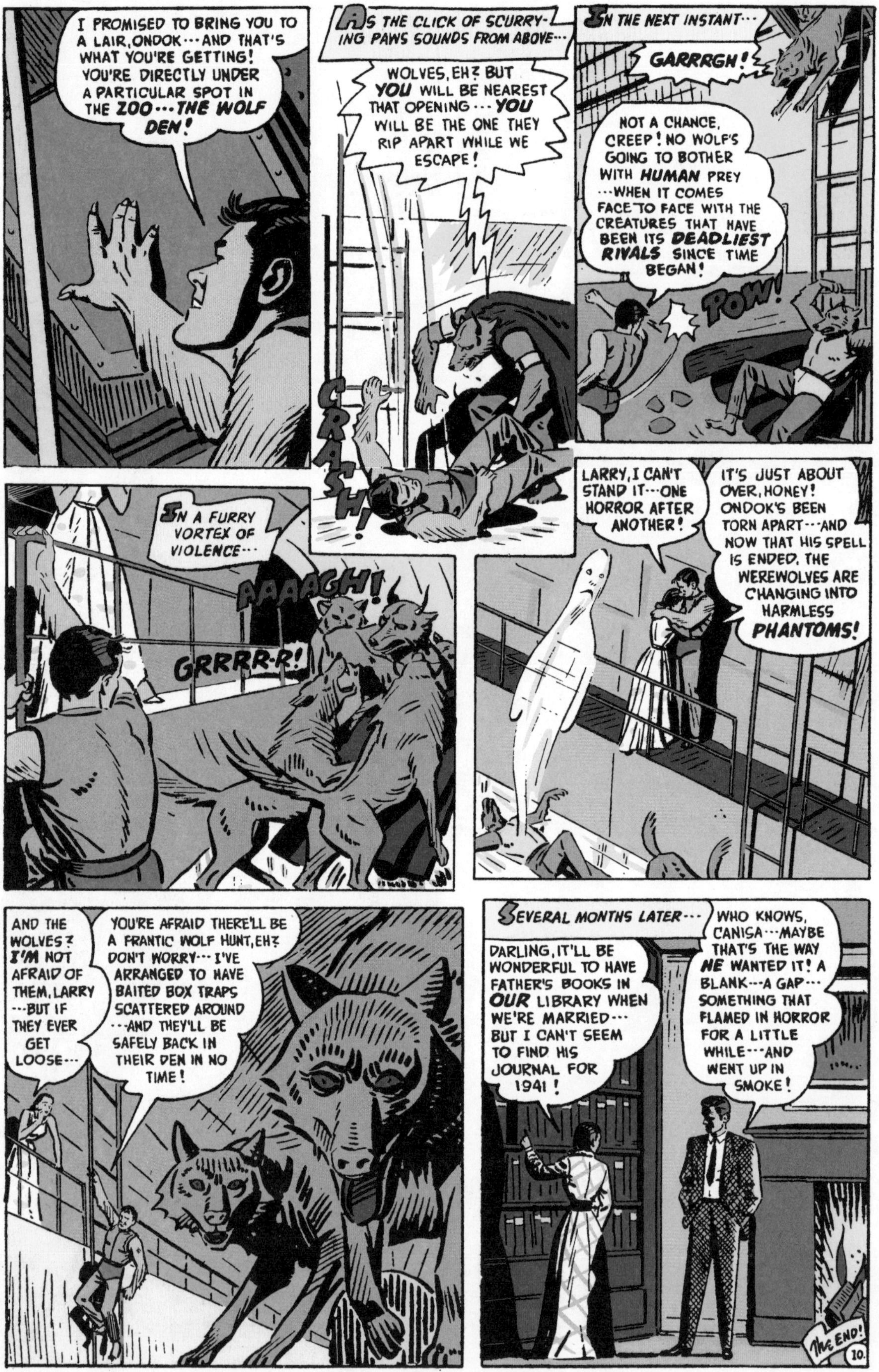
I PROMISED TO BRING YOU TO A LAIR, ONDOK --- AND THAT'S WHAT YOU'RE GETTING! YOU'RE DIRECTLY UNDER A PARTICULAR SPOT IN THE ZOO --- THE WOLF DEN!
AS THE CLICK OF SCURRYING PAWS SOUNDS FROM ABOVE ---
WOLVES, EH? BUT YOU WILL BE NEAREST THAT OPENING --- YOU WILL BE THE ONE THEY RIP APART WHILE WE ESCAPE!
CRASH!
IN THE NEXT INSTANT ---
GARRRGH!
NOT A CHANCE, CREEP! NO WOLF'S GOING TO BOTHER WITH HUMAN PREY --- WHEN IT COMES FACE TO FACE WITH THE CREATURES THAT HAVE BEEN ITS DEADLIEST RIVALS SINCE TIME BEGAN!
POW!
IN A FURRY VORTEX OF VIOLENCE ---
AAAAGH!
GRRRR-R!
LARRY, I CAN'T STAND IT --- ONE HORROR AFTER ANOTHER!
IT'S JUST ABOUT OVER, HONEY! ONDOK'S BEEN TORN APART --- AND NOW THAT HIS SPELL IS ENDED, THE WEREWOLVES ARE CHANGING INTO HARMLESS PHANTOMS!
AND THE WOLVES? I'M NOT AFRAID OF THEM, LARRY --- BUT IF THEY EVER GET LOOSE ---
YOU'RE AFRAID THERE'LL BE A FRANTIC WOLF HUNT, EH? DON'T WORRY --- I'VE ARRANGED TO HAVE BAITED BOX TRAPS SCATTERED AROUND --- AND THEY'LL BE SAFELY BACK IN THEIR DEN IN NO TIME!
SEVERAL MONTHS LATER ---
DARLING, IT'LL BE WONDERFUL TO HAVE FATHER'S BOOKS IN OUR LIBRARY WHEN WE'RE MARRIED --- BUT I CAN'T SEEM TO FIND HIS JOURNAL FOR 1941!
WHO KNOWS, CANISA --- MAYBE THAT'S THE WAY HE WANTED IT! A BLANK --- A GAP --- SOMETHING THAT FLAMED IN HORROR FOR A LITTLE WHILE --- AND WENT UP IN SMOKE!
THE END!
10.

"U.S." ROYAL
WITH HIS
JET-PROPELLED BIKE

43

Vampire's VICTIM

THE TIMES just weren't right for vampires, Rudolf thought bitterly as he drove his car up the lonely country road. Yes, he should have been living in 1700 or 1800, when a vampire didn't have to fear the modern police methods of the 20th century. Back in the olden days, the friends and relatives of a vampire's victim would never dare dream of hunting out the vampire and seeking vengeance... instead, they'd merely bolt their doors and cower in terror in the darkness, praying that the vampire would not pick *them* as his next victims. But when policemen of 1951 came across the white corpse of a vampire's victim, all the resources of modern science and criminology were brought to bear on the case.,,and the poor vampire had to flee and skulk in his hideout like a common, despicable thief!

Even Rudolf, the most cautious and cunning vampire of recent years, was now a fugitive from the police of eighteen states. His fingerprints, footprints, even teeth-marks, were on file in practically every police headquarters. That was why Rudolf was now driving along the lonely country lane looking for a potential victim. No city or town was safe for him now, not with all those "WANTED" circulars flooding the centers of crime enforcement.

Yes, from now on, he knew, he would have to lead a fugitive's life, living only in the thinly-populated rural areas, where the local police were less informed and efficient than their city colleagues. And he'd have to be very careful about his choice of victims...he'd have to rely on hoboes, wanderers, hitch-hikers...those without families or friends who would raise a hue and cry upon the disappearance or death of his victims.

Rudolf's burning, hungry eyes lit up suddenly as he spied the hitch-hiker down the road, thumbing for a ride. It was a girl... lovely and healthy-looking, with dark features and a flashing smile that showed strong white teeth.

"Hop in," Rudolf said as he pulled to a halt in front of her. "Visiting friends or relatives around here?"

The girl laughed, charmingly. "Oh, no...I have no friends or family...I'm just wandering around the country! But how about *you*...do you live around here?"

Rudolf smiled, an exultance welling up within his chest as he knew he had found the perfect victim.,,someone whose disappearance would not be noticed, whose death would not be mour. ed!

"No," he said, "I guess I'm a wanderer, just like you...we have at least that much in common. No family, no friends, no... *Yaaaghhh!*"

As the girl struck like a serpent, Rudolf knew, in his dying moment, that they had one *more* thing in common...and that *he* was about to become the victim of a vampire who had been wandering around the countryside for the same purpose!

"True" GHOSTS of HISTORY

The GHOSTLY ARMY of BETHUNE

EARLY IN 1918, THE GERMAN ARMIES MADE A LAST DESPERATE ATTACK NEAR THE SMALL BELGIAN TOWN OF BETHUNE...AND THE ALLIED LINES WERE SPLIT WIDE OPEN! ONLY A SMALL SQUAD OF BRITISH RIFLEMEN WERE LEFT BEHIND TO STEM THE VAST HUN HORDES...

WE CAN'T STOP 'EM...BUT WE'LL GO DOWN FIGHTING! FIX BAYONETS!

BUT SUDDENLY, AN ARMY OF GHOSTLY CAVALRY SEEMED TO APPEAR FROM NOWHERE IN FRONT OF THE GERMANS...AN ARMY CLAD IN WHITE, ALL MOUNTED ON WHITE HORSES WHOSE LEGS NEVER TOUCHED THE GROUND!

HIMMEL ...WAS IST?

WHILE THE KAISER'S MEN GAPED IN PETRIFIED ASTONISHMENT, THE GHOSTLY CAVALRY CHARGED!

FINALLY REGAINING THEIR SENSES, THE GERMANS POURED A TERRIFIC CONCENTRATION OF SHELL AND SHOT INTO THE RANKS OF THE GHOSTLY RIDERS...BUT NOT A WHITE HORSEMAN FELL!

BLAM!

BANG

BOOM!

THEN THE PRIDE OF THE KAISER'S ARMIES TURNED TAIL AND FLED IN SHEER TERROR... AND THE ALLIES WERE SAVED BY THE GHOSTLY ARMY OF BETHUNE! WERE THEY A FIGMENT OF THE FOG...OR...?

The END

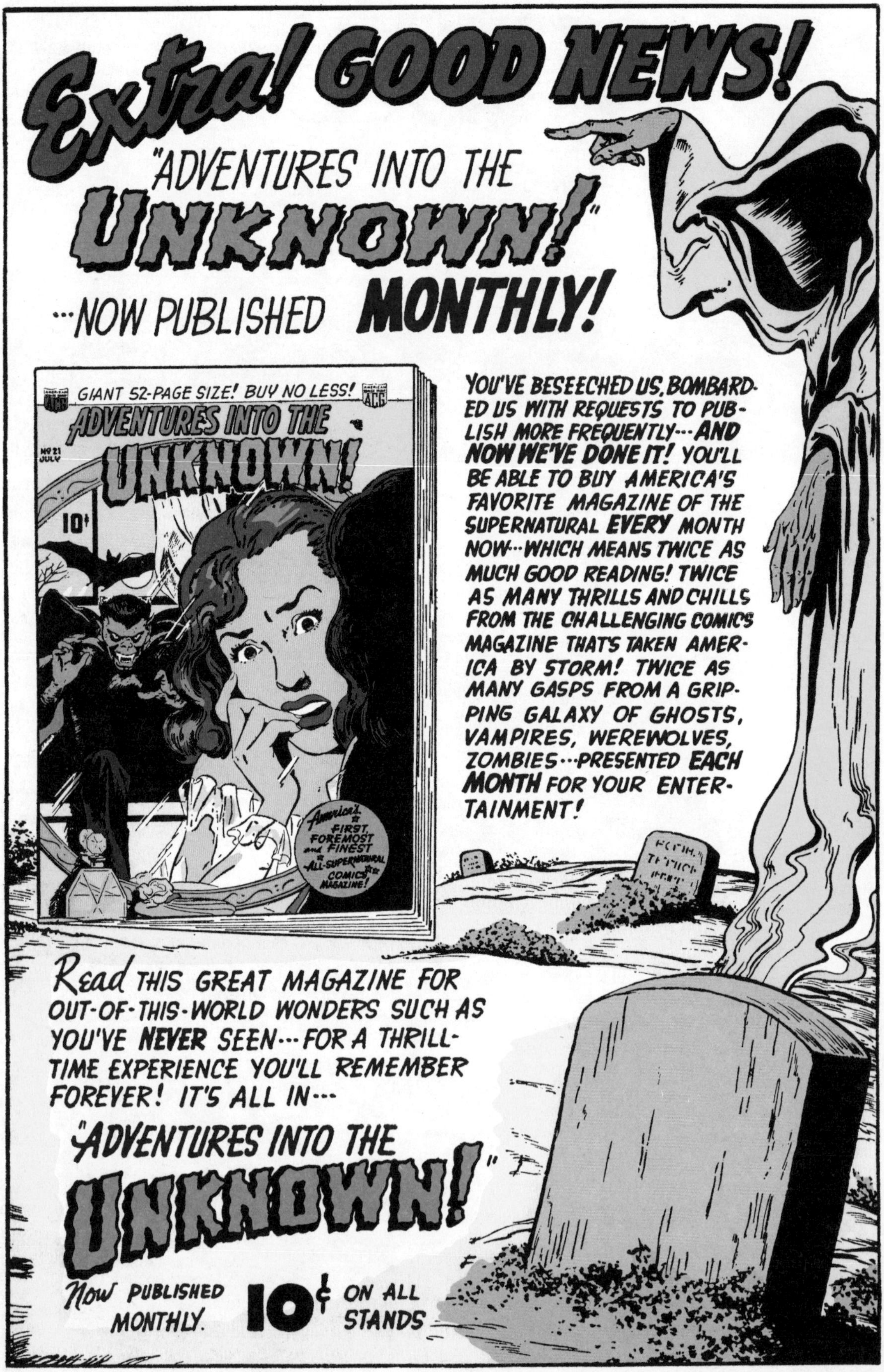

Extra! GOOD NEWS!
"ADVENTURES INTO THE UNKNOWN!"
...NOW PUBLISHED MONTHLY!
GIANT 52-PAGE SIZE! BUY NO LESS!
ADVENTURES INTO THE UNKNOWN!
Nº 21 JULY
10¢
America's FIRST, FOREMOST and FINEST ALL-SUPERNATURAL COMICS MAGAZINE!
YOU'VE BESEECHED US, BOMBARDED US WITH REQUESTS TO PUBLISH MORE FREQUENTLY--- AND NOW WE'VE DONE IT! YOU'LL BE ABLE TO BUY AMERICA'S FAVORITE MAGAZINE OF THE SUPERNATURAL EVERY MONTH NOW--- WHICH MEANS TWICE AS MUCH GOOD READING! TWICE AS MANY THRILLS AND CHILLS FROM THE CHALLENGING COMICS MAGAZINE THAT'S TAKEN AMERICA BY STORM! TWICE AS MANY GASPS FROM A GRIPPING GALAXY OF GHOSTS, VAMPIRES, WEREWOLVES, ZOMBIES---PRESENTED EACH MONTH FOR YOUR ENTERTAINMENT!
Read THIS GREAT MAGAZINE FOR OUT-OF-THIS-WORLD WONDERS SUCH AS YOU'VE NEVER SEEN--- FOR A THRILL-TIME EXPERIENCE YOU'LL REMEMBER FOREVER! IT'S ALL IN---
"ADVENTURES INTO THE UNKNOWN!"
Now PUBLISHED MONTHLY.
10¢ ON ALL STANDS

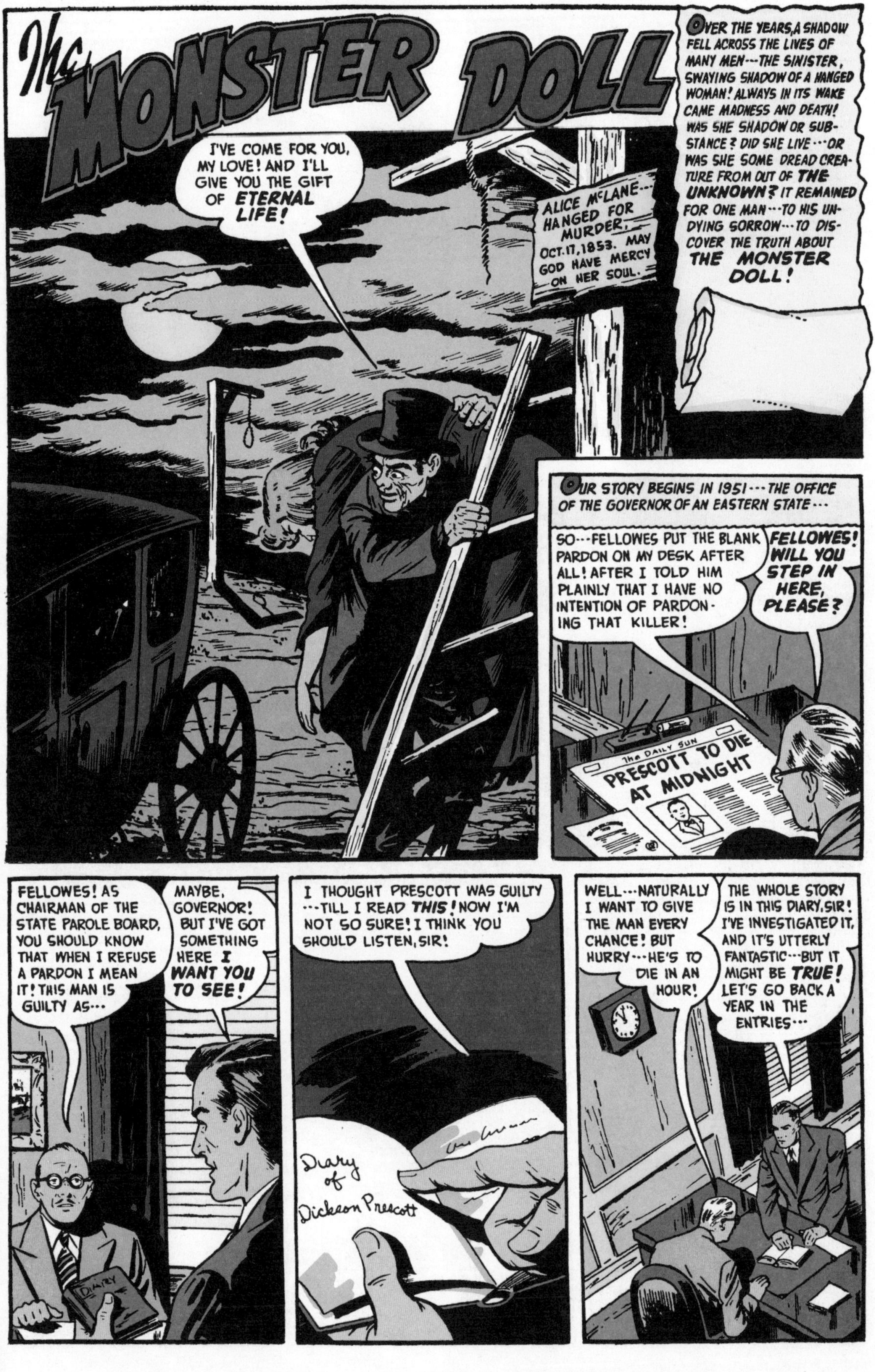
The MONSTER DOLL
OVER THE YEARS, A SHADOW FELL ACROSS THE LIVES OF MANY MEN---THE SINISTER, SWAYING SHADOW OF A HANGED WOMAN! ALWAYS IN ITS WAKE CAME MADNESS AND DEATH! WAS SHE SHADOW OR SUBSTANCE? DID SHE LIVE---OR WAS SHE SOME DREAD CREATURE FROM OUT OF THE UNKNOWN? IT REMAINED FOR ONE MAN---TO HIS UNDYING SORROW---TO DISCOVER THE TRUTH ABOUT THE MONSTER DOLL!
I'VE COME FOR YOU, MY LOVE! AND I'LL GIVE YOU THE GIFT OF ETERNAL LIFE!
ALICE McLANE--- HANGED FOR MURDER, OCT. 17, 1853. MAY GOD HAVE MERCY ON HER SOUL.
OUR STORY BEGINS IN 1951---THE OFFICE OF THE GOVERNOR OF AN EASTERN STATE---
SO---FELLOWES PUT THE BLANK PARDON ON MY DESK AFTER ALL! AFTER I TOLD HIM PLAINLY THAT I HAVE NO INTENTION OF PARDONING THAT KILLER!
FELLOWES! WILL YOU STEP IN HERE, PLEASE?
The DAILY SUN
PRESCOTT TO DIE AT MIDNIGHT
FELLOWES! AS CHAIRMAN OF THE STATE PAROLE BOARD, YOU SHOULD KNOW THAT WHEN I REFUSE A PARDON I MEAN IT! THIS MAN IS GUILTY AS---
MAYBE, GOVERNOR! BUT I'VE GOT SOMETHING HERE I WANT YOU TO SEE!
DIARY
I THOUGHT PRESCOTT WAS GUILTY---TILL I READ THIS! NOW I'M NOT SO SURE! I THINK YOU SHOULD LISTEN, SIR!
Diary of Dickson Prescott
WELL---NATURALLY I WANT TO GIVE THE MAN EVERY CHANCE! BUT HURRY---HE'S TO DIE IN AN HOUR!
THE WHOLE STORY IS IN THIS DIARY, SIR! I'VE INVESTIGATED IT, AND IT'S UTTERLY FANTASTIC---BUT IT MIGHT BE TRUE! LET'S GO BACK A YEAR IN THE ENTRIES---

JUST A YEAR AGO...AND WE SEE DICKSON PRESCOTT, BRILLIANT YOUNG SCIENTIST, TAKING A BUSMAN'S HOLIDAY...

GOOD AFTERNOON, DR. PRESCOTT! SURPRISED TO SEE *YOU* HERE! I MEAN...WHAT WITH YOUR *OWN* ROBOTS...

NOT AT ALL, BILL! GOT TO KEEP UP, YOU KNOW! SEE WHAT THE OTHERS ARE DOING IN THE FIELD!

INTERNATIONAL EXIBITION OF ROBOTS

HMM...MIGHT AS WELL HAVE STAYED IN MY OWN LAB! NOT MUCH HERE THAT'S NEW IN THE FABRICATION OF ROBOTS!

EXCUSE ME, MISTER! COULD YA TELL ME SOMETHING, PLEASE?

THE THINKER MODEL 9

WHO MADE *THAT* ONE, MISTER? GEE...AIN'T SHE *SWELL*? JUST AS LIFELIKE AS...

WHAT? I DON'T THINK I QUITE UNDERSTAND, YOUNG FELLOW! *SHE'S* NO ROBOT ...BUT A *BEAUTIFUL GIRL!*

THANK YOU, DR. PRESCOTT! YOU'RE VERY GALLANT!...OH, YES, I KNOW WHO YOU ARE! YOU SEE... *I'M* INTERESTED IN ROBOTS *MYSELF!*

HUH? SHE... SHE *IS* REAL!

SHE CERTAINLY IS, SON! NOW YOU'D BETTER RUN ALONG WHILE I MAKE OUR APOLOGIES!

NO APOLOGIES NECESSARY, DR. PRESCOTT --*IF* YOU'LL PROMISE TO SHOW ME ABOUT! MY NAME IS *JANE CROTHERS!*

INTERESTING... BUT A LITTLE *CRUDE*, DON'T YOU THINK? MORE PRIMITIVE THAN I EXPECTED!

PRIMITIVE? BUT MISS CROTHERS... JANE...THESE ARE THE VERY *LATEST* IN THINKING MACHINES AND ROBOTS! BUT MAYBE YOU'VE SEEN TOO *MANY* ROBOTS ...HOW ABOUT DINNER?

SO...

YOU KNOW SOMETHING, JANE...I'M AWFULLY GLAD I WENT TO THAT EXHIBIT TODAY! I WENT TO SEE ROBOTS ...AND FOUND *YOU!*

AND DO *YOU* KNOW SOMETHING, DICKSON... I FEEL *EXACTLY THE SAME WAY!*

A FEW WEEKS LATER, DICKSON PRESCOTT AND JANE CROTHERS WERE MARRIED! AFTER THE HONEYMOON---

IT'S BACK TO WORK FOR ME, DARLING! AFTER ALL, THE CYBERNETICS FOUNDATION EXPECTS RESULTS ON THE ROBOTS I DEVISE!

AND AT LAST I GET TO SEE THIS MYSTERIOUS MOUNTAIN LABORATORY OF YOURS!

DOCTOR PRESCOTT! DICKSON! OH, I'M SO GLAD YOU'RE BACK!

HELLO, SUE! THIS IS MY WIFE, JANE!

DICKSON TALKS ABOUT YOU ALL THE TIME, SUE! SAYS HE COULDN'T RUN THE LAB WITHOUT HIS INVALUABLE ASSISTANT!

I ALMOST FORGOT TO TELL YOU, DICKSON! THIS LETTER CAME SOME TIME AGO! IT LOOKS IMPORTANT---BUT I DIDN'T WANT TO DISTURB YOUR HONEYMOON!

LET'S SEE IT, SUE!

WHY---IT'S FROM ALAN MACCAMPBELL IN SCOTLAND! AND LISTEN TO THIS! HE THINKS HE'S DISCOVERED A CLUE TO A ROBOT MADE A HUNDRED YEARS AGO!

A---A HUNDRED YEARS? IS THAT POSSIBLE?

ALAN'S TALKING ABOUT THE BULMERE ROBOT--- BUT THAT'S ONLY A MYTH! STILL, I'M BETTING HE HAS SOMETHING! I'LL HAVE TO GO TO GLASGOW AT ONCE!

BUT, DICKSON, YOUR WIFE! YOU CAN'T JUST RUN OFF AND---

THAT NIGHT...

YOU DO UNDERSTAND, JANE? ALAN IS AN EXPERT---MUCH MORE SO THAN I AM---AND HE SEEMS TO HAVE EVIDENCE THAT SOMEONE BUILT A PERFECT ROBOT A HUNDRED YEARS AGO! I MUST GO AT ONCE!

I WON'T SAY I LIKE IT, DARLING! I DON'T! AFTER ALL, HOW COULD ANYONE BUILD A PERFECT ROBOT BEFORE ELECTRONICS WAS KNOWN? IT'S A WILD-GOOSE CHASE!

HOWEVER---GO CHASE YOUR WILD GOOSE AND THEN HURRY BACK TO ME! MEANTIME, I'LL TRY MY BEST TO LEARN TO LIKE THAT FUNNY LITTLE LAB ASSISTANT OF YOURS!

SUE? OH, YOU TWO WILL GET ALONG JUST FINE! SHE'S A TREASURE!

③.

49

NEXT DAY, AFTER PRESCOTT HAD GONE···

YOU'RE NOT FOOLING ME, MY DEAR! I KNOW YOU'RE IN LOVE WITH MY HUSBAND! YOU PROBABLY ENCOURAGED HIM TO GO ON THIS FOOL'S TRIP TO GET HIM AWAY FROM ME!

OHH! BUT I DIDN'T··· I'M NOT! HOW CAN YOU SAY SUCH THINGS!

BUT WHEN SUE IS ALONE···

SHE'S RIGHT! I D-DO LOVE HIM! AND I THOUGHT HE LOVED ME, TOO! THEN HE···BROUGHT HER HOME! AND SHE F-FRIGHTENS ME! SOMETHING ABOUT HER···

THE FOLLOWING WEEK···IN GLASGOW···

GLAD YOU COULD COME, DICKSON! BUT DON'T EXPECT TOO MUCH! WHAT I TOLD YOU WAS ONLY GUESS-WORK!

ALAN MacCAMPBELL! YOU KNEW ALL ALONG I'D COME SOON AS YOU MENTIONED THE BULMERE ROBOT! I CAN'T WAIT TO START TRACKING IT DOWN!

I CONTACTED YOU BECAUSE I GOT A LEAD TO IT···A LEAD WHICH CONVINCED ME IT MAY NOT BE A MYTH AFTER ALL!

I'VE HEARD THE STORY ALL MY LIFE···HOW POOR, CRAZY JULIAN BULMERE BUILT A ROBOT RIGHT HERE IN GLASGOW! YOU REALLY THINK IT MIGHT BE TRUE?

I NEVER DID TILL RECENTLY! THEN I DISCOVERED SOME NEW FRAGMENTS OF NOTES···AND FOUND THAT HE HAD DONE RESEARCH IN ELECTRONICS!

ELECTRONICS? A HUNDRED YEARS AGO? IF THAT'S POSSIBLE, THEN HE MIGHT HAVE BUILT A ROBOT AFTER ALL! BUT WHAT HAPPENED TO IT?

THAT NIGHT···

HERE'S ALL THE DATA I'VE BEEN ABLE TO FIND! THE FRAGMENTS OF BULMERE'S NOTES, OLD NEWSPAPERS, ETC! YOU KNOW THE GENERAL OUTLINE OF HIS STORY, DICKSON?

SOME OF IT I'VE FORGOTTEN! BETTER TELL ME AGAIN FROM THE BEGINNING!

JULIAN BULMERE WAS MAD, NO DOUBT OF IT! BUT HE HAD GENIUS, TOO! HE WAS AN UGLY, MALFORMED DWARF WHO LONGED FOR A WOMAN TO LOVE AND ADMIRE HIM! AND, AS THE STORY GOES, WHEN ALL WOMEN SPURNED HIM··· HE BUILT ONE THAT HE COULD IDOLIZE!

4.

"BUT HE NEEDED A WOMAN'S BODY TO SERVE AS THE FRAMEWORK FOR THIS STRANGE DEVICE HE HAD PLANNED! A HANGED MURDERESS ANSWERED THAT NEED!"

THERE, MY LOVELY! MY GENIUS WILL MAKE YOU LIVE AGAIN... I SWEAR IT!

THEY WOULD HANG ME TOO IF THEY CAUGHT ME! BUT THEY WON'T! THE FOOLS... HOW COULD THEY GUESS WHAT I'M GOING TO DO?

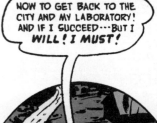

NOW TO GET BACK TO THE CITY AND MY LABORATORY! AND IF I SUCCEED... BUT I WILL! I MUST!

"LATER THAT NIGHT, ACCORDING TO BULMERE'S NOTES, HE BEGAN HIS FANTASTIC EXPERIMENT..."

SOON NOW, MY DEAR! SOON! AND THEN POOR, MAD, UGLY JULIAN BULMERE WILL HAVE AN INCOMPARABLE COMPANION! ONE WHO CAN NEVER LEAVE HIM... NEVER!

YOU CAN FEEL NOTHING! BUT SOON YOU BREATHE ... LIVE ...

I NEVER TIRE OF THAT STORY! BUT I ALWAYS THOUGHT IT WAS JUST THAT...A STORY WRITTEN BY A MADMAN TO AMUSE HIMSELF!

SO DID WE ALL ...AND IT STILL MAY BE THE CASE! BUT I HAVE POSITIVE PROOF NOW THAT BULMERE DID WORK IN ELECTRONICS, IN THINKING MACHINES...WORK THAT WAS FAR BEYOND HIS TIME! NOW, TAKE THIS NEXT NOTATION OF HIS THAT I DISCOVERED...

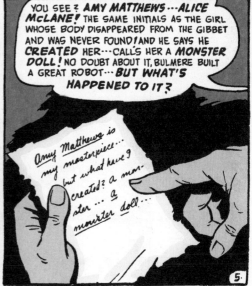

YOU SEE? AMY MATTHEWS ...ALICE McLANE! THE SAME INITIALS AS THE GIRL WHOSE BODY DISAPPEARED FROM THE GIBBET AND WAS NEVER FOUND! AND HE SAYS HE CREATED HER... CALLS HER A MONSTER DOLL! NO DOUBT ABOUT IT, BULMERE BUILT A GREAT ROBOT... BUT WHAT'S HAPPENED TO IT?

Amy Matthews is my masterpiece... but what have I created? a monster ... a monster doll...

5.

"THERE WERE OTHER PROOFS···EYEWITNESS REPORTS THAT BULMERE BEGAN TO BE SEEN WITH A GIRL WHO, APPARENTLY, HAD APPEARED FROM NOWHERE···"

SEE! THAT UGLY BULMERE HAS A SWEETHEART AT LAST!

THE NASTY LITTLE CREATURE! HOW CAN SHE ABIDE HIM?

I WONDER WHO SHE IS?

"THEN CAME RUMORS OF QUARRELS, BITTERNESS···"

YOU···YOU FILTHY LITTLE CREATURE! I HATE YOU···AND I'M GOING TO LEAVE YOU!

DON'T TRY IT, MY DEAR! YOU'RE MINE···ALL MINE, AND I'LL NEVER LET YOU GO! YOU KNOW WHAT I CAN DO TO YOU IF I CHOOSE!

"AND THEN···TRAGEDY! FOR BULMERE WAS FOUND DEAD ONE DAY···MURDERED!"

LOOKS AS THOUGH THE GIRL TRIED TO BURN ALL HIS PAPERS, SIR! NOT A VERY GOOD JOB OF IT, THOUGH!

NEVER MIND THE PAPERS, M'LAD! FINDING THAT GIRL IS THE THING! AND SHE'S VANISHED LIKE A GHOST!

SO THERE IT IS, DICKSON! EYE-WITNESS ACCOUNTS, BULMERE'S CHARRED NOTES, MY DISCOVERY THAT HE WAS THE EARLIEST ELECTRONIC EXPERT···ALL POINT TO THE FACT THAT HE REALLY BUILT A GREAT ROBOT···A MONSTER DOLL! IT DISAPPEARED···BUT THROUGH THE YEARS, IT'S LEFT A TRAIL! LOOK!

Le Étoile Soir 1867 MURDERED MAN GASPS WEIRD STORY OF ROBOT GIRL

Berlin 1888 LOVELY ROBOT RUNS AMOK, KILLS THREE!

The London Times 1876 DYING MAN CLAIMS WIFE WAS MACHINE

1888 WAS THE LAST REPORT···AND THEN THE TRAIL PETERED OUT! I SUPPOSE THAT MURDEROUS ROBOT HAS LONG SINCE CEASED TO EXIST···BUT IF YOU WANT TO TAKE UP THE HUNT FOR IT···

DO I! I'VE GOT A STRANGE FEELING THAT, SOMEWHERE, IT STILL EXISTS···AND I'LL TRACK DOWN BULMERE'S MONSTER DOLL IF IT'S THE LAST THING I DO!

FOR A MONTH DICKSON PRESCOTT DOGGEDLY PURSUED THE ELUSIVE SHADOW OF A DEADLY WOMAN ROBOT ACROSS EUROPE! BUT ALWAYS THE TRAIL ENDED IN A BLANK WALL! FINALLY, DISCOURAGED, HE GAVE UP THE HUNT, RETURNED TO GLASGOW···

I GAVE IT A GOOD TRY, ALAN, BUT I'M AFRAID WE'LL NEVER KNOW THE TRUTH NOW! THE WOMAN, OR ROBOT, OR WHATEVER SHE WAS, JUST DISAPPEARED INTO THIN AIR! AND I MUST GET BACK TO MY JOB AND WIFE!

I SUPPOSE YOU'RE RIGHT! BUT IT'S MADDENING NOT TO FIND THE CONCRETE PROOF THAT BULMERE REALLY SUCCEEDED IN MAKING A ROBOT FROM A DEAD WOMAN! WELL, SHE STILL MAKES A GOOD STORY···THIS MONSTER DOLL!

THE MONSTER DOLL! WHAT A CREATURE SHE MUST HAVE BEEN···IF SHE EVER EXISTED AT ALL! A ROBOT'S MACHINERY IN A WOMAN'S BODY! BULMERE WAS A GENIUS···IF HE DID IT!

IT WAS WONDERFUL, FINDING JANE WAITING FOR HIM AT THE AIRPORT...

OH, DICKSON, IT'S SO GOOD TO SEE YOU BACK! TELL ME, DID YOU FIND YOUR *ROBOT*?

I'M AFRAID YOU WERE RIGHT ALL ALONG, JANE ...IT WAS A WILD-GOOSE CHASE! BUT PLEASE DON'T SAY "*I TOLD YOU SO*"!

I WON'T GLOAT, DARLING! BUT YOU MUST DO ONE THING FOR ME... *FIRE SUE JACKSON!* I CAN'T STAND HER ANY LONGER! I'VE WAITED TILL YOUR RETURN... BUT NOW SHE HAS TO *GO*!

FIRE *SUE*? I ...I DON'T UNDERSTAND! I CAN'T PROMISE THAT, JANE, BUT I'LL TALK TO HER TONIGHT AND SEE WHAT'S WRONG!

That evening...

BUT WHAT'S *WRONG*, SUE? MY WIFE DISLIKES YOU... AND FROM YOUR ATTITUDE, YOU DISLIKE *HER*! IT'S PRETTY BAFFLING TO A MERE MAN!

I --- I CAN'T TELL YOU, DICKSON! I JUST CAN'T! BUT I'LL LEAVE FIRST THING IN THE MORNING!

HOW CAN I TELL HIM I LOVE HIM... AND THAT HIS WIFE KNOWS IT AND HATES ME FOR IT?

YOU'RE WANTED ON THE PHONE, DARLING! *IF* YOU CAN BREAK UP THAT LITTLE CONFERENCE...

I'LL BE RIGHT THERE!

IT WAS A SUMMONS TO AN URGENT CONFERENCE OF THE CYBERNETICS FOUNDATION!

DRIVE CAREFULLY, DICKSON! THE TRAFFIC IS BAD AND...

VERY TOUCHING, SUE! BUT I COULDN'T HELP OVERHEARING YOUR CONVERSATION JUST NOW IN THE LAB! WHY WAIT TILL MORNING? WHY NOT LEAVE *NOW*...BEFORE HE COMES BACK?

I REALLY THINK THAT WOULD BE BEST! JUST GO AWAY TONIGHT AND NEVER COME BACK AGAIN! *I'LL* EXPLAIN TO MY HUSBAND!

ALL RIGHT, MRS. PRESCOTT! BUT BEFORE I GO, I WANT TO TELL YOU WHAT I THINK OF YOU! YOU'RE NOT RIGHT FOR HIM! YOU'RE COLD, HEARTLESS, LACKING IN HUMAN EMOTION... ALMOST AS IF *YOU WERE A ROBOT YOUR-SELF*!

IT WAS THEN THAT A SUDDEN AND TERRIFYING CHANGE CAME OVER JANE PRESCOTT!

A ROBOT! HOW DARE YOU! I ---I'LL *KILL* ANY-ONE WHO TALKS TO ME LIKE THAT! DO YOU HEAR? *I'LL KILL*...

WHY...YOU'RE *INSANE*! GET AWAY FROM ME!

7.

GET AWAY? NO... I THINK I'LL DO IT NOW! AS I SHOULD HAVE DONE LONG AGO...*WITH MY BARE HANDS!*

NO! PLEASE ...*I'LL GO!* DON'T...

OH! SHE'S... FALLEN!

IN A FRENZY OF RAGE, JANE LUNGED... SLIPPED... AND...

AH-HHH...

SHE MAY BE...*BADLY HURT!* I'D BETTER CALL DICKSON AT THE CONFERENCE, THEN TAKE SOME X-RAYS ON OUR OWN MACHINE! THAT WILL SAVE TIME...

SUE SUMMONED PRESCOTT, THEN TOOK X-RAYS OF THE STILL UNCONSCIOUS WOMAN! BUT WHEN SHE EXAMINED THEM...

THERE MUST BE... SOME *MISTAKE!* THESE *CAN'T* BE THE PLATES... IT'S...TOO INCREDIBLE, TOO *HORRIBLE!* BUT WAIT A MINUTE! THIS WOULD *EXPLAIN* SO MUCH! THESE SHOW THAT...

BEHIND HER CAME A STEALTHY SOUND... THE LAST SHE EVER HEARD!

ARGH!

AND WHEN DICKSON PRESCOTT RETURNED...

GOOD HEAVENS! WHAT HAPPENED? NOT...NOT MY *WIFE!*

NO SIR! BUT IT'S *MURDER!* YOUR LAB ASSISTANT, MISS JACKSON! YOUR WIFE FOUND THE BODY AND CALLED US...

JANE! JANE, DARLING! WHAT...

OH, DICKSON! I'M SO GLAD YOU'RE HERE! IT WAS *TRAGIC, HORRIBLE!* I WAS ASLEEP UPSTAIRS AND HEARD A NOISE! WHEN I CAME DOWN, I FOUND HER *STRANGLED!*

8.

BUT···BUT SHE *CALLED* ME, JANE! SAID YOU TWO HAD QUARRELED AND YOU'D FALLEN DOWN THE STAIRS! AND THAT CRUCIBLE···SOMETHING HAS BEEN BURNT IN IT RECENTLY! I DON'T *UNDERSTAND* ALL THIS!

S-SHE PHONED YOU?

THIS FRAGMENT LOOKS LIKE THE NEGATIVE OF AN *X-RAY!* AND SUE TOLD ME SHE WAS GOING TO TAKE X-RAYS OF YOU, JANE! WHY SHOULD ANYONE *BURN* THEM?

DON'T DO IT, DICKSON! I WARN YOU! *DON'T LOOK AT THAT X-RAY!*

BUT THIS···THIS SHOWS THE MUSCULATURE AND BONE STRUCTURE OF A WOMAN! ONLY INSTEAD OF ORGANS THERE ARE···*MERCIFUL HEAVENS!*

YOU! ALL THIS TIME IT WAS *YOU!* THEN BULMERE DID SUCCEED! *YOU'RE THE MONSTER DOLL!*

AH, HOW RIGHT YOU ARE! AND NOW THAT YOU KNOW, DARLING, I'LL HAVE TO KILL YOU···AS I KILLED ALL THE OTHERS! I'M SORRY, BECAUSE I LOVED *YOU* BEST OF ALL!

HALF MAD WITH SHOCK AND FEAR, DICKSON PRESCOTT REACHED FOR SOME WEAPON OF DEFENSE! HIS HAND CLOSED UPON A BOTTLE OF DEADLY ACID···

LOVE? WHAT CAN *YOU* KNOW OF LOVE? YOU'RE NOT HUMAN! YOU'RE A ROBOT···A *THING!* YOU'VE KILLED A SCORE OF MEN···JUST AS YOU KILLED SUE!

I *HAD* TO DO IT! SHE *KNEW!* AND WHEN PEOPLE KNOW, I AM IN DANGER! I WANT TO LIVE AS MUCH AS YOU HUMANS! AND NOW···

NOW···I'VE GOT TO DESTROY *YOU*···AND UNDO THE FIENDISH WORK OF THE MADMAN WHO CREATED YOU!

NO··· *DON'T*···

IT'S···EXPLODED···MADE A LIVING TORCH OUT OF HER! HEAVEN FORGIVE ME FOR WHAT I HAD TO DO··· BUT SHE WASN'T ···HUMAN···

HELP! DON'T DESTROY ME AFTER ALL THESE YEARS! *AH-HH!*

DICKSON PRESCOTT WAS ARRESTED, ACCUSED OF MURDER! WHILE AWAITING TRIAL, HE SENT A CABLEGRAM---AND RECEIVED A STUNNING ANSWER!

ALAN MacCAMPBELL... DEAD OF A HEART ATTACK! *THE ONE WITNESS WHO MIGHT HAVE SAVED ME!*

AND AT HIS TRIAL---

YOU HAVE NOTHING TO SAY IN YOUR DEFENSE, MR. PRESCOTT?

HOW CAN I TELL THEM I MARRIED A *ROBOT*---AND THEN DESTROYED HER? THEY'D SEND ME TO THE INSANE ASYLUM---AND I'D *RATHER* DIE!

I'LL TELL YOU, GENTLEMEN, WHY THE PRISONER DOES NOT TALK! HE HAS NOTHING TO SAY! HE KNOWS HE IS *GUILTY!* I DEMAND THE *EXTREME PENALTY!*

YOU HAVE BEEN FOUND *GUILTY OF MURDER* IN THE FIRST DEGREE! IT IS THEREFORE MY DUTY TO IMPOSE A SENTENCE OF *DEATH* ON YOU! YOU WILL BE TAKEN FROM THIS PLACE AND---

HOW STRANGE ALL THIS SEEMS! SOME JUDGE MUST HAVE SAID ALMOST THE SAME WORDS TO *ALICE McLANE*---A CENTURY AGO, BEFORE BULMERE RESURRECTED HER AS THE *MONSTER DOLL!* NOW THEY'RE HANGING ME FOR *HER* DEATH!

THAT WAS THE STORY OF DICKSON PRESCOTT, AS TOLD TO THE GOVERNOR BY THE CHAIRMAN OF THE STATE PAROLE BOARD! WHEN THE STORY WAS ENDED, THERE WAS A SHORT, TENSE SILENCE IN THE GOVERNOR'S OFFICE! THEN---

FANTASTIC! DO YOU BELIEVE THIS---THIS CRAZY YARN?

I DON'T EXACTLY KNOW, SIR! BUT I INVESTIGATED! I CABLED SCOTLAND AND THEY BORE OUT SOME OF THE FACTS! PRESCOTT *DID* VISIT THERE, AND THERE *WAS* AN ALAN MacCAMPBELL! DEAD NOW!

BLAST IT, FELLOWES! DO YOU REALIZE THE LEGAL QUESTIONS ALL THIS RAISES? IF PRESCOTT IS INNOCENT, I CAN'T LET HIM DIE, OF COURSE! I'LL ADMIT I'M STUMPED!

BETTER MAKE UP YOUR MIND, SIR! *HE HAS ONLY TEN MINUTES LEFT!*

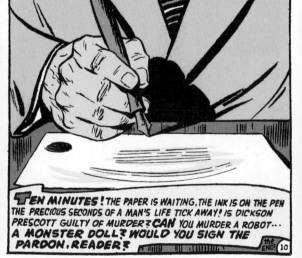

TEN MINUTES! THE PAPER IS WAITING, THE INK IS ON THE PEN THE PRECIOUS SECONDS OF A MAN'S LIFE TICK AWAY! IS DICKSON PRESCOTT GUILTY OF MURDER? *CAN* YOU MURDER A ROBOT--- A MONSTER DOLL? WOULD YOU SIGN THE PARDON, READER? *the END!* 10

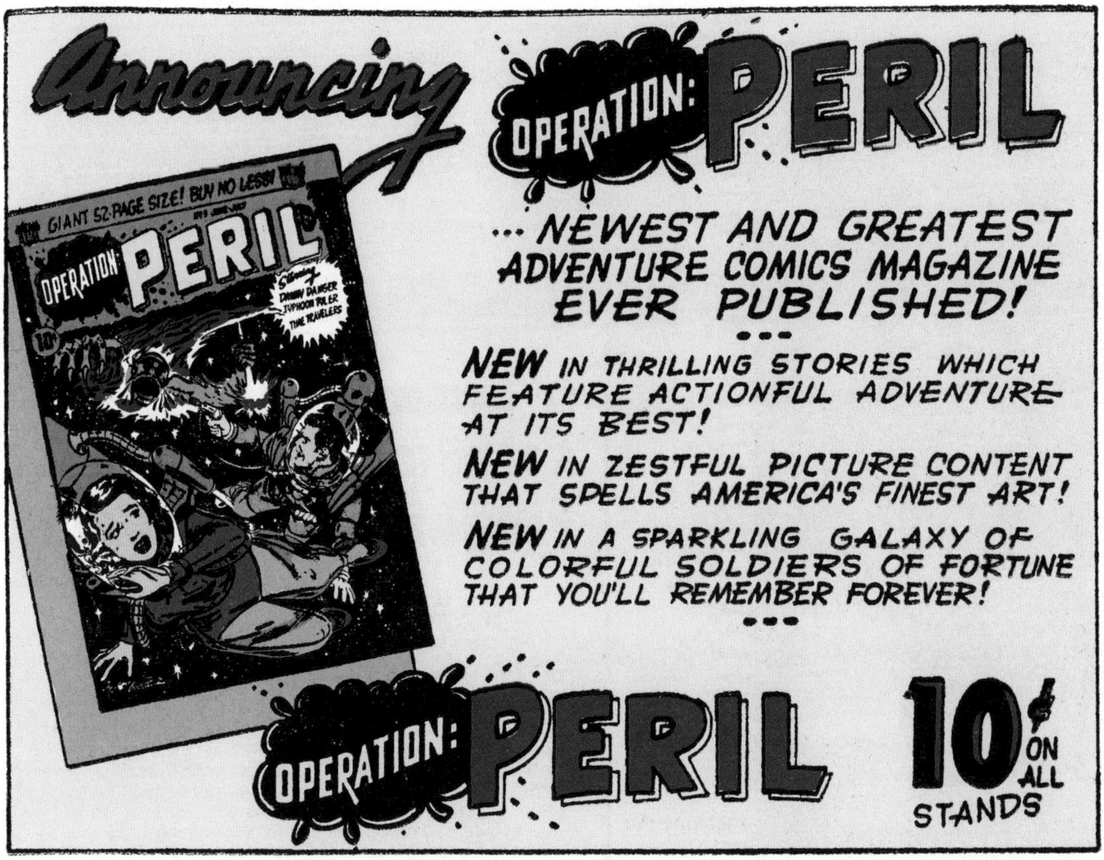

Announcing
OPERATION: PERIL
GIANT 52-PAGE SIZE! BUY NO LESS!
OPERATION: PERIL
10¢
...NEWEST AND GREATEST ADVENTURE COMICS MAGAZINE EVER PUBLISHED!
NEW IN THRILLING STORIES WHICH FEATURE ACTIONFUL ADVENTURE AT ITS BEST!
NEW IN ZESTFUL PICTURE CONTENT THAT SPELLS AMERICA'S FINEST ART!
NEW IN A SPARKLING GALAXY OF COLORFUL SOLDIERS OF FORTUNE THAT YOU'LL REMEMBER FOREVER!
OPERATION: PERIL
10¢ ON ALL STANDS

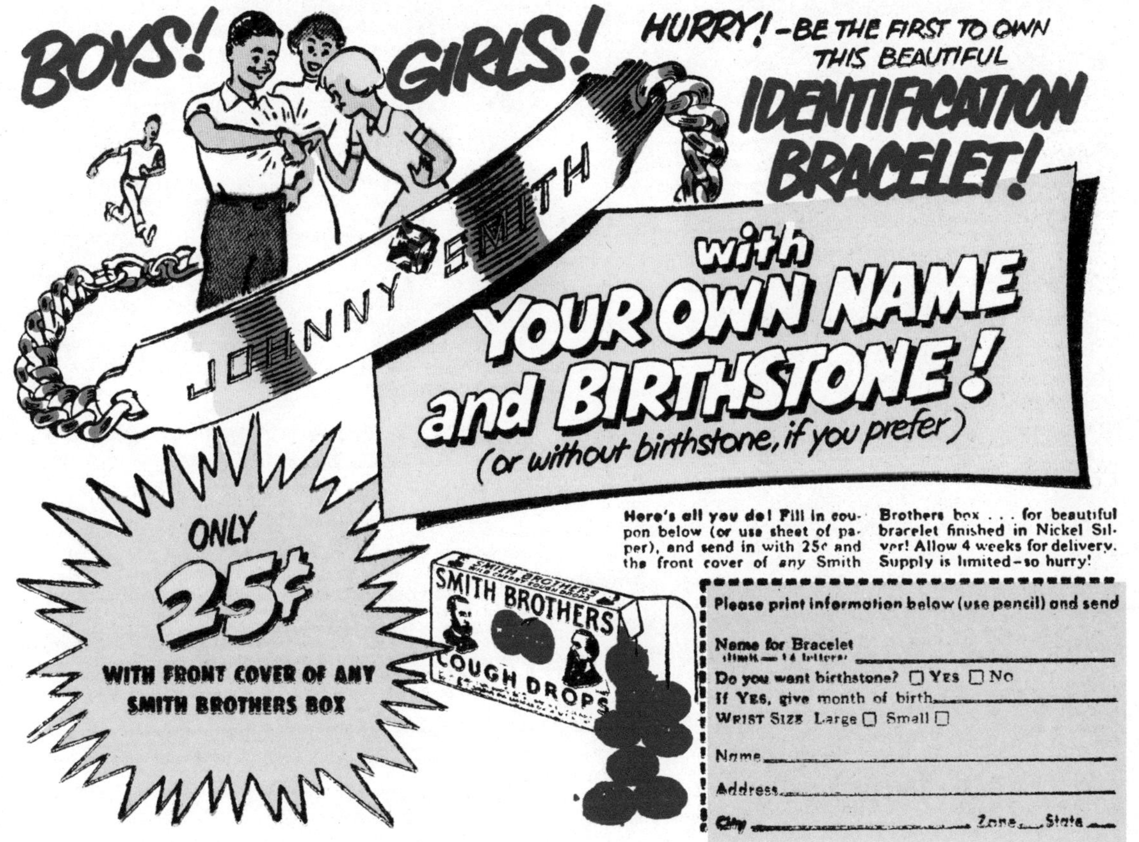

BOYS! GIRLS!
HURRY! - BE THE FIRST TO OWN THIS BEAUTIFUL
IDENTIFICATION BRACELET!
JOHNNY SMITH
with YOUR OWN NAME and BIRTHSTONE!
(or without birthstone, if you prefer)
ONLY 25¢
WITH FRONT COVER OF ANY SMITH BROTHERS BOX
SMITH BROTHERS
COUGH DROPS
Here's all you do! Fill in coupon below (or use sheet of paper), and send in with 25¢ and the front cover of any Smith Brothers box . . . for beautiful bracelet finished in Nickel Silver! Allow 4 weeks for delivery. Supply is limited—so hurry!
Please print information below (use pencil) and send
Name for Bracelet
Do you want birthstone? ☐ Yes ☐ No
If Yes, give month of birth
Wrist Size Large ☐ Small ☐
Name
Address
City Zone State

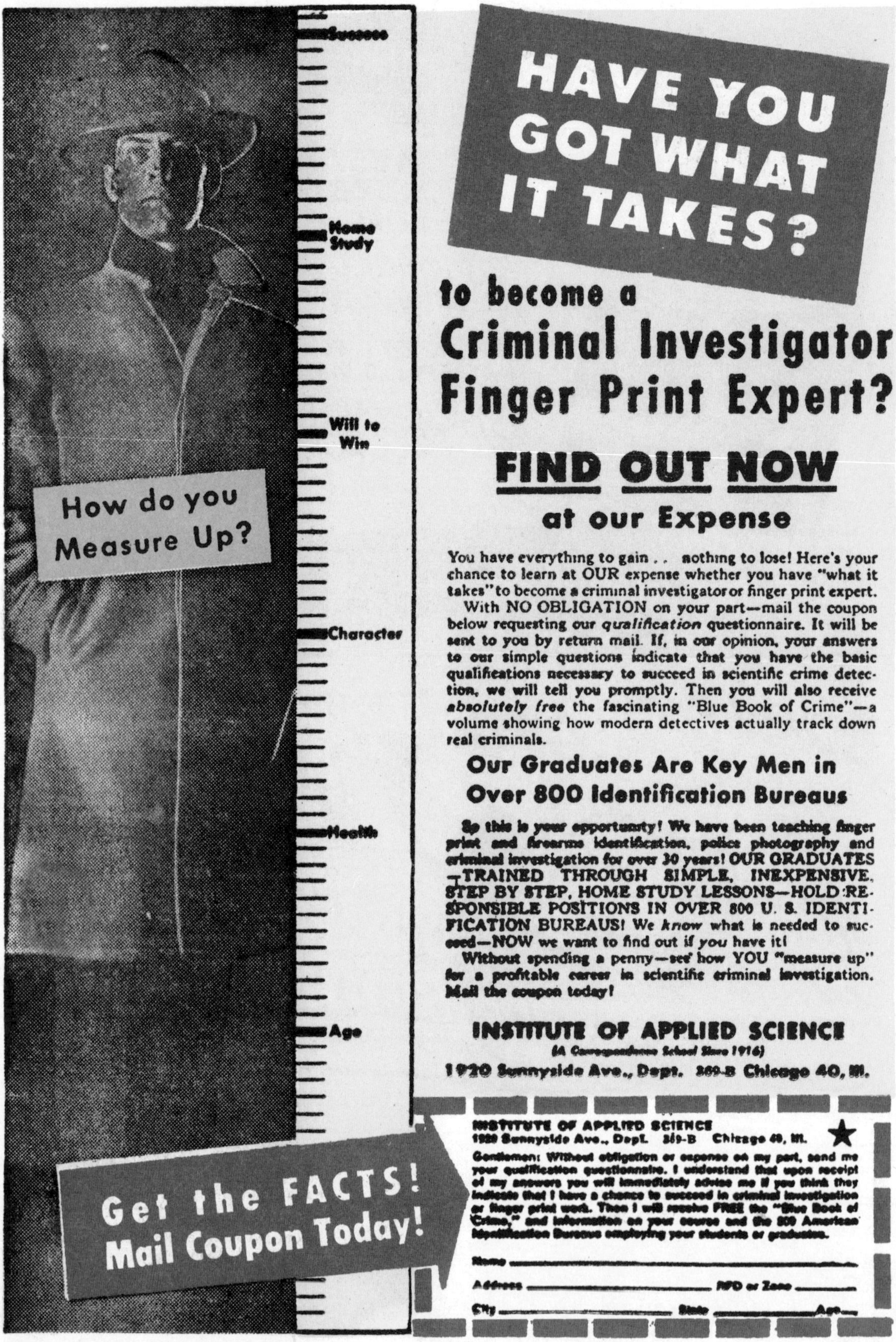
Success
Home Study
Will to Win
Character
Health
Age
How do you Measure Up?
Get the FACTS! Mail Coupon Today!
HAVE YOU GOT WHAT IT TAKES?
to become a
Criminal Investigator Finger Print Expert?
FIND OUT NOW
at our Expense
You have everything to gain .. nothing to lose! Here's your chance to learn at OUR expense whether you have "what it takes" to become a criminal investigator or finger print expert.
With NO OBLIGATION on your part—mail the coupon below requesting our *qualification* questionnaire. It will be sent to you by return mail. If, in our opinion, your answers to our simple questions indicate that you have the basic qualifications necessary to succeed in scientific crime detection, we will tell you promptly. Then you will also receive *absolutely free* the fascinating "Blue Book of Crime"—a volume showing how modern detectives actually track down real criminals.
Our Graduates Are Key Men in Over 800 Identification Bureaus
So this is your opportunity! We have been teaching finger print and firearms identification, police photography and criminal investigation for over 30 years! OUR GRADUATES—TRAINED THROUGH SIMPLE, INEXPENSIVE, STEP BY STEP, HOME STUDY LESSONS—HOLD RESPONSIBLE POSITIONS IN OVER 800 U. S. IDENTIFICATION BUREAUS! We *know* what is needed to succeed—NOW we want to find out if *you* have it!
Without spending a penny—see how YOU "measure up" for a profitable career in scientific criminal investigation. Mail the coupon today!
INSTITUTE OF APPLIED SCIENCE
(A Correspondence School Since 1916)
1920 Sunnyside Ave., Dept. 369-B Chicago 40, Ill.
INSTITUTE OF APPLIED SCIENCE
1920 Sunnyside Ave., Dept. 369-B Chicago 40, Ill.

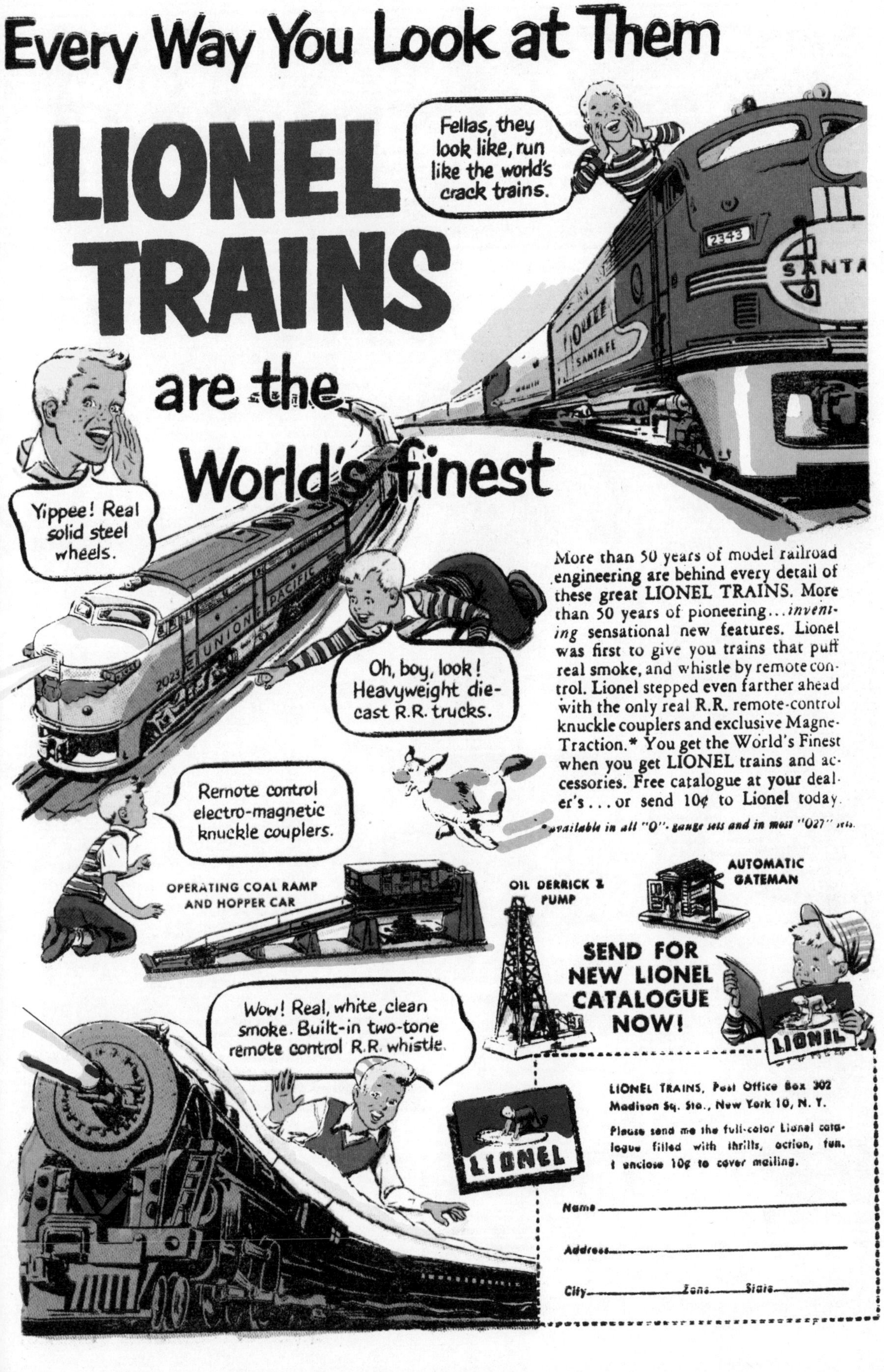

Every Way You Look at Them
LIONEL TRAINS
are the World's finest
Fellas, they look like, run like the world's crack trains.
Yippee! Real solid steel wheels.
Oh, boy, look! Heavyweight die-cast R.R. trucks.
More than 50 years of model railroad engineering are behind every detail of these great LIONEL TRAINS. More than 50 years of pioneering... *inventing* sensational new features. Lionel was first to give you trains that puff real smoke, and whistle by remote control. Lionel stepped even farther ahead with the only real R.R. remote-control knuckle couplers and exclusive Magne-Traction.* You get the World's Finest when you get LIONEL trains and accessories. Free catalogue at your dealer's... or send 10¢ to Lionel today.
*available in all "O"-gauge sets and in most "O27" sets.
Remote control electro-magnetic knuckle couplers.
OPERATING COAL RAMP AND HOPPER CAR
OIL DERRICK & PUMP
AUTOMATIC GATEMAN
SEND FOR NEW LIONEL CATALOGUE NOW!
Wow! Real, white, clean smoke. Built-in two-tone remote control R.R. whistle.
LIONEL
LIONEL TRAINS, Post Office Box 302
Madison Sq. Sta., New York 10, N. Y.
Please send me the full-color Lionel catalogue filled with thrills, action, fun. I enclose 10¢ to cover mailing.
Name
Address
City Zone State

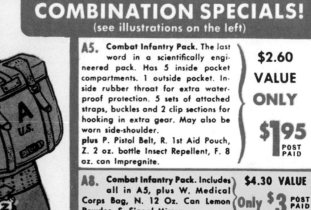
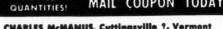

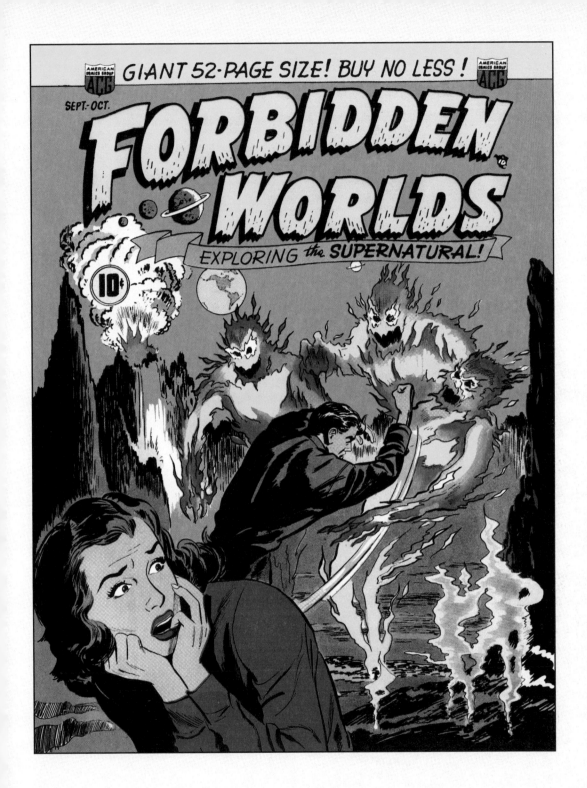

FORBIDDEN WORLDS #2 | September–October 1951

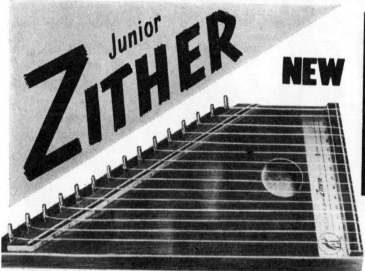

The MISTS of MIDNIGHT

The next time fog creeps over the countryside like a living shroud, peer into its restless depths -- and dare to speculate on what it hides! But first be sure you're in the right frame of mind -- because the hulking haze may hover toward you like an endless trap -- and enfold **YOU** among the victims of the **MISTS OF MIDNIGHT!**

LATE ONE NIGHT--
AUDREY--SOMETHING TELLS ME YOU'VE HAD FUN TONIGHT!

IT WAS A **WONDERFUL** SHOW, DARLING-- BUT I LIKE **THIS** EVEN BETTER -- STROLLING AROUND THE SPOT WHERE WE HAD OUR FIRST DATE!

WHAT BEATS **ME** IS HOW WE KEEP COMING BACK TO THIS QUIET LITTLE ROAD! MAYBE THAT'S WHAT LOVE IS -- A FIRST DATE THAT NEVER ENDS!

GOOD HEAVENS, NEIL, DID YOU **HAVE** TO STEP ASIDE -- AND LET THAT TREE COME BETWEEN US? YOU KNOW WHAT **THAT** MEANS -- **IT'S BAD LUCK!**

1

IT WOULD HAVE TO BE A PRETTY TOUGH JINX TO ROCK *OUR* LITTLE DREAMBOAT! GOSH, HONEY-- I THOUGHT YOU GOT OVER THIS *SUPERSTITIOUS* NONSENSE!

NONSENSE? I HAPPEN TO BELIEVE VERY FIRMLY IN THOSE THINGS -- AND I DON'T LIKE BEING RIDICULED!

LOOK, AUDREY-- NO MATTER *WHAT* YOU BELIEVE IN -- I DON'T SEE WHY IT SHOULD BECOME AN ISSUE!

DON'T WORRY-- IT *WON'T!* AND IF YOU DON'T MIND-- I'LL GO HOME BY *MYSELF!*

MINUTES LATER-- TOO LOST IN THOUGHT TO NOTICE THE STRANGE FOG CURLING OVER THE SILENT FIELDS--

MAYBE NEIL'S RIGHT ABOUT MY SUPERSTITIONS! IT WAS SILLY OF ME TO *EXPECT* BAD LUCK-- AND THEN BRING IT ABOUT WITH A QUARREL!

SUDDENLY-- FROM THE THICKENING MIST--

HELP! HELP!

WHATEVER'S WRONG-- THERE'S SOMETHING *QUEER* ABOUT THAT VOICE! I KNOW IT'S CLOSE-- AND YET IT SOUNDS SO FAINT AND FAR AWAY!

THEN-- AS A GROPING SHAPE REARS FROM THE CLAMMY BILLOWS--

WHAT'S THE MATTER? WHO ARE YOU?

FOR HEAVEN'S SAKE-- *DON'T BE AFRAID OF ME!* NO MATTER WHAT I *LOOK* LIKE, I'M ALIVE-- I'M *HUMAN!*

FOR JUST AN INSTANT-- AUDREY CATCHES A GLIMPSE OF THE WHITE, HAGGARD FACE PEERING FROM THE MIST--

THEY'RE COMING-- THEY'RE ALL AROUND US! GET ME AWAY FROM HERE-- *DON'T LET THEM DRAG ME BACK INTO THE MISTS!*

IN THE NEXT TERRIBLE MOMENT, THE WHITE EMPTINESS CHANGES INTO COWLED FIGURES-- HEMMING IN THEIR ANGUISHED VICTIM!

NO-- *NO!* NOT AGAIN-- NOT BACK *THERE!*

2

THEN-- IN A SHIFTING WAVE OF EVIL --

AGHHH!

GOOD HEAVENS-- HE'S DISAPPEARING-- THE FOG'S SWALLOWING HIM UP!

AND YET IT WASN'T FOG! THAT CREEPING VAPOR HARBORED THINGS-- ON THE TRAIL OF ESCAPING PREY!

BUT AN HOUR LATER--

I'VE GOT TO CALM DOWN-- IT DIDN'T REALLY HAPPEN! IT COULDN'T HAVE HAPPENED-- IT WAS JUST A HORRIBLE VISION CAUSED BY UPSET NERVES AFTER MY QUARREL WITH NEIL!

AT THAT MOMENT-- DEEP IN THE FORBIDDING HAZE--

UNTIL NOW-- NO ONE HAS GUESSED THE FATE OF THE THOUSANDS OF PEOPLE WHO HAVE VANISHED WITHOUT A TRACE! BUT WHAT THIS GIRL SAW CAN BE DANGEROUS-- THERE ARE HUMANS VERSED IN THE SUPERNATURAL WHO CAN DESTROY US IF SHE IS PERMITTED TO TALK!

BUT SHE WON'T! WE WILL LURE HER TO THE ECTOSPHERE-- SHE WILL BE THE NEXT VICTIM TO YIELD TO THE LIFE FORCE THAT MEANS OUR SURVIVAL!

THAT WILL NOT BE EASY! ONE LOOK SHOWED THAT THE GIRL LEADS A FULL AND CONTENTED LIFE-- AND THE HUMANS WE PREY ON ARE THOSE SO LADEN WITH TROUBLES THAT THEY GROW UNWARY OF THE FORCES READY TO ENGULF THEM!

BUT SUPPOSE WE BLIGHT THE CONTENTED LIFE OF AUDREY CLARK? SUPPOSE SHE IS BURDENED WITH ALL THE MISFORTUNE WE CAN DEVISE-- WHAT COULD SAVE HER FROM THE ECTOSPHERE THEN?

NEXT DAY-- AT AUDREY'S HOME --

HONEY, LET'S FORGET ABOUT THOSE CREEPS YOU *THINK* YOU SAW IN THE FOG LAST NIGHT! YOU NEEDN'T GO *THAT* FAR TO GAIN MY SYMPATHY-- I'M AS ANXIOUS TO MAKE UP, AS YOU ARE!

AND YET YOU'RE READY TO SHRUG OFF THE WHOLE STORY AS JUST ANOTHER SUPER-STITIOUS FANTASY! YES, I WAS JOLTED BY WHAT I *SAW* -- BUT WHAT *REALLY* TERRIFIES ME IS THE *PROOF* THAT IT ACTUALLY HAPPENED!

NEIL, *THIS* IS THE MAN WHO BEGGED ME TO HELP HIM-- *THE MAN CLAIMED BY THE PHANTOMS OF THE MIST!*

CLIN DAY NEW
NO TRACE OF MAN
MISSING FOR 5 DAYS!

BABY, I *KNOW* YOU'RE CERTAIN ABOUT THIS-- BUT CAN'T YOU SEE WHERE SUCH THOUGHTS LEAD TO? OKAY, YOU'VE GOT PROOF -- YOU WERE TERRIFIED AND NERVE-WRACKED -- BUT YOU'VE GOT TO PROMISE YOU'LL STOP THINKING ABOUT IT!

NEIL-- I'LL *TRY!* MAYBE IT WAS SOMETHING I'LL NEVER EX-PERIENCE AGAIN-- SOMETHING I CAN DRIVE OUT OF MY HEAD BY THINKING OF *YOU!*

BUT THAT NIGHT-- A PROWLING SHAPE IS READY TO OPEN THE EVIL CAMPAIGN OF DOOM!

AUDREY CLARK MAY BE SAFE FROM THE ECTOSPHERE *NOW* -- BUT WAIT! FROM THIS HOUR ON -- HER BROODING WILL BE THE LURE THAT LEADS HER TO *US!*

AS THE COWLED FIGURE HOVERS THROUGH THE GLOOMY HUSH--

OHH! IT'S ONE OF THOSE THINGS I SAW IN THE FOG!

I HAVE COME WITH A WARNING FROM THE BEYOND!

BEWARE-- BEWARE OF WHAT LIES AHEAD FOR YOU! YOU ARE FATED TO LOSE ALL YOU HAVE LOVED-- AND ALL YOU HAVE WORKED FOR!

AS THE SPECTRAL FORM FADES IN A GLOWING HAZE --

I'VE GOT TO PHONE NEIL! NOW HE *WILL* BELIEVE ME-- I CAN COUNT ON HIM--*HE'LL* FIND A WAY TO HELP ME!

4

WHAT--*AGAIN!* SWEETHEART, I THINK A PHONE CALL IN THE MIDDLE OF THE NIGHT IS CARRYING THIS GHOST BUSINESS A LITTLE TOO FAR!

IS *THAT* ALL YOU CAN SAY AT A TIME WHEN I NEED YOUR PROTECTION MOST! ALL RIGHT, NEIL-- I WON'T BOTHER YOU AGAIN-- *EVER!*

I'M *THROUGH* WITH NEIL-- I'VE LOST ALL I LOVED! IF THE PHANTOM WAS RIGHT ABOUT *THAT*-- WHAT ABOUT *ALL I HAVE WORKED FOR?* DOES THAT MEAN MY ADVERTISING JOB-- THE ONLY *OTHER* THING THAT MEANS ANYTHING TO ME?

NEXT DAY--

I KNOW I'M BEHIND SCHEDULE ON THIS LAYOUT, MR. FLETCHER-- BUT I'M STYMIED! I CAN'T CONCENTRATE!

I'M AFRAID YOU'LL HAVE TO WORK OVERTIME, AUDREY-- IT'S AN IMPORTANT ACCOUNT!

HOURS LATER--FRANTICALLY TRYING TO FORGET THE GNAWING TERROR OF THE PROPHECY--

OH, MURDER-- THERE GOES THE BOTTLE OF WHITE INK! IT'S RUINED EVERYTHING!

THEN--

OHH!

GREAT SCOTT, AUDREY-- WHAT'S *WRONG?*

NEIL WOULDN'T BELIEVE ME-- AND I DON'T EX- PECT *YOU* TO-- BUT *THERE'S* ONE OF THE THINGS I'VE SEEN FOR THE PAST TWO NIGHTS-- AS PLAINLY AS I SEE YOU!

WELL--THERE'S NO USE TRYING TO GET THOSE LAYOUTS FINISHED *NOW!* BY TOMORROW MORNING WE'LL HAVE LOST OUR BIGGEST ACCOUNT-- AND I HOPE I DON'T HAVE TO EXPLAIN WHAT *THAT* MEANS!

MR. FLETCHER-- WHAT ARE YOU TRYING TO SAY? YOU NEEDN'T PULL ANY PUNCHES!

5

IT'S A TOUGH BREAK, KID-- BUT YOU JUST HAVEN'T HELD UP IN A PINCH-- WHEN WE NEEDED YOU MOST! AND IN THIS GAME--IT HAPPENS ONLY ONCE!

YOU'RE NOT SAYING WHAT YOU REALLY THINK-- THAT I'M NOT ONLY UNRELIABLE-- BUT VERY POSSIBLY HALF-CRACKED! BUT NEVER MIND-- YOU NEEDN'T FIRE ME -- I KNEW THIS WAS GOING TO HAPPEN!

BROKENLY, AUDREY WALKS AIMLESS-LY THROUGH THE DESERTED STREETS -- HER THOUGHTS SHADOWED BY A BLEAK CONVICTION --

NOW THAT I'VE LOST BOTH NEIL AND MY CAREER--THERE'S ONLY ONE CERTAINTY LEFT! I DID SEE THOSE PHANTOMS-- AND IT'S A PORTENT OF A DOOM I CAN'T ESCAPE!

AN HOUR LATER -- WITH STREAMERS OF FOG DRIFTING AMONG THE BARE TREES --

IT'S A STRANGE, HAZY NIGHT-- BUT WHY SHOULD I MIND -- WHEN IT MATCHES MY MOOD?

ORDINARILY, I'D SHRINK FROM THIS GREY, SHAPELESS MOTION AROUND ME -- BUT NOW I KNOW THAT FEAR IS A LUXURY-- FELT ONLY BY PEOPLE WITH SOMETHING TO LOSE!

SLOWLY, THE MISTS OF MIDNIGHT THICKEN AROUND THE SOLITARY FIGURE-- AND THE MUFFLED SILENCE IS BROKEN BY WEIRD LAUGHTER-- RISING AND FADING IN THE CLAMMY PALL!

HA! HA! HA!

GUESS I'M NOT ALONE AFTER ALL! BUT IF THERE ARE PEOPLE OUT THIS LATE -- WHERE ARE THEY!

WITH MOUNTING DREAD --

I-- I DON'T LIKE THIS! I'VE GOT THE FEELING THAT EACH STEP IS TAKING ME TOWARD SOMETHING FROM WHICH THERE'S NO RETURN -- AS COLD AND CLINGING AS DEATH ITSELF!

THEN, AS THE FOG LOOMS CLOSER -- AND ITS HOVERING DEPTHS EDDY INTO COWLED AND CACKLING FORMS ---

ROAD-- TREES -- EVERYTHING'S BLOTTED OUT! THERE'S NOWHERE TO TURN-- I DON'T KNOW WHERE I AM!

HA! HA!

6

FROM ALL SIDES -- SOUNDLESS AND STARING -- THE PHANTOMS MOVE TOWARD AUDREY IN A CHILL WHITE WAVE --

I CAN'T SEE ANYTHING -- NOTHING BUT *THEM!* NOW I KNOW WHAT HAPPENED TO THAT MAN THE OTHER NIGHT! I'M BEING CAUGHT IN THE MISTS -- *FOREVER!*

DON'T STRUGGLE -- YOU CAN'T ESCAPE THE HALF-DEATH OF THE ECTOSPHERE! WHY *SHOULD* YOU -- WHAT HAS THE WORLD TO OFFER YOU?

AND WHAT CAN *YOU* OFFER ME? YOU'RE EVIL -- EVERYTHING IN ME SENSES IT AND SHRINKS FROM IT!

THERE ARE NO *THOUGHTS* IN THE ECTOSPHERE! ALL THAT IS GONE AND ALL THAT IS LOST WILL NEVER MATTER AGAIN!

YOU WILL FORGET IN OUR QUIET GREY WORLD! THERE WILL BE NO DAYS AND NO NIGHTS -- NOTHING BUT A HUSHED ETERNITY!

TO FORGET... THEN I WOULDN'T MIND ANY MORE -- THERE'D BE NO GRIEF -- NO LONELY BROODING!

THAT IS THE WAY IT WILL BE IN THE ECTOSPHERE! IT'S WHAT YOU WANT -- COME WITH US!

SUDDENLY, THE HUDDLED FIGURES ARE TOUCHED BY FAINT POINTS OF TWINKLING LIGHT -- AND A WEIRD AMBER GLOW FILTERS THROUGH THE VEIL OF TERROR --

WHAT DOES THAT FLASH MEAN? NOW THAT I'VE BEEN LULLED INTO A FEELING OF SAFETY -- WILL I HAVE TO FACE A NEW OUTBURST OF HORROR?

I HEAR A VOICE! IT'S NOT LIKE *YOURS* -- IT'S *HUMAN!*

NO -- YOU HEAR NOTHING! IT IS ONLY AN ECHO OF WHAT YOU HAVE LOST -- A MEMORY THAT WILL DIE OUT AS WE APPROACH THE ECTOSPHERE!

THEN -- THROUGH THE FOG-STREAKED GLOOM --

7

AUDREY-- AUDREY! IT'S ME-- NEIL!

NEIL! FOR HEAVEN'S SAKE, HELP ME-- THEY WON'T LET ME GO!

YE GODS-- THEY DO EXIST!

WHOEVER YOU ARE-- KEEP BACK! SHE HAS BEEN CHOSEN-- AND NOTHING CAN DISPUTE OUR CLAIM!

WITH A FEARLESS RUSH--

DON'T WORRY, SWEETHEART-- THEY CAN'T CLAIM YOU UNLESS YOU'RE AT THE VERY BOTTOM OF DESPAIR-- AND THAT'S NEVER HAPPENED YET TO SOMEONE WHO'S IN LOVE!

IN LOVE! THAT WAS SUPPOSED TO BE OVER-- WE SCHEMED TO WRECK IT-- AND WE FAILED!

NEIL-- I'M TERRIFIED! THE MURK IS SWARMING WITH THOSE CREATURES-- SUPPOSE THEY CAPTURE BOTH OF US?

THEY'VE LOST THEIR CHANCE, AUDREY-- AND THEY KNOW IT! LOOK AT THE MIST-- IT'S STREAMING PAST US!

SLOWLY, THE PHANTOMS FADE-- BECOMING ONE WITH THE WHITENESS THAT ROLLS OVER THE GLISTENING COUNTRYSIDE!

GOOD HEAVENS! HERE'S WHERE I WALKED WITHOUT EVEN KNOWING IT-- TO THE VERY LANE WHERE WE HAD OUR FIRST DATE!

I WENT AROUND TO YOUR OFFICE TO PATCH THINGS UP-- AND WHEN JIM FLETCHER TOLD ME WHAT HAD HAPPENED, I KNEW THIS WAS THE PLACE YOU'D GO!

THERE'S NO USE SAYING I WAS A CHUMP-- THAT I SHOULD HAVE LISTENED TO YOU IN THE FIRST PLACE! BUT THANK HEAVEN I GOT HERE SOON ENOUGH TO SAVE YOU FROM BEING SWEPT INTO OBLIVION BY THOSE DEMONS!

I'M LUCKY YOU FOUND ME FOR MORE REASONS THAN ONE! THERE'S NO WAY TO EXPLAIN THE MISTS OF MIDNIGHT, NEIL-- THEY'VE GOT TO BE SEEN-- AND THAT'S WHY I WONDER HOW I'LL EVER SET THINGS STRAIGHT WITH JIM FLETCHER!

YOU NEEDN'T WORRY ABOUT THAT, HONEY-- I'VE FIXED IT! I TOLD HIM THAT ANY GIRL WAS LIKELY TO GO SLIGHTLY DAFFY OVER A PROPOSAL OF MARRIAGE-- AND HE AGREED!

NEIL-- DARLING!

The End

8

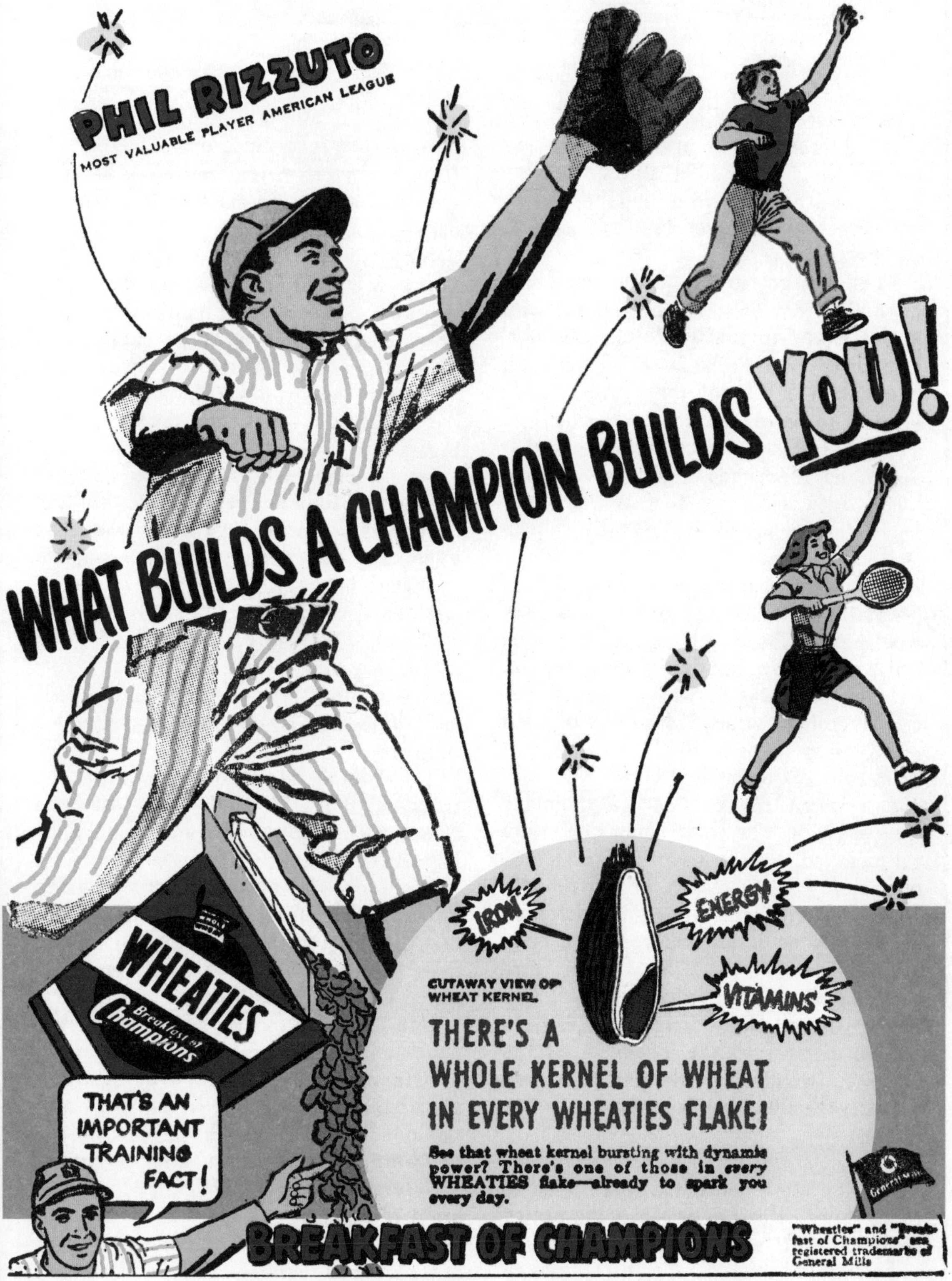
PHIL RIZZUTO
MOST VALUABLE PLAYER AMERICAN LEAGUE
WHAT BUILDS A CHAMPION BUILDS YOU!
IRON
ENERGY
VITAMINS
WHEATIES
Breakfast of Champions
CUTAWAY VIEW OF WHEAT KERNEL
THERE'S A WHOLE KERNEL OF WHEAT IN EVERY WHEATIES FLAKE!
See that wheat kernel bursting with dynamic power? There's one of those in every WHEATIES flake—already to spark you every day.
THAT'S AN IMPORTANT TRAINING FACT!
BREAKFAST OF CHAMPIONS
"Wheaties" and "Breakfast of Champions" are registered trademarks of General Mills

POSTSCRIPT to DEATH

SYLVIA SUDDENLY FOUND herself running breathlessly towards the house. She had a strange feeling that something terrible had happened, and she prayed fervently that her husband was all right.

When she got to the house, she flung open the front door and called out with a desperate intensity, "John...*John!*" But there was no answer. Fearfully, she began a tour of the rooms, which seemed to be overcast with the hush of death. The conviction struck her that John had died, and she was about to burst into grieving tears, when she heard the sound of a car pulling up in front of the house.

Looking through the window, Sylvia uttered a heartfelt cry of relief as she saw her husband get out of the car. But...what was he doing in a *funeral* car...and why was he wearing those dismal mourning clothes? Had any of their relatives or friends died? Why hadn't John told *her* about it?

She raced to the door, a thousand questions on her lips. But they were all unasked, as she saw the stark lines of tragedy etched into her husband's face. There was something lifeless about him, as if all emotions had been drained from him, as if he were no more than a hollow shell from which all life and spirit had fled. Frightened, Sylvia shrank back into the shadows of the hallway, wondering whether this was actually the laughing John she'd always known.

As he swept by her with unseeing eyes, she stretched out a timid hand to touch him. But he went up the stairs as if he'd felt nothing at all. Was this a horrible nightmare she was having? Desperately, Sylvia pinched her arm with all her strength, feeling the sharp pain as her long nails dug into the soft flesh...and the bright red mark her fingers had made told her that this was no dream, but awful reality.

Slowly she followed John up the stairs, watched him enter her room with the stiff tread of the sleepwalker. She stood in the doorway as he opened one of her closets and stared at her clothes. Suddenly he was on his knees, his hands clutching at her dresses, crying.

For a moment, Sylvia stood there in stunned astonishment, dumbly thinking that this was the first time she had ever seen him weep. But then she ran towards him with outstretched arms, her heart wracked by his sobs.

"John, John! What's wrong?" she cried, dropping to her knees beside him and enfolding him in her arms. "Tell me what's the matter, darling. Let me help you!"

John didn't seem to have heard her. Instead, he clenched his fists and cried out, "Why...why did it have to happen to *her?*"

His face now raised, he was staring up at the ceiling. Sylvia bent over him, looking right into his pain-filled eyes that gazed right through her, as if she weren't even there. *"John!"* Sylvia cried, terror growing in her heart. *"Talk* to me...*look* at me!"

"He can't, my dear," a quiet voice said behind her. "The living can't see the dead. Come, you have many years to wait until he can talk to you."

Sylvia whirled, and gasped at the sight of her mother, who had died years before. Slowly, Sylvia advanced to take her mother's outstretched hand, aware of the truth at last.

The LEAGUE of VAMPIRES

THERE ARE NIGHTS WHEN A CHILL WIND SENDS DEAD LEAVES DANCING AGAINST THE LAST STREAKS OF SUNSET--WHEN A DARTING BLACK FORM SKIMS THROUGH THE WHISPERING TREES! AND ON SUCH A NIGHT, IT'S EASY TO BELIEVE THAT A FACE WILL APPEAR AT THE FROSTY WINDOW-- A FACE WITH BEADY EYES AND FANGS THAT WARN OF EVIL --A FACE THAT CAN SUMMON THE FLAPPING *LEAGUE OF VAMPIRES!*

ONE NIGHT--AT THE HOME OF NANCY LEWIS--

WITH ALL THE PAPERS REPORTING MY ENGAGEMENT TO ROY, IT'S A LITTLE HARD TO REALIZE THAT HIS EXPERIMENTS KEEP HIM ISOLATED--TOO BUSY TO SEE EVEN *ME!* BUT LONELY AS I AM, I CAN'T INTERRUPT HIS WORK--NOT AT A TIME WHEN HE'S TURNING EVERYONE *ELSE* AWAY FROM HIS LABORATORY!

UNEXPECTEDLY--

THAT'S STRANGE! WHAT COULD ANYONE WANT AT *THIS* HOUR?

NOK! NOK!

OH!

DON'T BE ALARMED! I'VE COME TO SEE YOU ABOUT SOMEONE IN WHOM WE'RE *BOTH* INTERESTED--ROY CARLSON!

IN A WORD--I'M PLACED IN A DIFFICULT POSITION BY THE FACT THAT DR. CARLSON WON'T PERMIT VISITORS AT HIS LABORATORY! MY BUSINESS THERE IS *URGENT*--AND YOU'VE GOT TO HELP ME!

BUT THAT'S AN UNUSUAL REQUEST --WHEN THIS IS THE FIRST TIME I'VE SET EYES ON YOU!

AND THIS IS THE FIRST TIME I'VE SET EYES ON *YOU!* WATCH THEM-- WATCH THEM *CLOSELY*-- AND YOU WILL SEE HOW EASY IT IS TO DO WHAT I ASK!

SLOWLY, THE STRANGE FIGURE FADES --WITH ONLY HIS RESTLESS EYES FLUTTERING IN THE GLOOM!

DID YOU EVER SEE EYES LIKE *THESE?* DO YOU BEGIN TO THINK THAT MAYBE THEY *AREN'T* EYES?

IT'S SOME KIND OF TRICK-- I'M NOT GOING TO LET MYSELF BE *AFRAID!*

THEN, AS THE BLACK ORBS COME CLOSER--AND THEIR EVIL TWINKLE CHANGES INTO MOVEMENT--

THEY'RE STILL SIDE BY SIDE-- THEY'RE STILL LOOKING AT ME-- *BUT THEY'RE BATS!*

IN A FLASH, THE FURRY FORMS MERGE--INTO A SINGLE SQUEAKING CREATURE THAT SWOOPS DIZZILY BEFORE ITS VICTIM!

CAN *YOU* RESIST-- AFTER THOUSANDS OF OTHERS HAVE WATCHED ME IN A HELPLESS TRANCE?

I'M FACE TO FACE WITH SOMETHING HIDEOUSLY EVIL, BUT NOT EVEN TERROR CAN SAVE ME --*I'VE GOT TO OBEY!*

WITH A GLIDE THAT RUSTLES ITS SILKEN BLACK WINGS--

YOU KNOW WHERE I WISH TO GO! *TAKE ME THERE!*

THE LABORATORY! YES, YOU WILL ENTER --*WITH ME!*

2.

A HALF-HOUR LATER--

WE'RE HERE! HAVE YOU ANY OTHER COMMANDS?

TAKE ME INSIDE-- I CAN DO THE REST!

NANCY! GOSH--FOR A MOMENT I COULDN'T BELIEVE MY EYES!

PLEASE DON'T BE CROSS WITH ME, ROY--I JUST HAD TO SEE YOU!

YOU COULDN'T HAVE PICKED A BETTER TIME, HONEY! I'VE JUST COMPLETED A RESEARCH-PROJECT THAT WILL GIVE WORLD AGRICULTURE THE THING IT NEEDS MOST--A PERFECT SOIL!

I'VE LEARNED THAT MUCH ALREADY--BY FLUTTERING OUTSIDE THE LOCKED WINDOWS! YES, IT'S A PERFECT SOIL--FOR VAMPIRES!

AT ONE TIME, NANCY, THE WORLD WAS AMAZINGLY FERTILE--AND THE ENTIRE GLOBE HAD JUST ONE TYPE OF SOIL! WIND, EROSION, AND OTHER FACTORS CHANGED ALL THAT--BUT I'VE MIXED TOGETHER ONE-POUND SAMPLES OF SOIL FROM FIFTY DIFFERENT LOCATIONS ALL OVER THE WORLD! THE BLEND IN THIS BOX IS VERY SIMILAR TO THE ORIGINAL SOIL THAT ONCE COVERED THE EARTH--AND ANALYSIS SHOWS IT CAN BE MASS-PRODUCED BY ARTIFICIAL MEANS!

HONEY, I WAS TOO EXCITED TO NOTICE IT BEFORE, BUT THERE'S SOMETHING STRANGE IN YOUR MANNER --IT ISN'T NATURAL!

I--I CAN'T EXPLAIN! YOU SEEM SO FAR AWAY-- JUST AS IF THERE WAS NOTHING HERE BUT MYSELF-- AND THOSE EYES!

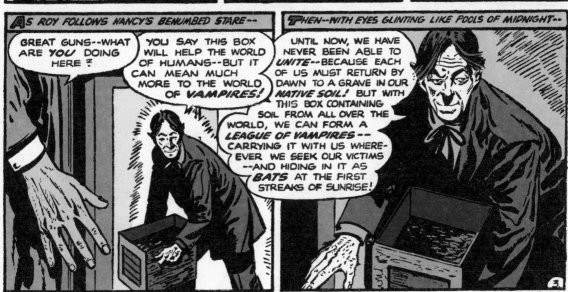

AS ROY FOLLOWS NANCY'S BENUMBED STARE--

GREAT GUNS--WHAT ARE YOU DOING HERE?

YOU SAY THIS BOX WILL HELP THE WORLD OF HUMANS--BUT IT CAN MEAN MUCH MORE TO THE WORLD OF VAMPIRES!

THEN--WITH EYES GLINTING LIKE POOLS OF MIDNIGHT--

UNTIL NOW, WE HAVE NEVER BEEN ABLE TO UNITE--BECAUSE EACH OF US MUST RETURN BY DAWN TO A GRAVE IN OUR NATIVE SOIL! BUT WITH THIS BOX CONTAINING SOIL FROM ALL OVER THE WORLD, WE CAN FORM A LEAGUE OF VAMPIRES-- CARRYING IT WITH US WHEREVER WE SEEK OUR VICTIMS --AND HIDING IN IT AS BATS AT THE FIRST STREAKS OF SUNRISE!

3.

FOR AN INSTANT, ROY IS CHECKED BY THE MURKY HOLD OF THE STARING EYES--STIFLING HIS RESISTANCE IN WAVES OF EVIL!

NOW I KNOW WHAT'S WRONG WITH NANCY! SHE MAY NOT BE ABLE TO RESIST THIS FIEND--BUT I'VE GOT TO!

THEN-- THERE'S NO TELLING WHAT'LL HAPPEN TO ME IF YOU START SLUGGING BACK, CREEP--BUT YOU'LL HAVE TO DROP THE BOX FIRST!

DO YOU THINK I NEED TO WASTE MY STRENGTH ON A MERE HUMAN? VAMPIRES--- COME FORTH!

IN THE NEXT SECOND--

ROY! IT'S JUST AS IF I'VE BEEN SLEEPWALKING THROUGH A HORRIBLE NIGHTMARE--BUT THAT BLOW SNAPPED ME OUT OF IT!

YE GODS, LOOK--COMING THROUGH THE DOOR!

WITH A HURTLING IMPACT--

CRASH!

WHAM!

ROY! YOU SHOULDN'T HAVE DEFIED HIM--NOT A CREATURE LIKE THAT!

CAN YOU SEE NOW WHY I WANTED THIS BOX OF EARTH, DR. CARLSON?

IT WILL BE A HAVEN--A GATHERING PLACE--FOR DOZENS OF VAMPIRES NOW SCATTERED AROUND THE WORLD! THANKS TO YOU, WE NEED NO LONGER BE CONTENT WITH RANDOM VICTIMS--NOW THERE WILL NOT BE A SLEEPER ANYWHERE WHO CANNOT BE REACHED BY THE LEAGUE OF VAMPIRES!

4

As a chill, taunting laugh ripples through the darkness--

HA HA HA!

GREAT GUNS--HE'S SPROUTING IMMENSE BAT WINGS!

Then--with his black demons wheeling around him--

BE CAREFUL, DR. CARLSON! REMEMBER THIS NIGHT--AND REMEMBER THE LEAGUE OF VAMPIRES!

DARLING, I WOULD RATHER HAVE BEEN A VICTIM MYSELF THAN HELP THAT FIEND--BUT IT'S JUST AS IF I HAD BEEN TURNED INTO A MERE MACHINE--MANIPULATED BY THOSE HIDEOUS, STARING EYES!

DON'T BLAME YOURSELF, NANCY--I'M GLAD YOU MANAGED TO ESCAPE UNHARMED! BUT WHEN I THINK OF THE UNBRIDLED TERROR THAT LIES AHEAD--WITH FLOCKS OF FLUTTERING DEMONS CONVERGING ON A SINGLE DISTRICT--THERE'S JUST ONE THING TO DO! I'VE GOT TO FIND THAT BOX!

Three days pass--marked by the looming shadow of impending terror!

IT'S NO USE, SWEETHEART--THE PAPERS DON'T CARRY SO MUCH AS A HINT AS TO THE WHEREABOUTS OF THOSE VAMPIRES!

MAYBE IT'S A MISTAKE TO TRY TO DO ANYTHING ALONE, ROY! CONSIDERING THE GRISLY HORROR THOSE CREATURES CAN WREAK--WE'VE GOT TO CALL ON THE POLICE FOR HELP!

NATURALLY, I'VE THOUGHT OF THAT--BUT DON'T YOU SEE THE VAMPIRES WILL REALLY HIDE ONCE THEY GET WIND OF AN ORGANIZED SEARCH? ON THE OTHER HAND, IF WE COULD ONLY TRICK THEM INTO THINKING WE KNOW WHERE THEY ARE--IT MIGHT GET RESULTS!

HONEY--I'VE GOT IT! THE VAMPIRE LEADER NEVER ACTUALLY RELEASED YOU FROM THAT HYPNOTIC SPELL--AND AS FAR AS HE KNOWS--YOUR MIND IS STILL UNDER HIS CONTROL!

THANK HEAVEN IT ISN'T--BUT WHAT'S THE TIE-UP?

IT'S JUST A SHOT IN THE DARK, BUT I'M GOING TO SEE MY FRIEND STAN ADAMS--OVER AT THE FEDERAL BROADCASTING STUDIOS! HE'S GOING TO SEND OUT A NEWS FLASH--THE FANTASTIC KIND THAT FEW PEOPLE WILL TAKE SERIOUSLY--EXCEPT THE VAMPIRES!

That night--nearing the end of a grim journey from the ends of the world--

My summons has been answered--they're coming from EVERYWHERE! Sunrise will find them all safely inside the box--and by tomorrow night--THE LEAGUE OF VAMPIRES will be ready for its first wave of terror!

It isn't likely anyone noticed the bats making their way HERE--but I'll tune in on the late news bulletins just to play safe!

CLIK!

Folks, this is Stan Adams--with a local item proving how whacky some people can get! A girl named Nancy Lewis claims she was hypnotized by a lunatic who thinks he's a vampire! What's more, she claims she's still subject to his will--and she's ready to lead victims to the vampire's lair!

People may really think Nancy Lewis is crazy--but the POLICE aren't that easily fooled! Once they get wind of this, they'll KNOW she's really hypnotized--and she'll be leading THEM here!

Get Nancy Lewis! There's ONE way to end this dangerous hypnotic state-- DEATH!

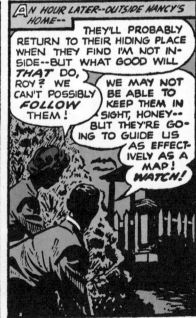

An hour later--outside Nancy's home--

They'll probably return to their hiding place when they find I'm not inside--but what good will THAT do, Roy? We can't possibly FOLLOW them!

We may not be able to keep them in sight, honey--but they're going to guide us as effectively as a MAP! WATCH!

6.

A MOMENT LATER--AS THE BATS CIRCLE AWAY FROM THE HOUSE--

I'M NOT SORRY TO SEE THEM GO, ROY-- BUT I'M *STILL* PUZZLED ABOUT WHAT YOU'RE UP TO!

THESE THREADS CAUGHT ON THE BATS' WINGS, JUST AS I EXPECTED --AND THEY WERE TREATED WITH A *RADIOACTIVE SOLUTION* STRONG ENOUGH TO REGISTER ON THIS EXTRA-SENSITIVE DETECTOR! IT MAY TAKE TIME--BUT THE DEVICE WILL HUM LOUDER AND LOUDER AS WE APPROACH THE VAMPIRES' RETREAT!

THROUGHOUT THE NIGHT, NANCY AND ROY FOLLOW THE TELLTALE HUM ALONG LONELY BACK ROADS--AND FINALLY--

THE DETECTOR SIGNAL HAS REACHED ITS MAXIMUM PITCH, NANCY! NO MISTAKE ABOUT IT--*THIS IS THE PLACE!*

THE LEAGUE OF VAMPIRES! WHO'D EVER DREAM THAT SO MUCH HIDEOUS, FLAPPING EVIL COULD BE GATHERED UNDER ONE ROOF?

WAIT--I CAN'T LET YOU FACE THOSE FIENDS A *SECOND* TIME! I'M NOT SURE YET OF HOW MUCH *I'LL* BE ABLE TO DO--BUT I'VE GOT TO MEET THE PROBLEM *ALONE!*

AT THAT INSTANT--IN ONE OF THE MURKY CHAMBERS OF HORROR--

THAT'S STRANGE...THE BATS WOULDN'T FLUTTER RESTLESSLY WITHOUT A REASON--CAN IT BE THAT THEY SENSE THE PRESENCE OF *PREY?*

AHH--THIS EXPLAINS THAT RADIO BULLETIN--*THEY'VE TRIED TO TRICK ME!* BUT NOW THE TABLES WILL BE TURNED--*NOW* THEY *WILL* LEARN WHAT IT MEANS TO BE UNDER A VAMPIRE'S SPELL!

SECONDS LATER--AS THE RUSH OF IMMENSE WINGS CUTS THR-OUGH THE BLACK SILENCE--

ALL RIGHT, ROY! I HATE TO SEE YOU RUN THE RISKS *ALONE*--BUT I'LL WAIT IN THE CAR!

I WISH YOU *HAD*, BABY--BUT IT'S TOO LATE NOW! *HERE HE COMES!*

THEN--WITH A FIXED AND LUMINOUS STARE--

THOSE EYES AGAIN! ROY --CAN YOU FEEL IT?

GOOD LORD-- IT'S A NUMBING WAVE OF EVIL-- *I CAN'T FIGHT IT OFF!*

7.

YARD BY YARD --THE VAMPIRE'S VICTIMS STAGGER HELPLESS-LY TOWARD THE PORTALS OF DOOM!

HA HA! YOU TWO LONGED TO FIND THE HIDING-PLACE OF EVIL--I WAITED IMPATIENTLY FOR PREY--AND NOW WE'LL ALL BE SATISFIED!

THERE'S NO NEED WAITING UNTIL TOMORROW NIGHT TO SEARCH FOR VICTIMS! TONIGHT THE VICTIMS HAVE COME TO US!

I CAN'T GIVE UP LIKE THIS! I'VE GOT TO SUMMON EVERY IOTA OF WILL POWER --AND RESIST!

AS THE FLUTTERING WINGS BEAT CLOSER--

NANCY--DON'T YOU SEE THEM? NO--NO--I CAN'T LET THEM TOUCH YOU!

DESPERATELY--ROY FIGHTS OFF THE PARALYZING CLUTCH OF THE VAMPIRE'S WILL!

WHATEVER ELSE HAPPENS-- I KNOW ONE THING THAT WILL DRAW THEM AWAY FROM NANCY!

POW!

THE BOX! MAY ALL THE BLACK CURSES OF PERDITION BE ON HIS HEAD--STOP HIM!

MAYBE YOU FLITTING FIENDS CAN STOP ME--BUT EVERY MINUTE COUNTS--AND I'M READY TO FIGHT RIGHT DOWN TO THE LAST SECOND!

WHAM!

8.

THIS IS **ONE** WAY TO GET MYSELF CORNERED--BUT AS LONG AS THEY'RE AFTER **ME**--NANCY WILL BE SAFE!

BODILY INJURY DOESN'T MEAN A THING TO CREEPS LIKE THESE--IT'S JUST A QUESTION OF HOW LONG I CAN KEEP THEM CHECKED!

CRAK!

THEN--IN AN UNEXPECTED SWOOP--

THAT WAS CLOSE ENOUGH! BUT THE FACT THAT I SPOTTED THE VAM-PIRE JUST IN TIME PROVES IT'S GETTING LIGHTER--**IT'S WITHIN A FEW MINUTES OF DAWN!**

FOOL--HOW OFTEN CAN YOU DODGE? WE'LL COME AT YOU FROM ALL SIDES--**WE'LL WEAR YOU OUT!**

AS THE VAMPIRE CIRCLES FOR ANOTHER DIVE--

HOLY SMOKE-- I'M LOSING MY BALANCE!

POW!

MAYBE **I'M** DONE FOR--BUT THEY'RE NOT GETTING **THIS!**

IN THE NEXT INSTANT--

CRASH!

9.

81

THIS TIME HE *WON'T* DODGE! FOLLOW ME, VAMPIRES--*FOR THE FINAL POUNCE!*

YOU'D BETTER MAKE IT A QUICK ONE, CREEP! THE EARTH THAT SHELTERS YOU IS SCATTERED FOR YARDS--*AND YOU WON'T HAVE TIME TO GATHER IT TOGETHER!*

THE BOX--*HE DRAGGED IT DOWN WITH HIM!* GET THE SOIL--*FAST--FAST!*

TAKE A LOOK AT THE HORIZON, BUD! WHAT DO YOU SEE--*WHAT DOES IT MEAN?*

THAT BURST OF LIGHT...IT'S THE SUN--*IT'S DAWN!*

THEN--IN AN UNCHECKED PLUNGE--

WE'RE TRAPPED--DAYLIGHT HAS CAUGHT US WITHOUT A REFUGE! YAAAGH!

FIFTY FEET BELOW--THE LEAGUE OF VAMPIRES MEETS ITS DOOM!

BLAM!

THAT FINISHES 'EM, NANCY! THOSE WINGS THAT RUSTLED AT MIDNIGHT--THE EVIL SPELL THAT CLAIMED THOUSANDS OF VICTIMS--THEY'VE VANISHED FOREVER!

NOW THAT *THEY'RE* GONE, DARLING --MAYBE I'LL BE ABLE TO GET YOU UNDER A LITTLE SPELL OF MY OWN!

The End

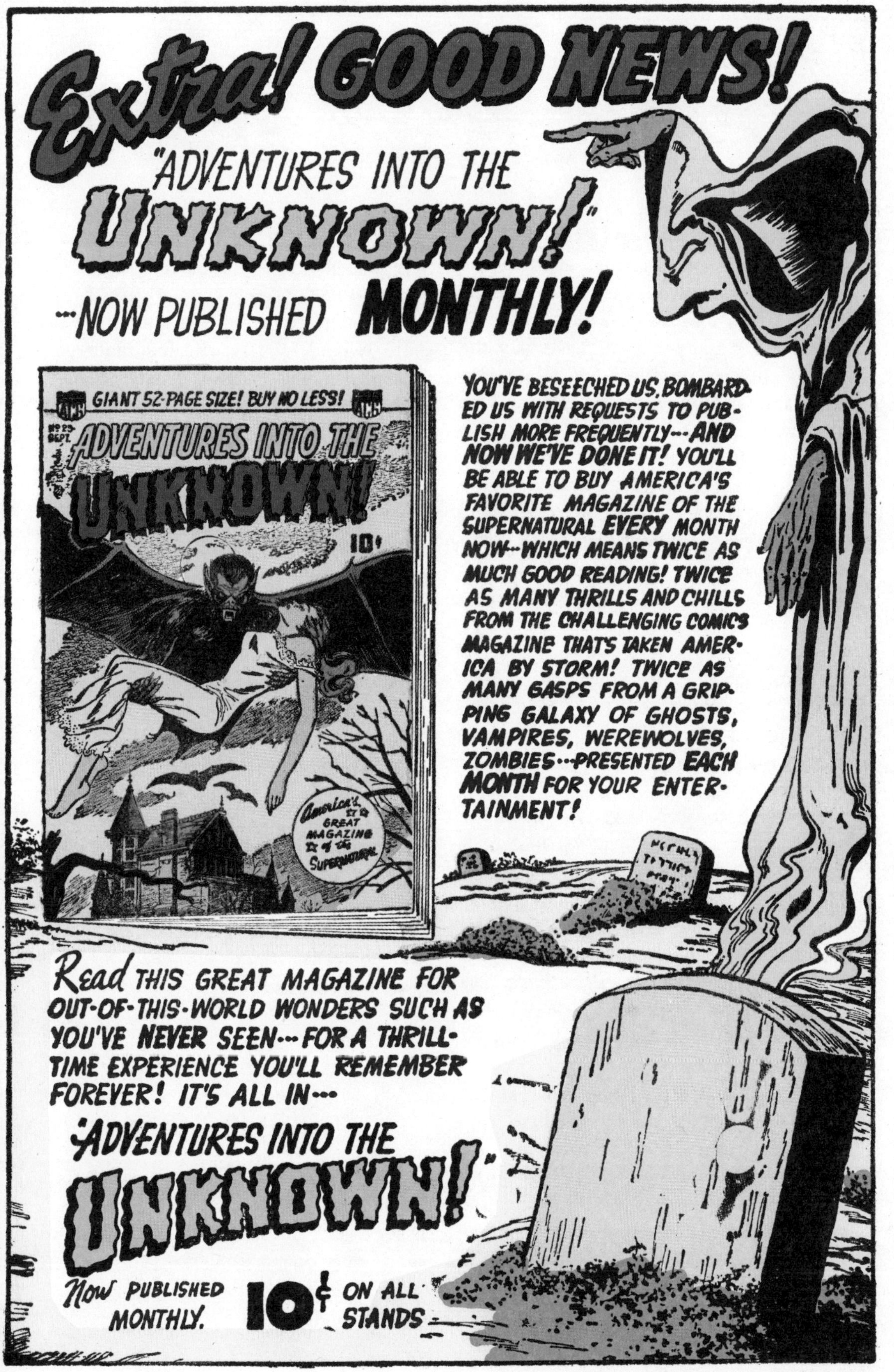

Extra! GOOD NEWS!
"ADVENTURES INTO THE UNKNOWN!"
---NOW PUBLISHED MONTHLY!
GIANT 52-PAGE SIZE! BUY NO LESS!
ACG
No 23 SEPT.
ADVENTURES INTO THE UNKNOWN!
10¢
America's GREAT MAGAZINE of the SUPERNATURAL
YOU'VE BESEECHED US, BOMBARDED US WITH REQUESTS TO PUBLISH MORE FREQUENTLY---AND NOW WE'VE DONE IT! YOU'LL BE ABLE TO BUY AMERICA'S FAVORITE MAGAZINE OF THE SUPERNATURAL EVERY MONTH NOW---WHICH MEANS TWICE AS MUCH GOOD READING! TWICE AS MANY THRILLS AND CHILLS FROM THE CHALLENGING COMICS MAGAZINE THAT'S TAKEN AMERICA BY STORM! TWICE AS MANY GASPS FROM A GRIPPING GALAXY OF GHOSTS, VAMPIRES, WEREWOLVES, ZOMBIES---PRESENTED EACH MONTH FOR YOUR ENTERTAINMENT!
Read THIS GREAT MAGAZINE FOR OUT-OF-THIS-WORLD WONDERS SUCH AS YOU'VE NEVER SEEN---FOR A THRILL-TIME EXPERIENCE YOU'LL REMEMBER FOREVER! IT'S ALL IN---
"ADVENTURES INTO THE UNKNOWN!"
Now PUBLISHED MONTHLY.
10¢ ON ALL STANDS

From YOUR EDITOR - to YOU!

GREETINGS, READERS! This is an important meeting between us---since it marks the second issue of *"Forbidden Worlds"*. Which means that many of you have had the opportunity of reading our first number---and seeing exactly what it was that we were trying to bring you. For the benefit of newcomers, we're going to repeat that aim. What we plan for every issue is to bring you the breathtaking forbidden worlds of the supernatural---of the great *Unknown*. We'll touch on forbidden knowledge, and lay bare the secret mysteries of the occult. And we're going to do this through bringing you a constant succession of truly outstanding stories---strange and challenging stories---the products of the best in research, art and writing. That's our pledge to you---and it's a pledge we're going to keep! We feel that our first issue served to launch us far along our chosen path---if reader reaction is any criterion! For letters have been pouring in---and they've been letters that have warmed our hearts. Yes, it seems that you like what we've done---and want more of the same!

To you from us, then, this current issue---in which we've tried to follow your expressed desires by featuring a lineup of tense, gripping tales that'll leave you calling for more! Take our opening story, *"Mists of Midnight"*, for instance. We'll wager you've never read anything like *this* one! For suspenseful gasps--- for out-of-this-world chills---it's tops! *"League of Vampires"* sheds a new and eerie light on the ancient vampire legend, and it will fascinate you! Then there's *"Dead Man's Doom"*, for our money one of the weirdest, most spine-tingling yarns ever to come across an editor's desk. *"True Witches of History"* packs a novel punch and reveals some surprising facts, as does *"True Ghost Tales"*, wherein you're sure to enjoy meeting *"The Boy Who Talked With Spirits"*! Lastly, you're sure to enjoy the intriguing *"Magic Coin"*---your passport to a brand new world!

Beginning next issue, we plan to feature as many letters from our readers as space will allow. You'll be able to learn what others think--- and they'll get your viewpoint, too! As a step in this direction, we urge you to write to us, telling what you think of our stories---what you like or don't like---what you'd like to see us carry in future issues. Address your mail to:

The Editor
"FORBIDDEN WORLDS"
45 West 45 Street
New York 19, N. Y.

We'll be waiting for your letter! Remember, it's a date for our next issue---and meanwhile, don't fail to read our companion magazine---*"Adventures Into The Unknown"*!

DEAD MAN'S DOOM

YOU'VE HEARD BEFORE OF CORPSES THAT RISE TO METE OUT JUSTICE···OF VENGEFUL SPIRITS WHOSE MIDNIGHT VISITS ARE MARKED BY STRANGLED CRIES FROM BEHIND LOCKED DOORS! BUT NO HORROR CAN SURPASS THE BLACK SHAPE THAT ANSWERED THE WILD SUMMONS OF A CORNERED KILLER···THE DARK AND DRIPPING WREAKER OF THE *DEAD MAN'S DOOM!*

IF FATE IS A WITNESS TO HUMAN DEEDS···AND MANY PEOPLE THINK IT *IS*···IT WOULD HAVE BEEN WATCHING HERE TONIGHT···IN THE GLOOMY SEANCE CHAMBER OF PHANTO, THE SPIRITUALIST!

NOK! NOK!

AH···MY WELL-HEELED CLIENT IS RIGHT ON TIME! TONIGHT I'LL NICK HIM FOR *ANOTHER* FIVE THOUSAND DOLLARS!

FOUR-TIME KILLER STILL AT LARGE MORE HOLDUPS FEARED

EVERYTHING O.K., PHANTO? ANYONE IN THERE WITH YOU?

YOU NEEDN'T FEAR THE SPIRITS I SUMMON, MY FRIEND! ENTER AND BE AT EASE---THEY ARE READY TO *HELP* YOU!

HERE'S YOUR FEE, PHANTO---BUT I WANT MORE DEFINITE RESULTS THAN *LAST* TIME, SEE? I'VE GOT TO KNOW WHAT THE FUTURE HOLDS FOR ME---*AND I WANT IT IN BLACK AND WHITE!*

AND TONIGHT YOU *WILL* KNOW! TONIGHT THE *POWERS OF THE UNKNOWN* WILL APPEAR TO YOU---*AND SPEAK!*

*B*IT BY BIT, THE LIGHTS FADE---AND AS THE VISITOR'S EYES STRAIN IN THE DEEPENING DARKNESS---

OUT OF THE TOMB AND OUT OF THE BIER--- GHOSTS OF THE FUTURE--- GATHER HERE!

*T*hen---AS A DISTANT THROB CREEPS ALONG THE MUFFLED WALLS---

I SEE 'EM---BUT THAT NOISE ---*IT'S GETTING LOUDER!*

WOOO---OO!

*L*OUDER---AND *LOUDER*---LIKE A WAIL FROM A STRICKEN GRAVEYARD!

PHANTO---THE LIGHTS! THEY'RE COMING---*THEY'RE AFTER ME!*

WOOO---OO!

GET AWAY FROM THE SWITCH! THE SPIRITS WON'T HURT YOU ---*AS LONG AS THEY'RE IN DARKNESS!*

KEEP BACK! DO YOU THINK I'M AFRAID OF *THEM?*

POW!!

2.

Then ···in a sudden flood of light···

JUST AN AUTOMOBILE SIREN ··· AND SOME PIECES OF PHOSPHORESCENT GAUZE LOWERED FROM OPENINGS IN THE CEILING! **YOU SIDE-SHOW PHONY!**

I GOT MY MONEY THE HARD WAY, PHANTO ··· AND I WANT BACK EVERY DOLLAR! **FORK IT OVER!**

YOU THINK I'LL GIVE IT UP **THAT** EASILY ··· AT GUN-POINT? WATCH ··· LOOK AT MY EYES ··· **AND SEE HOW FAR YOU GET!**

AGAIN, THE DARKNESS SEEMS TO FALL IN SLOW, HEAVING WAVES ··· AND PHANTO'S GLINTING STARE BECOMES AN ENORMITY THAT FILLS THE ROOM!

SOMETHING'S HIT ME! I CAN'T THINK ··· I **CAN'T MOVE!**

YOU THINK A FEW TRICKS DON'T RATE THE TEN THOUSAND DOLLARS YOU GAVE ME, EH? BUT I'M READY TO DO **MORE** FOR THE MONEY ··· **MUCH MORE ··· INCLUDING MURDER!**

YES ··· IF FATE WERE WATCHING ··· THERE WOULD BE NO NEED FOR CRUDE DEVICES LIKE FLOATING GAUZE! THERE WOULD BE HORROR ENOUGH IN ITS LURKING SHAPE ··· IN THE LOW CHUCKLE THAT FORESAW THE **DEAD MAN'S DOOM!**

AAAGH!

BANG!

PHANTO ··· GIVE ME A BREAK! I WON'T TELL A SOUL WHO PLUGGED ME ··· YOU CAN KEEP THE MONEY ··· **BUT GET ME TO A DOCTOR!**

DO YOU EXPECT A SWINDLER LIKE ME TO TAKE **ANYBODY'S** WORD? AH, NO ··· YOU'RE FINISHED!

WE THINK OF HORROR IN TERMS OF GHOSTS ··· BUT WHAT TERROR COULD MATCH **THIS** MIDNIGHT SCENE ··· A HUMAN FIEND WITH A HUMAN BURDEN?

PHANTO ··· I'LL DO ANYTHING! FOR HEAVEN'S SAKE ··· **DON'T KILL ME!**

AT LEAST IT WON'T BE WITH A **GUN!** AFTER YEARS OF DABBLING IN BLACK MAGIC ··· I HAVE A TASTE FOR THE **HORRIBLE!**

3.

PHANTO---I WARN YOU! YOU'LL REGRET IT---RIGHT DOWN TO THE LAST SECOND OF YOUR LIFE!

THIS IS WHAT I HAVE IN MIND ---SOFT, STIFLING TAR!

DO YOU THINK YOU SCARE ME? WHAT WILL I HAVE TO FEAR--- FROM A DEAD MAN?

AAAGH!

THAT'S MY LAST GLIMPSE OF YOU! WHOEVER YOU WERE---THANKS FOR THE TEN THOUSAND DOLLARS!

AS THE WIND RISES---FLINGING A DARK VEIL OF CLOUDS ACROSS THE MOON---

IT'S A STRANGE, FORBID-DING NIGHT---BUT THERE'S NOTHING ON MY CONSCIENCE! THAT STRANGER WANTED TO KNOW HIS FUTURE---AND HE LEARNED IT!

MINUTES LATER---

HA-HA---A THREAT FROM A DEAD MAN! I'LL LAUGH ABOUT THAT ONE---WHILE I'M SPENDING HIS MONEY!

Then ---SUDDEN AS A THUNDERCLAP---

FOOTPRINTS ---BLACK ONES!

YES, TAR---BUT THERE'S NOTHING ON MY SHOES! HOW DID THOSE TRACKS GET HERE--- WHO LEFT THEM?

4.

I MUSTN'T LOSE MY HEAD! THERE MUST BE *SOME* EXPLANATION--- HE *COULDN'T* HAVE FOLLOWED ME---HE'S A *DEAD MAN!*

*M*INUTES LATER---

IT'S JUST NERVES---THAT'S ALL! EVEN AT THIS HOUR, THERE'LL BE *PEOPLE* DOWNTOWN--- THERE'LL BE RESTAURANTS WHERE I CAN GET A GOOD DINNER TO PICK ME UP!

THIS IS MORE LIKE IT! LET'S SEE A DEAD MAN LEAVE HIS STICKY FOOT-PRINTS *HERE*---IN A PLACE THRONGING WITH LIFE!

POLICE CLOSING IN ON BANK ROBBERY KILLER

*A*ND SO PHANTO JOINS THE THINNING CROWDS--- ONCE MORE BEARING A BURDEN---THE INVISIBLE CURSE OF A MIND SADDLED WITH FEAR!

HE *CAN'T* BE TRAILING ME---WHY DO I KEEP LOOKING AROUND? AND NO WONDER I'M LIGHT-HEADED---I HAVEN'T EATEN!

AH---LOBSTER! SORRY I'M YOUR ONLY CUSTOMER, WAITER--- I'LL NEED SOME TIME TO HANDLE *THIS!*

QUITE ALL RIGHT, SIR! THERE'S JUST ONE THING I'D LIKE TO KNOW---

---CAN YOU TAKE CARE OF THE DEAD MAN BY YOURSELF?

DEAD MAN! *HERE?*

CRASH!

5.

NO···I DON'T WANT TO SEE HIM! BLACK··· DRIPPING···HE DID FOLLOW ME!

WHAT IN BLAZES HAPPENED TO HIM···IS HE NUTS?

YOU TELL ME! I BROUGHT HIM A LOBSTER AND WONDERED IF HE COULD REMOVE THE DEAD MAN···YOU KNOW, THE INEDIBLE PART THAT'S SO HARD TO GET OUT OF THE SHELL···AND HE WENT COMPLETELY HAYWIRE!

SOON AFTERWARD···ALONG A LONELY ROAD OVERLOOKING THE MOURNING SEA···

I CAN'T GIVE WAY LIKE THIS···IT'S JUST A STATE OF MIND! A DEAD MAN IN A RESTAURANT···A DEAD MAN IN A BARREL OF TAR···IT'S CRAZY!

THOSE FISHERMEN HAVE JUST BROUGHT IN THEIR NIGHT'S CATCH···AND A QUIET CHAT WITH THEM WILL SOOTHE MY NERVES! THOSE FELLOWS LIKE ME··· THEY THINK I'M SOME KIND OF SCHOLAR!

EVENING, PHANTO! WE'VE GOT SOMETHING THAT OUGHT TO INTEREST YOU!

HE'LL KNOW WHAT IT IS! PHANTO'S SEEN THIS BEFORE!

YAAAGH! WHAT'S THAT?

GOSH, PHANTO···DON'T YOU RECOGNIZE IT? IT'S A DEAD MAN'S FINGERS!

6.

DEAD MAN...DEAD MAN! I CAN'T GET AWAY FROM HIM!

BY GEORGE ...THAT BEATS EVERYTHING!

SURE DOES! IMAGINE BEING SCARED BY SEAWEED...JUST BECAUSE IT HAS A SPOOKY NAME!

UP THE FROWNING ROCKS... WITH FEAR TIGHTENING AROUND HIM LIKE A CLAMMY NET...

HE MAY BE CLOSING IN...BUT I KNOW HOW TO GET THE BEST OF HIM! YOU DEAD MAN WITH YOUR BLACK, STICKY CORPSE...SEE HOW YOU FARE AGAINST WHAT I CAN CONJURE UP!

IF EVER I HAVE KNOWN EVIL...LET IT TAKE SHAPE NOW! COME FORTH, ENCRUSTED WITH HORROR... AND BE THE DEAD MAN'S DOOM!

The DARKNESS ROLLS IN LIKE A SILENT SEA...AND FROM ITS BROODING PALL...

MY SUMMONS HAS BEEN ANSWERED...IT'S COMING! YOU'RE BEATEN, DEAD MAN... YOU'LL NEVER GET ME... WITH THAT AROUND!

SHAPELESS ...GUMMY WITH A STRANGE AND GLISTENING JET...

THE FIEND I EXPECTED SHOULD BE BLACK... THERE'S NO REASON TO THINK IT'S TAR! IT'S EVIL...THAT'S WHAT I ASKED FOR... THAT'S WHAT IT LOOKS LIKE!

Then ...AS THE WIND SWEEPS UP A NEWSPAPER THROWN ASIDE BY A LATE FERRY PASSENGER...

AM I DREAMING...OR DID I CATCH A GLIMPSE OF SOMETHING FAMILIAR IN THAT HEADLINE?

HOLDUP KILLER! YE GODS, HE'S THE ONE I KILLED...HE'S THE DEAD MAN I'VE BEEN FLEEING...

FIND BODY OF HOLDUP KILLER IN TAR DRUM!

...AND HE'S THE EVIL I SUMMONED!

THEN...WITH A YELL THAT IS SMOTHERED IN THE TARRY DARKNESS...

AAAAGHH...

SPLASH!

FOR JUST A SECOND, PHANTO GROPES ABOVE THE THICK, CLINGING BLACKNESS THAT ENGULFS HIM... AND THEN SINKS, A DARK AND WRITHING FORM, INTO THE DEAD MAN'S FINGERS THAT CHOKE THE MOON-LIT TIDE!

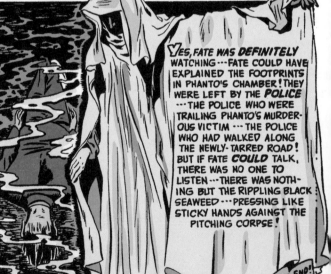

YES, FATE WAS DEFINITELY WATCHING...FATE COULD HAVE EXPLAINED THE FOOTPRINTS IN PHANTO'S CHAMBER! THEY WERE LEFT BY THE POLICE ...THE POLICE WHO WERE TRAILING PHANTO'S MURDER-OUS VICTIM...THE POLICE WHO HAD WALKED ALONG THE NEWLY-TARRED ROAD! BUT IF FATE COULD TALK, THERE WAS NO ONE TO LISTEN...THERE WAS NOTH-ING BUT THE RIPPLING BLACK SEAWEED...PRESSING LIKE STICKY HANDS AGAINST THE PITCHING CORPSE!

The END!

8.

"TRUE" WITCHES of HISTORY

KATE, the WITCH, vs. ANDREW JACKSON

THE MOST CELEBRATED WITCH IN AMERICAN HISTORY WAS THE ONE THAT WAS REPORTED TO HAVE APPEARED BEFORE ANDREW JACKSON IN 1821! GENERAL JACKSON HIMSELF, THE GREAT DUELLIST, STATESMAN, AND HERO OF THE WAR OF 1812, ACTUALLY *VOUCHED* FOR THIS EXPERIENCE!

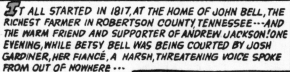

IT ALL STARTED IN 1817, AT THE HOME OF JOHN BELL, THE RICHEST FARMER IN ROBERTSON COUNTY, TENNESSEE---AND THE WARM FRIEND AND SUPPORTER OF ANDREW JACKSON! ONE EVENING, WHILE BETSY BELL WAS BEING COURTED BY JOSH GARDINER, HER FIANCÉ, A HARSH, THREATENING VOICE SPOKE FROM OUT OF NOWHERE---

BETSY BELL, DON'T MARRY JOSH GARDINER!

OHH! WHO--- WHO'S THERE--- WHERE ARE YOU?

I'M *KATE, THE WITCH*--- AND I'M RIGHT HERE! ONCE *I* WAS HAPPY, JUST LIKE YOU, UNTIL I CAME UNDER AN EVIL SPELL! AND NOW I'M GOING TO MAKE SURE THAT *YOU'LL* ALWAYS BE UNHAPPY, JUST LIKE ME!

NO---DON'T---DON'T BEWITCH ME! I *WON'T* MARRY JOSH---I'LL GIVE HIM BACK HIS RING!

BUT THE VENGEFUL WITCH REFUSED TO LET BETSY ALONE---AND IN THE DAYS THAT FOLLOWED, WOULD TORMENT THE POOR GIRL UNMERCIFULLY!

OH, STOP ---PLEASE STOP!

GREAT HEAVENS! SOMETHING'S STRIKING HER--- BUT *WHAT?*

SLAP!

THE IMPRINT OF A SUPERNATURAL HAND WAS CLEAR ON THE GIRL'S FACE---BUT IT DIDN'T STOP THERE! HER GOLDEN HAIR WAS RENDED---

HA-HA -HA!

WHEN JOHN BELL CALLED IN SOME TRUSTED NEIGHBORS TO ASK THEIR ADVICE, THE WITCH REACTED IN AWFUL RAGE··· AND PANDEMONIUM ENSUED!

PEOPLE FLOCKED TO VIEW THE UNCANNY GOINGS-ON, UNTIL THE ENTIRE COUNTY KNEW ABOUT THE WITCH THAT WAS PLAGUING THE BELL HOUSEHOLD! BUT WHEN TOO MANY CURIOSITY-SEEKERS BEGAN POURING INTO THE HOUSE, THE WITCH TURNED ON *THEM*!

FINALLY, IN 1821, THE NEWS OF HIS FRIEND'S TROUBLE REACHED ANDREW JACKSON AT THE HERMITAGE, NEAR NASHVILLE ···BUT THE HARDHEADED, REALISTIC GENERAL REFUSED TO BELIEVE WHAT HE'D HEARD!

I'VE KNOWN JOHN BELL ALL MY LIFE···THERE NEVER WAS A SANER MAN! BUT HE MUST HAVE GONE *CRAZY* IF HE SAYS A *WITCH* IS HAUNTING HIS HOUSE!

BUT ANDREW, DOZENS OF PEOPLE HAVE SEEN HER···THEY CAN'T *ALL* HAVE GONE MAD!

WELL, RACHEL, THIS WITCH CAN'T BE ANY WORSE THAN THE INDIANS AND POLITICIANS AND BRITISH I'VE FACED! I THINK I'LL GO SEE HER FOR *MYSELF*!

IF YOU DO, ANDREW, YOU'D BETTER TAKE ALONG THAT FAMOUS WITCH-DESTROYER WHO LIVES NEAR THE RIVER! HE'S GOT SILVER BULLETS IN HIS GUN, AND IF HE GETS TO USE THEM ON THAT CREATURE, SHE'LL VANISH FOR GOOD!

UPON HIS WIFE'S INSISTENCE, JACKSON TOOK THE "WITCH-DESTROYER" ALONG TWO DAYS LATER ON THE TRIP TO ROBERTSON COUNTY! THE RIDE WAS UNEVENTFUL UNTIL THE GENERAL'S COACH NEARED THE BELL HOME ···

WHAT'S WRONG, DRIVER···WHY AREN'T WE MOVING?

I···I DON'T KNOW, GENERAL···THE HORSES ARE STRAINING, BUT THEY DON'T SEEM TO BE ABLE TO STIR! AND THERE'S NO MUD FOR US TO BE STUCK IN···THERE'S SOMETHING *UNCANNY* ABOUT THIS!

JACKSON ORDERED HIS FOLLOWERS TO PUT THEIR SHOULDERS TO THE WHEEL AND TRY TO MOVE THE COACH···

WE···WE CAN'T BUDGE IT!

IT'S *INCREDIBLE* ···THAT WITCH MUST'VE PUT A *HEX* ON THE COACH!

THAT'S RIGHT, GENERAL··· BUT NOW I'LL TAKE THE HEX OFF!

AS THE COACH SUDDENLY LURCHED FORWARD···

SEE YOU AGAIN TONIGHT, GENERAL!

2.

At the Bell home, Jackson began the vigil of waiting for the witch... and he soon became annoyed at the witch-destroyer's boasting...

This pistol's never been known to misfire ...and my silver bullets have killed over a dozen of the old hags! And when THIS one appears, I'll...

I think you'll RUN! The only reason you're talking so much is to keep up your courage!

You're right, General ...he IS a coward!

THE WITCH!

Yes, here I am... SHOOT, COWARD!

THE --- THE GUN WON'T FIRE!

CLICK

The witch-destroyer pulled the trigger again, and when it failed to fire this time...

NOW IT'S MY TURN!

NO, NO ... LET ME OUT OF HERE!

HAW-HAW-HAW! I KNEW he was a coward!

Jackson wanted to stay on at the Bell household, to continue his investigations of the witch, but was unfortunately called away on urgent official business...

GOODBYE, JOHN --- THANKS FOR ENTERTAINING ME WITH THE WITCH! She gave me the best laugh I've had in years ---and was the funniest-looking thing I've EVER seen!

LAUGH AT ME, WILL HE? I'LL FIX HIM --- THROUGH HIS FRIEND!

As soon as Jackson left...

YOU'RE GOING TO DIE, JOHN BELL ---VERY SOON!

Bell became seriously ill, and nothing the doctors did seemed to help him! One day---

ALL YOUR MEDICINES ARE USELESS --- I GAVE HIM MY MEDICINE! HE'LL NEVER GET UP FROM THAT BED AGAIN!

The witch's prophecy came true ---and when John Bell died, she left with the promise that she would be back in seven years, when she would visit every house in the neighborhood! This she did in February, 1828... and then disappeared forever! Legend ---or fact?

3.

95

Strange STAIRCASE

YIIIPE!
Billy began to run as he heard the terrified yelp of his dog. When he reached the front door of his house, his heart sank, for his stepfather was brutally kicking Roger.

"Keep that mutt out of my way," his stepfather roared, shaking his fist at Billy, "or I'll slit his throat one o' these days!"

The screen door slammed, and Billy gathered the trembling Roger into his arms. "Easy, boy, easy," Billy murmured. "I know just how you feel. He kicks *me* every now and then, too! C'mon, we'll go down to your favorite romping place. Maybe finding a fieldmouse in the barn will help you forget that kick."

By the time they got near the barn, Roger was his usual frisky self. Watching the dog race ahead, Billy thought sadly, "Golly, if only Roger and me could *always* be happy. If...if only we could go someplace where we were never kicked or beaten, where everyone was kind and..."

Roger's sudden outburst of excited barking from the barn interrupted Billy's reverie, and he dashed inside. "What's wrong, Roger?" he asked as he entered the barn. "Oh, there's someone here!"

The little man grinned up at Billy. "Don't be afraid," he said in a high, squeaky voice. "I'm just the repair man. I fix troubles and staircases. Right now, I'm putting the finishing touches on this new staircase I built up to the barn's attic."

But Billy couldn't tear his eyes away from the little man to look at the new staircase. "I...I'm not afraid of you. Why, you're even smaller than me, even though you've got a long, white beard. Are you an elf? Why do you wear those funny clothes? Who asked you to build a new staircase? Why..."

The strange little man cackled with glee. "You're not afraid, and you're curious. Good! And I see your dog is just like you...*he's* already climbing up the stairs. Go on, Billy...follow him up!"

Billy hesitated, watching Roger scamper up the strange-looking staircase that hadn't been there before. And a moment later, *Roger* wasn't there!

"He...he just disappeared!" Billy gasped. "He went up to the top step... and *vanished!*"

"Heh, heh. Sure, he's in *my* world now," the little man said. "And it's the kind of world *you* said you wanted, Billy...a place where everyone is always kind and happy and wise. Go on up. Your new friends are waiting for you. You'll love it up there. But hurry, I've got other calls to make."

Billy stared at the little man, eager to believe that such a world could actually exist, but still doubtful. Excited barking from the staircase made him look up again, and he saw Roger materialize from nothingness on the top step. The dog bounded down the stairs, and began tugging at Billy's overalls, urging him to follow.

"He...he's acting just like he does when he wants to show me something new or wonderful," Billy said.

"Well, it's not so new," the little man said, "but it *is* wonderful, more wonderful than all the fairy tales you ever read. Follow him up and take a peek at it. If you don't like it, you can come right on down."

Quickly Billy followed Roger up the strange staircase. From below, the little man smilingly watched Billy's head disappear. Then he heard the boy say delightedly, *"Golleee!* Wait for me, Roger...I'm coming!"

When Billy had completely disappeared, the strange little man began dismantling his strange staircase. Moments later, he was on his way, looking for more troubles to repair.

The MAGIC COIN

MYSTERY SURROUNDED THE STAID OLD COSMOPOLITAN MUSEUM-- FOR FROM WITHIN ITS GREY WALLS, THE RENOWNED ARCHEOLOGIST, DR. AMOS BROWN, HAD VANISHED! IN VAIN, POLICE INVESTIGATORS HAD QUESTIONED AND SEARCHED! THE CASE SEEMED HOPELESS UNTIL DR. BROWN'S YOUNG ASSISTANT, KEN HAVERS, HUNTING DOGGEDLY FOR A CLUE, STUMBLED ON THE KEY TO THE MYSTERY -- A KEY WHICH BROUGHT THE PAST AND PRESENT TOGETHER IN ONE TERRIFYING FLASH!

WHY DON'T YOU GO HOME AND GET SOME REST, MR. HAVERS? IT'S WAY PAST CLOSING TIME-- AND USELESS TO SEARCH ANY MORE!

BUT THERE **MUST** BE AN EXPLANATION! A MAN JUST DOESN'T VANISH WITHOUT A TRACE! YOU RUN ALONG, MISS SEELY! I'LL LOOK AROUND DR. BROWN'S OFFICE AGAIN!

I DON'T LIKE TO READ HIS PERSONAL DIARY-- BUT PERHAPS HE WROTE **SOMETHING** THAT'LL GIVE ME A LEAD!

WONDER WHAT PLANS HE MEANT? HE CERTAINLY DIDN'T TELL ME--AND HE'D EXAMINED THAT COIN THOROUGHLY ANY NUMBER OF TIMES!

Tonight I shall further examine the Roman coin. I must remember to tell Ken my plans.

WHY, HERE IT IS-- UNDER THE MICROSCOPE! IT'S A RARE COIN FROM THE TIME OF **MARCUS AURELIUS**-- BUT **THAT** CAN'T EXPLAIN DR. BROWN'S STRANGE INTEREST IN IT!

1

THIS MICROSCOPE SURE IS *POWERFUL!* BRINGS OUT THE DETAILS LIKE... *HOLY NELLY!* THOSE RAISED PARTS LOOK LIKE *HILLS!* AND THAT APPEARS TO BE A *ROAD* LEADING INTO THEM!

THERE'S SOMETHING *MOVING...* IT'S-- IT'S A LITTLE MAN! WHY... WHY... HIS FACE-- *IT'S DR. BROWN!*

HE'S LOOKING UP AT ME-- WAVING HIS HANDS! SIGNALING IN SEMAPHORE! HE'S TELLING ME TO--

I'M BEGINNING TO GET IT! HE'S TELLING ME TO MIX CERTAIN RARE CHEMICALS TOGETHER-- AND LET A SINGLE DROP OF THE MIXTURE FALL ON THE COIN!

IT'S CRAZY-- I KNOW I'M GOING TO WAKE UP AND FIND THIS IS ALL A DREAM! BUT SOMEHOW-- I FEEL I OUGHT TO DO WHAT HE SAYS!

NOW-- TO LET A SINGLE DROP FALL-- AS HE INSTRUCTED! BUT-- BUT WHAT'S GOING TO HAPPEN!

GOOD LORD! HE'S DIVING RIGHT INTO IT!

DR. BROWN! YOU'RE... YOU'RE...

YES, I'M HERE, KEN! THANK GOODNESS YOU LOOKED AT THE COIN AND RECEIVED MY MESSAGE! I'D *NEVER* HAVE GOT OUT IF YOU HADN'T!

GOT OUT! BUT I DON'T UNDERSTAND-- WHAT--

RELAX, LAD, AND I'LL EXPLAIN! YOU KNOW I'VE BEEN STUDYING THAT COIN FOR SOME TIME -- BUT I DIDN'T DARE TELL ANYONE THAT I SUSPECTED IT CONTAINED A *MINIATURE WORLD* ALL ITS OWN! EVEN TO AN ARCHEOLOGIST, IT SEEMED TOO *FANTASTIC!*

BUT THE MORE I INSPECTED IT, THE MORE I WAS STRUCK WITH THE RESEMBLANCE BETWEEN THE HILLS ON THE COIN AND THE SEVEN HILLS OF ROME! THEN ONE DAY I SAW THROUGH THE MICROSCOPE A TROOP OF *ROMAN SOLDIERS* MARCH ALONG THAT ROAD-- AND I WAS *SURE* I WAS RIGHT!

AN ANCIENT WORLD-- RIGHT THERE UNDER MY MICROSCOPE! I WAS POSSESSED WITH THE DESIRE TO GET *INTO* THE COIN! IT SEEMED IMPOSSIBLE-- UNTIL I RECALLED DECIPHERING AN ANCIENT GREEK PALIMPSEST WHICH PURPORTED TO GIVE THE FORMULA FOR REDUCING ALL MATTER TO INFINITESIMAL SIZE!

"I INTENDED TELLING YOU OF MY PLAN, KEN, SO YOU COULD HAVE THE ANTIDOTE READY! BUT FIRST I PREPARED THE FORMULA-- IT ACTED QUICKER THAN I THOUGHT--FUMES GUSHED AROUND ME..."

"AND THEN-- I FOUND MYSELF ON THE COIN-- DRASTICALLY REDUCED IN SIZE! AND WITH EACH SECOND I GREW SMALLER-- *SMALLER!*"

I TRAVELED ALONG THE ROAD, THROUGH THE HILLS, INTO THE VERY HEART OF THE COIN-- TO *ANCIENT ROME!* OH, IF ONLY I'D BROUGHT CAMERAS AND RECORDING EQUIPMENT ALONG!

IT'S AN ARCHEOLOGIST'S GOLD MINE, KEN! THAT'S WHY I RETURNED-- TO GET FULLY EQUIPPED, AND TO TAKE YOU BACK WITH ME-- *IF* YOU'D LIKE TO COME!

WHY-- IT'S THE CHANCE OF A LIFETIME!

FIRST LET ME WARN YOU! WE MAY RUN INTO DANGER--THE ROMANS OF THAT PERIOD WERE RUTHLESS-- REMEMBER, HUMAN LIFE MEANT NOTHING TO THEM!

JUST TRY TO KEEP ME FROM GOING!

3

KEEPING DR. BROWN'S REAPPEARANCE A SECRET, THEY QUICKLY PREPARED FOR THE TRIP! ONLY ONE OTHER PERSON WAS LET IN ON THE SECRET...

SMITHERS, JUST KEEP AN EYE ON THE COIN THROUGH THE MICROSCOPE! AND WHEN WE SIGNAL, LET A DROP OF THIS FLUID FALL ON THE COIN! JUST A *SMALL DROP*-- UNDERSTAND?

SURE, DOC! I'LL DO IT!

KEEP YOUR EYES ON THE COIN, KEN! I'M TAKING THE STOPPER OUT OF THE FLASK-- ALL SET?

LET'S GO!

JUMPIN' SPHINXES! *THEY'RE GONE!*

AND WITHIN MOMENTS-- A MAGIC WORLD!

WE'RE HERE, KEN! ASSEMBLE THE MOTORBIKE, AND WE'RE OFF FOR *ANCIENT ROME!*

I--I CAN'T *BELIEVE* IT!

I MADE FRIENDS WITH A ROMAN PHILOSOPHER NAMED DECIMUS-- HE LIVES OUTSIDE THE CITY! WE'LL GO TO HIS HOUSE FIRST!

LOOK! *ROMAN SOLDIERS!*

A CENTAUR! FLEE FOR YOUR LIVES!

NEVER BEFORE HAVE I BEHELD A *TWO-HEADED* CENTAUR! 'TIS BEST THAT I FOLLOW THIS STRANGE THING!

JUST AHEAD IS DECIMUS' HOUSE! AND BEYOND IT, FEAST YOUR EYES, KEN-- *THE CITY OF ANCIENT ROME!*

JUST WAIT TILL WE TELL THE WORLD ABOUT *THIS!*

WELL, DECIMUS, I CAME BACK AS I PROMISED! THIS IS MY YOUNG ASSISTANT, KEN HAVERS!

WELCOME TO ROME, GOOD FRIENDS OF THE TWENTIETH CENTURY! LET ME INTRODUCE MY DAUGHTER, SABINA! SHE HAS BEEN MOST IMPATIENT TO SEE YOU!

WHILE DR. BROWN AND DECIMUS TALKED--

IT IS HARD TO FIND WORDS WITH SOMEONE -- FROM ANOTHER WORLD' TELL ME, DO YOU NOT FIND OUR LAND FAIR TO BEHOLD?

ALMOST... ALMOST AS BEAUTIFUL AS YOU, SABINA!

SO THESE STRANGERS ARE FRIENDS OF DECIMUS, WHO IS SUSPECTED OF PLOTTING AGAINST THE EMPEROR! THEY MUST BE SPIES FROM ABROAD! I SHALL REPORT THIS!

CENTURIES AND WORLDS APART -- BUT WHAT A PAIR THEY MAKE!

YES! I HATE TO BREAK IT UP, BUT WE MUST GET ON TO ROME -- KEN! COME ALONG! TEMPUS FUGIT!

LEAVING THE MOTORBIKE BEHIND, KEN AND DR. BROWN SET OUT FOR ROME--

YOU WILL RETURN SOON, KENNETH?

WE SURE WILL, HONEY!

MEANWHILE, IN THE AUDIENCE CHAMBERS OF THE TYRANNICAL EMPEROR, MARCUS AURELIUS--

YOU MEAN THESE STRANGERS PLOT WITH THE TRAITOR DECIMUS?

YES, MY EMPEROR -- THEY CAME ON A STEED WITH NO HEAD AND NO TAIL! WIZARDS, THEY ARE! THEY DOUBTLESS PLAN TO SPY ON YOUR MILITARY INSTALLATIONS!

THERE ARE THE STRANGERS, SIRE! THEY HAVE ENTERED ROME ITSELF!

FOLLOW AND SEIZE THEM!

GOOD THING WE BROUGHT ALONG LOTS OF FILM! GOLLY-- WHAT A BREAK THIS'LL BE-- IF WE CAN COMPLETE OUR INSPECTION WITHOUT AROUSING SUSPICION!

5

UNAWARE OF PURSUIT, KEN AND DR. BROWN ENTERED THE COLOSSEUM --

TO THINK WE'RE ACTUALLY IN THE FLAVIAN AMPHITHEATER -- *WOW!* IF THIS SHOT COMES OUT, IT'LL BE THE PICTURE OF THE CENTURY!

HEY, WAIT A MINUTE, BUD!

CAPTURED -- AND BROUGHT BEFORE THE EMPEROR --

LOOKS BAD, DOC!

IT SURE DOES! THEY DON'T BELIEVE A WORD OF WHAT I TOLD THEM!

YOU ARE BOTH JUDGED GUILTY OF HIGH TREASON -- AND SENTENCED TO *DEATH IN THE ARENA!*

IF I REMEMBER MY HISTORY RIGHTLY -- THAT MEANS WE'RE TO BE *DINNER FOR A BUNCH OF LIONS!*

SHORTLY AFTER -- WHILE THE EXCITED ROMAN CROWDS WATCHED --

IF ONLY WE'D BROUGHT ALONG OUR *PISTOLS,* WE MIGHT HAVE A CHANCE -- BUT NOW ---

WE AREN'T LICKED *YET,* DOC! BUT GET SET -- *HERE COME THE LIONS!*

KEN WAITED UNTIL THE SNARLING BEASTS WERE ALMOST UPON THEM -- AND THEN -- TRIPPED THE RELEASE OF HIS FLASH GUN!

POP!

THE WIZARDS MAKE *LIGHTNING!*

FLEE! THE LIONS ARE UPON US!

TAKING ADVANTAGE OF THE PANDEMONIUM, KEN AND DR. BROWN HEADED FOR AN EXIT --

GET GOING, DOC, WHILE THE GOING'S GOOD!

SPARE MY LIFE, GODS! I PRAY YOU, *SPARE ME!*

6

OUTSIDE -- A CAPTURED CHARIOT --

SHIFT THIS THREE HORSE-POWER JOB INTO HIGH! WE'VE GOT TO GET TO THE MOTORCYCLE OR WE'LL BE SUNK!

IN THE NAME OF THE EMPEROR, PURSUE THEM! THEY MUST DIE!

MOMENTS LATER -- BACK AT DECIMUS' HOUSE --

THE EMPEROR'S SOLDIERS ARE AFTER US! YOU'D BETTER HIDE!

BE OFF, BEFORE IT IS TOO LATE!

GOOD-BYE, SABINA! GOSH, IF ONLY--

OH, KENNETH!

THROTTLE PUSHED WIDE OPEN, KEN SENT THE MOTORCYCLE TEARING BACK UP THE ROAD THROUGH THE MOUNTAINS --

THEY CAN'T CATCH US NOW, DOC! WE'RE IN THE CLEAR!

PROVIDED SMITHERS IS LOOKING INTO THE MICROSCOPE -- AND REMEMBERS TO DROP THE FLUID!

BUT BACK IN THE MUSEUM --

I GUESS IT'S O.K. TO TAKE A SHORT NAP -- THE DOC AND KEN AREN'T LIABLE TO SHOW UP FOR A WHILE!

MEANWHILE, AS THE MOTORCYCLE RACED ACROSS THE FACE OF THE COIN --

WHAT THE -- A BLOWOUT!

POW!

I'M ALL IN, KEN! YOU -- RUN FOR IT! THERE'S THE CONTACT PLACE AHEAD!

AND LEAVE YOU TO THOSE BABIES? NOTHING DOING!

HERE THEY COME -- THE WHOLE BLASTED ROMAN ARMY!

7

IT WAS A MAD RACE TO THE POINT OF CONTACT WITH THE MICROSCOPE-- BUT THERE--

THAT IDIOT SMITHERS! I'VE SIGNALED! WHY DOESN'T HE *DO* SOMETHING?

IT HAD BETTER BE *SOON*-- OR IT'LL BE ALL UP WITH US!

HO-HUM! MAYBE I'D BETTER TAKE ANOTHER LOOK BEFORE I DROP OFF--

GREAT GUNS! THERE THEY ARE-- AND A BUNCH OF SOLDIERS ARE AFTER THEM! THE FLUID-- *I MUST DROP THE FLUID!*

HASTILY, SMITHERS FILLED THE DROPPER WITH THE SPECIAL FLUID! THEN, HIS FINGERS SHAKING FROM EXCITEMENT, HE SQUEEZED THE BULB -- BUT TOO HARD!

THE FOOL! HE'S LET *TOO MUCH* OF THE LIQUID COME OUT!

THE NEXT INSTANT--

THANK GOODNESS YOU'RE BACK!

MORE THAN JUST *US!* GET OUT OF SIGHT IF YOU *WANT* TO STAY ALIVE!

GOSH ALMIGHTY! HOW'D *THEY* G-GET HERE?

AS THE BEWILDERED ROMANS SURGED OUT INTO FIFTH AVENUE --

IT'S AN INVASION FROM MARS!

SEND FOR THE RIOT SQUAD!

WE'RE IN *ANOTHER WORLD!*

THE STREETS ARE FILLED WITH *ARMORED BEASTS!* LET US FLEE TO WHENCE WE CAME!

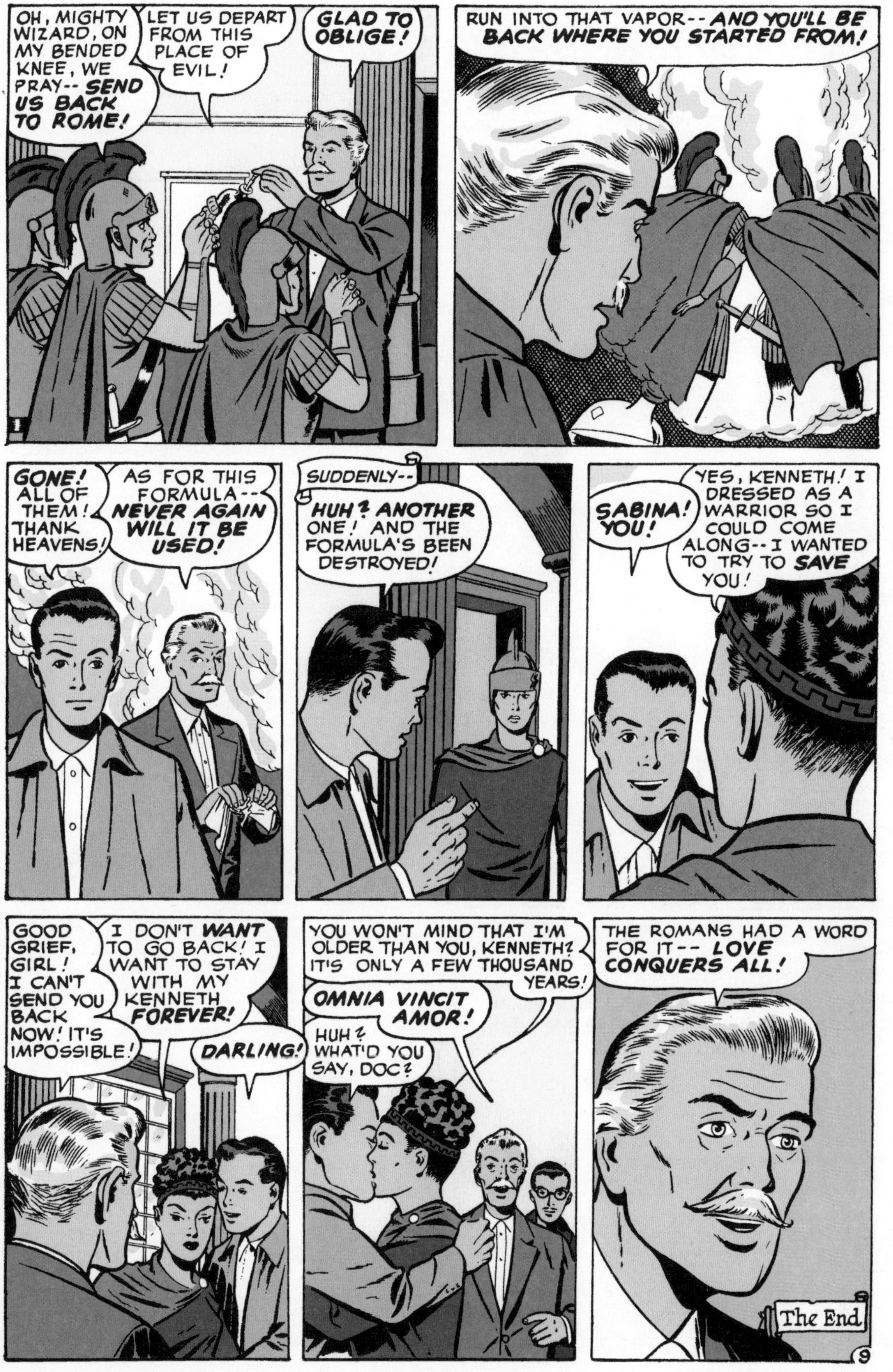
OH, MIGHTY WIZARD, ON MY BENDED KNEE, WE PRAY-- SEND US BACK TO ROME!
LET US DEPART FROM THIS PLACE OF EVIL!
GLAD TO OBLIGE!
RUN INTO THAT VAPOR-- AND YOU'LL BE BACK WHERE YOU STARTED FROM!
GONE! ALL OF THEM! THANK HEAVENS!
AS FOR THIS FORMULA-- NEVER AGAIN WILL IT BE USED!
SUDDENLY--
HUH? ANOTHER ONE! AND THE FORMULA'S BEEN DESTROYED!
SABINA! YOU!
YES, KENNETH! I DRESSED AS A WARRIOR SO I COULD COME ALONG-- I WANTED TO TRY TO SAVE YOU!
GOOD GRIEF, GIRL! I CAN'T SEND YOU BACK NOW! IT'S IMPOSSIBLE!
I DON'T WANT TO GO BACK! I WANT TO STAY WITH MY KENNETH FOREVER!
DARLING!
YOU WON'T MIND THAT I'M OLDER THAN YOU, KENNETH? IT'S ONLY A FEW THOUSAND YEARS!
OMNIA VINCIT AMOR!
HUH? WHAT'D YOU SAY, DOC?
THE ROMANS HAD A WORD FOR IT-- LOVE CONQUERS ALL!
The End
9

UNCANNY MYSTERIES

The SPECTRAL SKY-SHIP

IN JANUARY, 1646, THE VESSEL *FELLOWSHIP* SAILED FROM THE COLONY OF NEW HAVEN FOR ENGLAND, WITH AN ENORMOUSLY RICH CARGO AND A DISTINGUISHED PASSENGER LIST! THE WATCHERS ON SHORE JOINED IN THE MINISTER'S HEARTFELT WORDS...

> LORD, IF IT BE THY PLEASURE TO BURY THESE OUR FRIENDS IN THE BOTTOM OF THE SEA, THEY ARE THINE! BUT WE PRAY THEE-- *SPARE THEM!*

BUT THE MONTHS LENGTHENED INTO A YEAR, WITHOUT WORD FROM THE FELLOWSHIP! EACH TIME ANOTHER SHIP ARRIVED FROM ENGLAND, ITS CAPTAIN WAS EAGERLY QUESTIONED BY THE WORRIED COLONISTS...

> THE *FELLOWSHIP!* SHE COULDN'T HAVE REACHED ENGLAND ---OR I WOULD HAVE HEARD OF HER!

> THEN SHE MUST HAVE BEEN LOST, WITH ALL HANDS ABOARD! LET US PRAY THAT WE MAY BE GIVEN SOME INDICATION OF WHAT HAPPENED TO OUR SHIP AND LOVED ONES!

THEN, THE FOLLOWING SUMMER, AFTER A VIOLENT THUNDERSTORM HAD PASSED OVER NEW HAVEN---

> LOOK--UP IN THE SKY---IT'S THE FELLOWSHIP!

CROWDS POURED OUT INTO THE STREETS TO WITNESS THE ASTONISHING SIGHT OF THE LOST SHIP SAILING ON A CLOUD THROUGH THE SKY! THE CLOUD SEEMED TO DROP, AND THE SHIP SAILED IN CLOSE, IT ALMOST BRUSHED THE CHURCH STEEPLE!

> THAT'S THE *FELLOWSHIP*, ALL RIGHT---JUST AS WE SAW HER TWO WINTERS AGO!

> YES--AND THERE'S CAP'N LAMBERTON ON THE QUARTERDECK! THIS *IS* A MIRACLE!

BUT SUDDENLY, WITHOUT WARNING, THE BILLOWING CLOUDS RUSHED OVER THE *SPECTRAL SHIP* LIKE STORM WAVES! ITS RIGGING WAS BLOWN AWAY---THE MASTS FELL ON TOP OF THE SEAMEN---AND WITHIN A FEW MINUTES, THE VESSEL WAS REDUCED TO A BATTERED HULK!

MINUTES LATER, THE GHOSTLY *FELLOWSHIP* SANK SLOWLY INTO THE CLOUD, AS IF SINKING INTO THE BRINY DEEP--WHILE THE NEW HAVEN COLONISTS LOOKED ON IN HORROR AND AWE!

> NOW WE *KNOW* THE FATE OF THE *FELLOWSHIP!*

THE END..

TRUE GHOST TALES

The BOY who TALKED with SPIRITS

HOW WOULD YOU LIKE TO TALK WITH GHOSTS, READER-- TO BE TAKEN INTO THEIR CONFIDENCE, HAVE THEM WHISPER SECRETS OF THE UNKNOWN INTO YOUR EARS? WELL, JUST THAT HAPPENED TO A NINE YEAR-OLD LAD OF RENO, NEVADA-- TO EDDIE HARKNESS, THE BOY WHO TALKED WITH GHOSTS!

IT ALL STARTED WHEN THE HARKNESSES MOVED INTO A LONG-VACANT FARMHOUSE OUTSIDE RENO...

GOSH, THIS IS A **WONDERFUL** OLD HOUSE! IT LOOKS AS IF MAYBE IT'S **HAUNTED!**

DON'T BE SILLY, EDDIE--THERE'RE NO SUCH CREATURES AS GHOSTS! YOU'VE BEEN READING TOO MANY SPOOK STORIES!

IT JUST LOOKS STRANGE BECAUSE NO ONE'S LIVED IN IT FOR SO LONG --BUT WE'LL CHANGE **THAT!**

THE FAMILY SOON MADE THEMSELVES AT HOME, AND ASSIGNED ONE OF THE SPARE ROOMS TO EDDIE AS A PLAYROOM...

PLEASE, LAD--- **STOP THAT RACKET!**

BANG! BANG! BANG!

HUH? WHO... WHO ARE YOU?

ISN'T IT **OBVIOUS?** FOR **28** YEARS, EVER SINCE WE DIED IN THIS ROOM, WE'VE HAD ALL THE PEACE AND QUIET WE WANT ...UNTIL **NOW!**

NOW, JOSIAH, THE BOY JUST DIDN'T **KNOW** ABOUT OUR BEING HERE! DON'T BE HARSH WITH HIM!

I... I CAN SEE RIGHT THROUGH YOU--- YOU **ARE** GHOSTS! GOSH, I'M GOING RIGHT DOWN AND TELL MOM AND DAD THAT--

NO---YOU **MUSTN'T** TELL THEM ABOUT US! WE KNEW THAT **YOU** WOULDN'T BE FRIGHTENED, THAT YOU'D ACCEPT US WITHOUT QUESTION! BUT IF **ADULTS** SAW US, THEY'D EITHER THINK THEY'D GONE CRAZY OR ELSE CALL IN A WHOLE ARMY OF SO-CALLED PSYCHIC EXPERTS WHO'D **NEVER** GIVE US ANY PEACE!

SO YOU SEE, WE DON'T *DARE* APPEAR TO ANYONE IN THIS HOUSE-- EXCEPT *YOU*!

I...I UNDERSTAND--AND I'LL BE CAREFUL NEVER TO MAKE NOISE, HERE! BUT YOU *WILL* APPEAR TO ME OFTEN, WON'T YOU?

SURELY, MY BOY--- WE'LL MATERIALIZE AND TALK TO YOU *EVERY DAY*!

A FEW NIGHTS LATER... EDDIE, WE'RE WORRIED! SPIRITS CAN SEE INTO THE FUTURE--AND WE JUST FOUND OUT THAT YOUR AUNT EMILY IS PLANNING A SURPRISE VISIT! WE'RE AFRAID YOUR FOLKS MIGHT PUT HER UP IN *OUR* ROOM-- HERE!

GOSH--AND SHE *SNORES*! I'LL GO RIGHT DOWN AND TRY TO MAKE MOM PROMISE TO PUT HER UP SOME- PLACE ELSE!

BUT I TELL YOU SHE *IS* COMING HERE ON A SURPRISE VISIT--- THE TWO GHOSTS WHO LIVE IN MY PLAYROOM *TOLD* ME! AND YOU *MUSTN'T* PUT HER UP IN THAT ROOM!

YOU'VE JUST HAD A BAD DREAM, DARLING! BUT IF IT'LL HELP YOU GO BACK TO SLEEP, I PROMISE NOT TO PUT AUNT EMILY UP THERE --*IF* SHE COMES!

BUT THE NEXT DAY...

WHY, IT...IT'S *EMILY*!

HA, HA---I KNEW YOU'D BE SURPRISED! I DIDN'T TELL A *SOUL* ABOUT THE VISIT I WAS PLANNING!

WE'LL HAVE TO LIVE UP TO THE PROMISE I MADE EDDIE-- AND PUT HER UP HERE IN THE LIVING ROOM!

YES---BUT HOW DID HE KNOW SHE WAS COMING? I'M BEGINNING TO *BELIEVE* IN THOSE GHOSTS OF HIS!

BUT THERE WAS MORE *TO COME---FOR A FEW NIGHTS LATER...*

EDDIE, THE HORSE IN YOUR BARN IS GOING TO KICK OVER THE OIL LAMP IN FIFTEEN MINUTES! BUT IF YOUR FATHER GETS OUT THERE IN TIME, HE CAN SAVE THE BARN FROM BURNING DOWN!

GOLLY, IT'S AFTER MIDNIGHT NOW! I'LL HAVE TO WAKE HIM UP!

BUT DAD---THE GHOSTS WERE *RIGHT* ABOUT AUNT EMILY, WEREN'T THEY? THEN THEY'RE PROBABLY RIGHT ABOUT THE BARN ---YOU'VE GOT TO HURRY OUT THERE!

ALL RIGHT, SON... ALL RIGHT! I'LL GO DOWN AND TAKE A LOOK AT OLD DOBBIN ---BUT I'M SURE THERE'S NO RUSH!

2

BY THE TIME MR. HARKNESS REACHED THE BARN...

GREAT SCOTT---IT HAPPENED JUST THE WAY EDDIE SAID!

LUCKY I GOT HERE WHEN I DID---OR THE WHOLE BARN WOULD HAVE BURNED DOWN! THANK HEAVENS I'VE GOT A SON WHO *TALKS WITH GHOSTS!* I'LL NEVER *DOUBT THEIR EXISTENCE AGAIN!*

THEN, IN OCTOBER, 1950.....

EDDIE, I'VE GOT SOME BAD NEWS! THE TRUCKEE RIVER IS GOING TO OVERFLOW NEXT MONTH---AND WASH THIS HOUSE CLEAN AWAY! YOU'D BETTER TELL YOUR DAD TO GET OUT *FLOOD INSURANCE!*

GOSH, THANKS ---I'LL TELL HIM RIGHT NOW!

EDDIE'S GHOST FRIENDS HAVE BEEN RIGHT TWICE BEFORE ---WE'D BETTER DO AS THEY SUGGEST!

YES, WE CAN'T TAKE ANY CHANCES! WE'LL KEEP OUR EYES OPEN---AND BE READY TO EVACUATE AT THE FIRST SIGN OF DANGER!

SURE ENOUGH, TORRENTIAL RAINS SOON BEGAN, AND THE TRUCKEE RIVER OVERFLOWED ITS BANKS IN ONE OF THE WORST FLOODS IN NEVADA'S HISTORY! BUT ONE FAMILY, AT LEAST, DIDN'T LOSE ALL THEIR POSSESSION...

COME ON, THE HOUSE IS ABOUT TO BE WASHED AWAY! WE SAVED EVERYTHING WE WANTED--- AND NOW IT'S TIME FOR *US* TO GET OUT!

NO! WAIT FOR THE GHOSTS--- THEY'LL *DROWN* IF WE LEAVE THEM HERE!

LOOK, THERE THEY ARE---I *SEE* THEM!

DON'T WAIT FOR US, EDDIE--- WE'LL NEVER LEAVE THIS HOUSE UNTIL IT FALLS APART IN THE FLOOD WATERS! WE'LL MEET YOU AGAIN WHEN *YOUR* LIFE- TIME'S THROUGH---AND WE'LL HAVE A HOUSE WAITING FOR *YOU* UP ABOVE!

AND SO IT WAS THAT THE FEW FAMILIES AFLOAT IN THAT DISASTROUS FLOOD SAW A STRANGE SIGHT--- TWO GHOSTLY FIGURES CLINGING TO A WRECK OF A HOUSE UNTIL THE FLOOD WATERS RIPPED IT APART---AND FORCED THEM TO FIND ANOTHER HOME IN THE GREAT *UNKNOWN!*

..THE END..

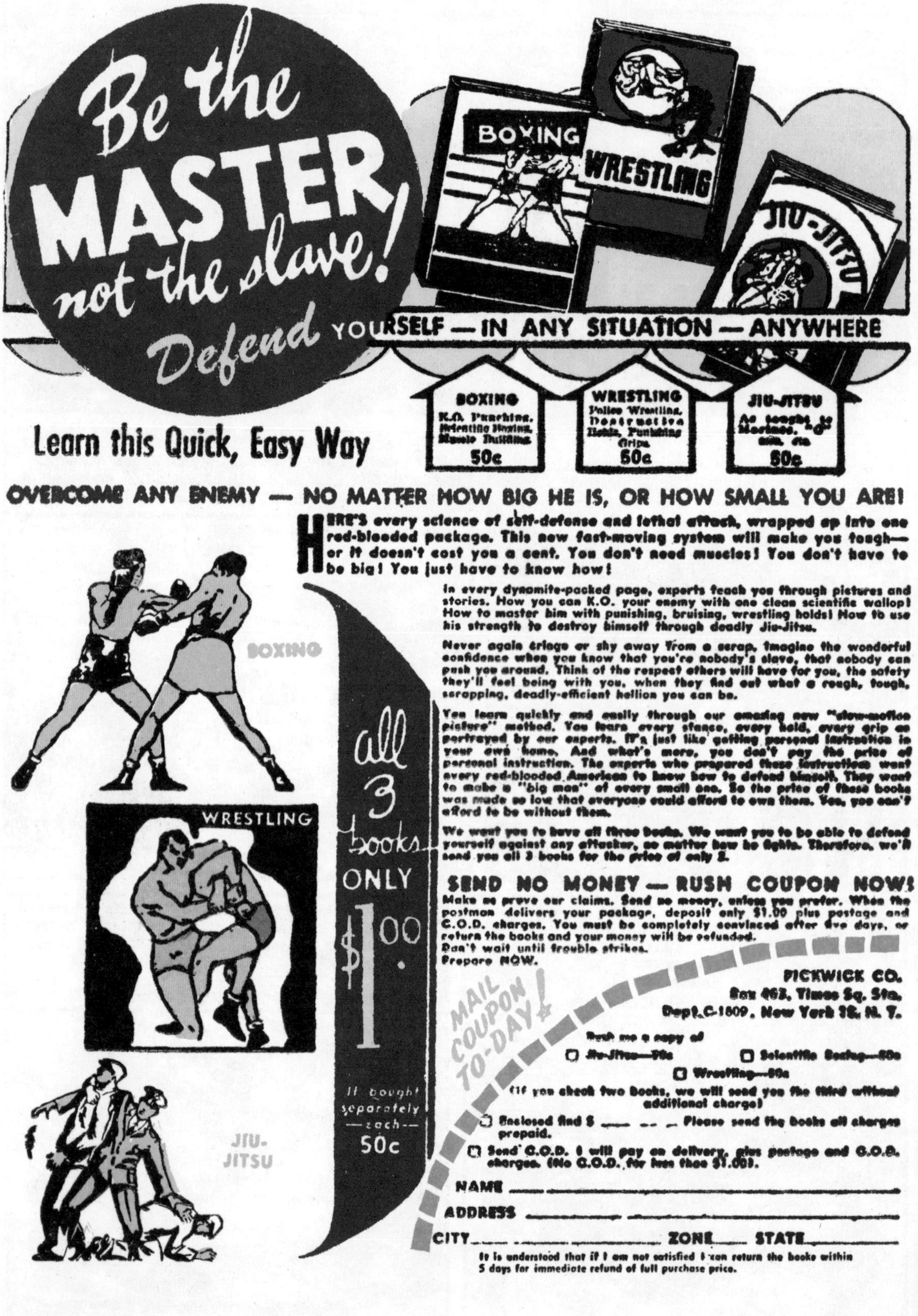
Be the MASTER not the slave!
Defend YOURSELF — IN ANY SITUATION — ANYWHERE
BOXING
WRESTLING
JIU-JITSU
BOXING
K.O. Punching, Scientific Boxing, Muscle Building
50c
WRESTLING
Police Wrestling, Destructive Holds, Punishing Grips
50c
JIU-JITSU
As taught to Marines, "G" men, etc.
50c
Learn this Quick, Easy Way
OVERCOME ANY ENEMY — NO MATTER HOW BIG HE IS, OR HOW SMALL YOU ARE!
HERE'S every science of self-defense and lethal attack, wrapped up into one red-blooded package. This new fast-moving system will make you tough—or it doesn't cost you a cent. You don't need muscles! You don't have to be big! You just have to know how!
In every dynamite-packed page, experts teach you through pictures and stories. How you can K.O. your enemy with one clean scientific wallop! How to master him with punishing, bruising, wrestling holds! How to use his strength to destroy himself through deadly Jiu-Jitsu.
Never again cringe or shy away from a scrap. Imagine the wonderful confidence when you know that you're nobody's slave, that nobody can push you around. Think of the respect others will have for you, the safety they'll feel being with you, when they find out what a rough, tough, scrapping, deadly-efficient hellion you can be.
You learn quickly and easily through our amazing new "slow-motion picture" method. You learn every stance, every hold, every grip as portrayed by our experts. It's just like getting personal instruction in your own home. And what's more, you don't pay the price of personal instruction. The experts who prepared these instructions want every red-blooded American to know how to defend himself. They want to make a "big man" of every small one. So the price of these books was made so low that everyone could afford to own them. Yes, you can't afford to be without them.
We want you to have all three books. We want you to be able to defend yourself against any attacker, no matter how he fights. Therefore, we'll send you all 3 books for the price of only 2.
BOXING
WRESTLING
JIU-JITSU
all 3 books ONLY $1.00
If bought separately —each— 50c
SEND NO MONEY — RUSH COUPON NOW!
Make us prove our claims. Send no money, unless you prefer. When the postman delivers your package, deposit only $1.00 plus postage and C.O.D. charges. You must be completely convinced after five days, or return the books and your money will be refunded.
Don't wait until trouble strikes.
Prepare NOW.
MAIL COUPON TO-DAY!
PICKWICK CO.
Box 463, Times Sq. Sta.
Dept. C-1809, New York 18, N. Y.
Rush me a copy of
☐ Jiu-Jitsu—50c ☐ Scientific Boxing—50c
☐ Wrestling—50c
(If you check two books, we will send you the third without additional charge)
☐ Enclosed find $ ____ Please send the books all charges prepaid.
☐ Send C.O.D. I will pay on delivery, plus postage and C.O.D. charges. (No C.O.D. for less than $1.00).
NAME ____
ADDRESS ____
CITY ____ ZONE ____ STATE ____
It is understood that if I am not satisfied I can return the books within 5 days for immediate refund of full purchase price.

BLACKHEADS "PET HATE"
Say Men, Girls in Choosing Date

What a "black mark" is the blackhead ... according to men and girls popular enough to be choosy about dates!

"Nobody's dreamboat!" "Nobody's date bait!" And that's not all that's said of those who are careless about blackheads. But blackheads ARE ugly! Blackheads ARE grimy! And they DON'T look good in close-ups!

So can you blame the fellow who says, "Sure, I meet lots of girls who look cute at first glance. But if, on that second glance, I see dingy blackheads, it's *good night!*"

Or can you blame the girl who confesses, "I hate to go out with a fellow who has blackheads. If he's careless about that you're sure he'll embarrass you in other ways, too!"

But you — are YOUR ears burning? Well, you've company and, sad to say, good company. There are lots of otherwise attractive fellows and girls who could date anyone they like if they'd only realize how offensive blackheads are ... and how easily and quickly they could get rid of them ... if they *want to!*

"He-Man" Often Guilty of Blackhead Crime

Take your "he-man" ... super at track, games, sports of all kinds ... who thinks that after just a shower he's ready to go anywhere! And won't the girls all admire his muscles!

Sure they would! But not many dance floors are set up for hurdle races! You can't show off your snappy left hook when only cokes are in the ring. The "he-man" who's also clean-cut, will get the breaks wherever he is.

Even Cute Girls Become Careless

Easy, too easy, for a girl to think that if she has the latest in clothes and hair-do she needn't bother about blackheads. A little more make-up, she guesses, will take care of that. BUT MAKE-UP WON'T HIDE BLACKHEADS! Not unless it's plaster of paris, maybe! And even good make-up "slips" at a dance! So don't take chances, cute though you may be!

TAKE THESE TIPS TO BANISH BLACKHEADS

Keep skin clean by washing morning and night with warm, almost hot, water Use good soap and plenty of it. And finish with cool water.

Extract every blackhead as soon as you see it — with a SAFE extractor Don't use finger nails. Don't squeeze. That may mean infection, injured tissues, a marred skin.

Just be clean! Be quick! And be safe! That's easy! And that's ALL!

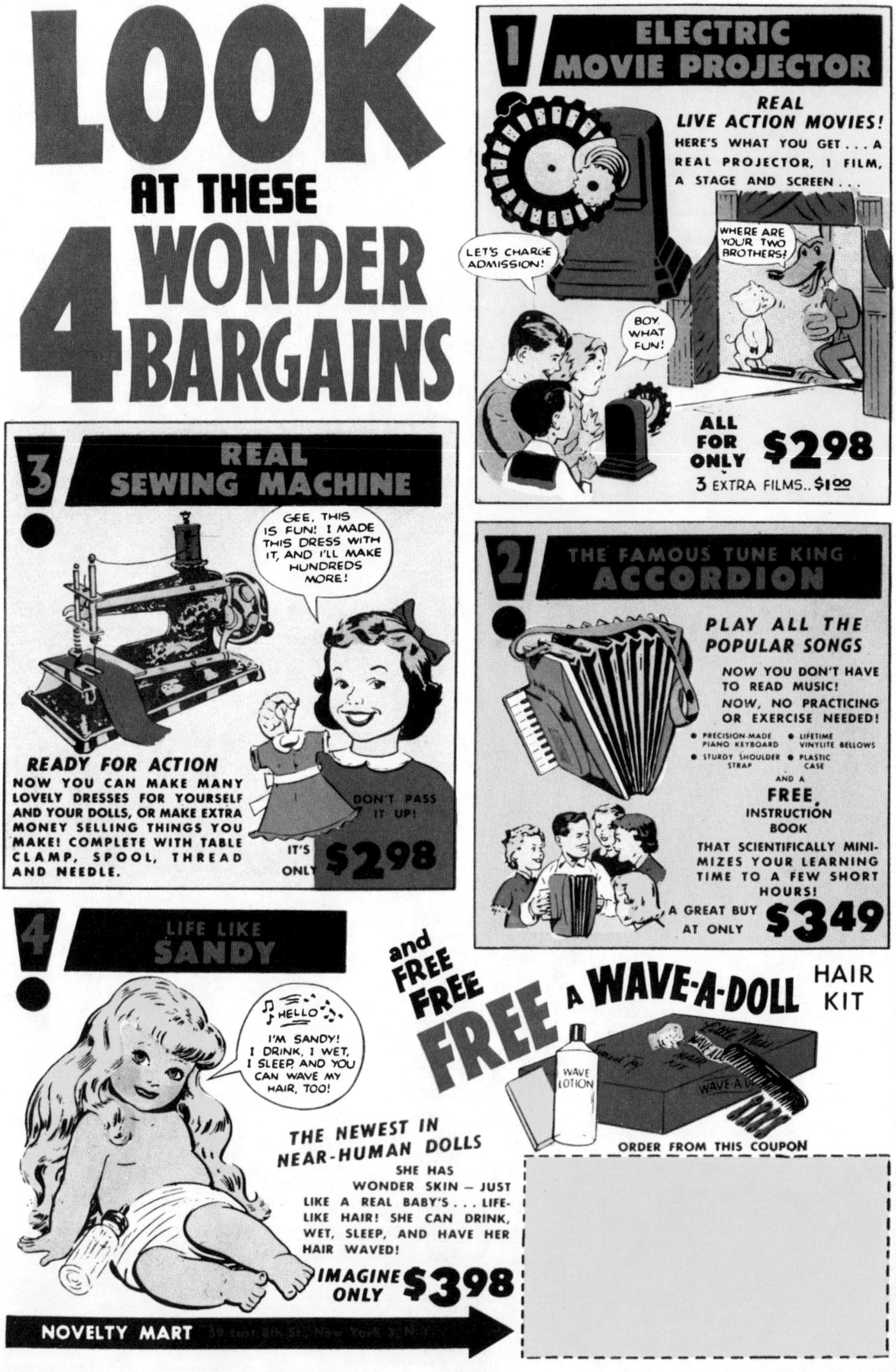
LOOK
AT THESE
4 WONDER BARGAINS
1 ELECTRIC MOVIE PROJECTOR
REAL LIVE ACTION MOVIES!
HERE'S WHAT YOU GET . . . A REAL PROJECTOR, 1 FILM, A STAGE AND SCREEN . . .
LET'S CHARGE ADMISSION!
WHERE ARE YOUR TWO BROTHERS?
BOY. WHAT FUN!
ALL FOR ONLY $2.98
3 EXTRA FILMS.. $1.00
3 REAL SEWING MACHINE
GEE, THIS IS FUN! I MADE THIS DRESS WITH IT, AND I'LL MAKE HUNDREDS MORE!
READY FOR ACTION
NOW YOU CAN MAKE MANY LOVELY DRESSES FOR YOURSELF AND YOUR DOLLS, OR MAKE EXTRA MONEY SELLING THINGS YOU MAKE! COMPLETE WITH TABLE CLAMP, SPOOL, THREAD AND NEEDLE.
DON'T PASS IT UP!
IT'S ONLY $2.98
2 THE FAMOUS TUNE KING ACCORDION
PLAY ALL THE POPULAR SONGS
NOW YOU DON'T HAVE TO READ MUSIC!
NOW, NO PRACTICING OR EXERCISE NEEDED!
• PRECISION-MADE PIANO KEYBOARD
• LIFETIME VINYLITE BELLOWS
• STURDY SHOULDER STRAP
• PLASTIC CASE
AND A FREE, INSTRUCTION BOOK
THAT SCIENTIFICALLY MINIMIZES YOUR LEARNING TIME TO A FEW SHORT HOURS!
A GREAT BUY AT ONLY $3.49
4 LIFE LIKE SANDY
HELLO
I'M SANDY! I DRINK, I WET, I SLEEP, AND YOU CAN WAVE MY HAIR, TOO!
and FREE FREE FREE A WAVE-A-DOLL HAIR KIT
WAVE LOTION
THE NEWEST IN NEAR-HUMAN DOLLS
SHE HAS WONDER SKIN – JUST LIKE A REAL BABY'S . . . LIFE-LIKE HAIR! SHE CAN DRINK, WET, SLEEP, AND HAVE HER HAIR WAVED!
IMAGINE ONLY $3.98
ORDER FROM THIS COUPON
NOVELTY MART

FORBIDDEN WORLDS #3 | November–December 1951

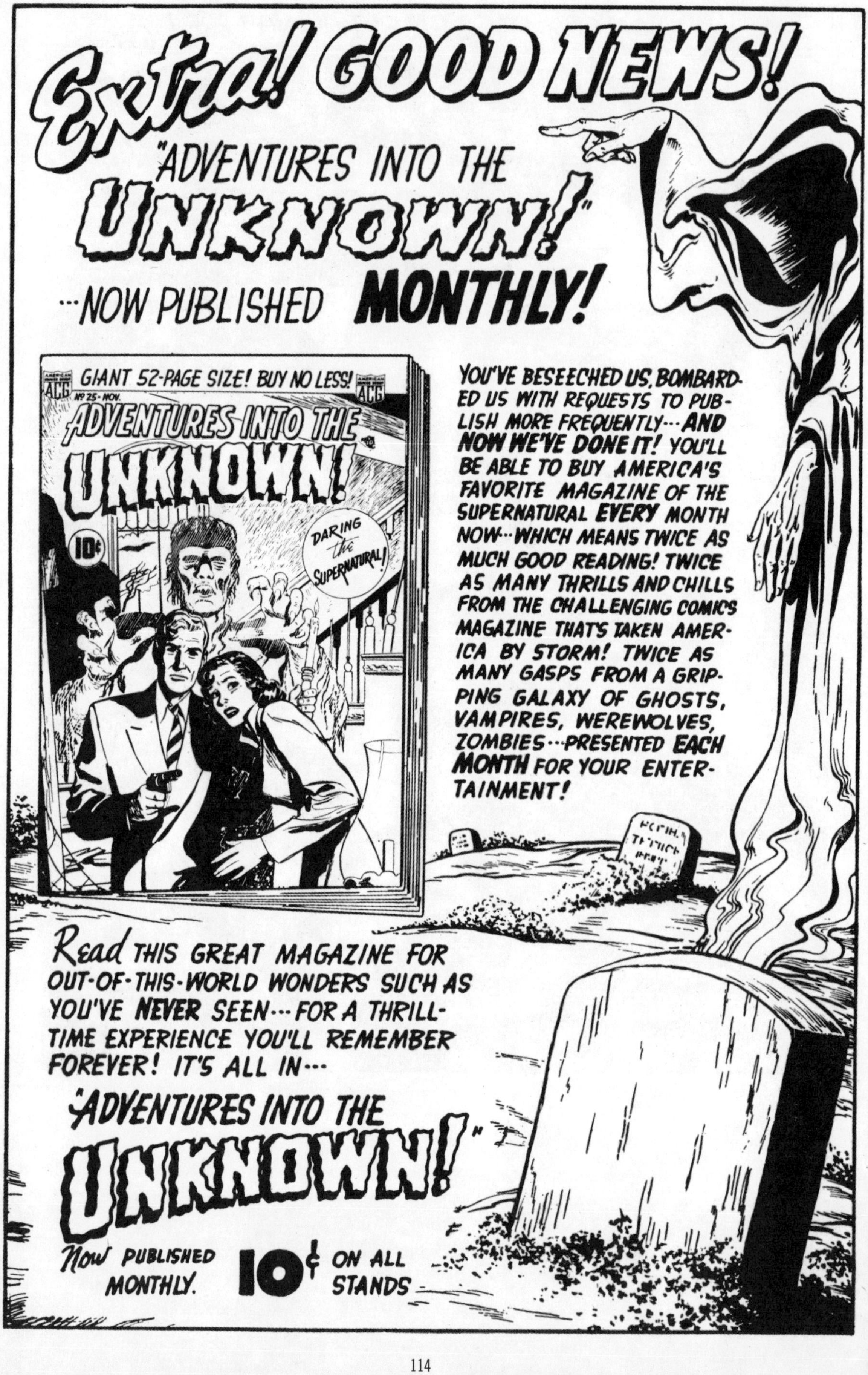

Extra! GOOD NEWS!
"ADVENTURES INTO THE UNKNOWN!"
...NOW PUBLISHED MONTHLY!
GIANT 52-PAGE SIZE! BUY NO LESS!
ACG
No 25 - NOV.
ADVENTURES INTO THE UNKNOWN!
10¢
DARING the SUPERNATURAL!
YOU'VE BESEECHED US, BOMBARDED US WITH REQUESTS TO PUBLISH MORE FREQUENTLY--- AND NOW WE'VE DONE IT! YOU'LL BE ABLE TO BUY AMERICA'S FAVORITE MAGAZINE OF THE SUPERNATURAL EVERY MONTH NOW--- WHICH MEANS TWICE AS MUCH GOOD READING! TWICE AS MANY THRILLS AND CHILLS FROM THE CHALLENGING COMICS MAGAZINE THAT'S TAKEN AMERICA BY STORM! TWICE AS MANY GASPS FROM A GRIPPING GALAXY OF GHOSTS, VAMPIRES, WEREWOLVES, ZOMBIES--- PRESENTED EACH MONTH FOR YOUR ENTERTAINMENT!
Read THIS GREAT MAGAZINE FOR OUT-OF-THIS-WORLD WONDERS SUCH AS YOU'VE NEVER SEEN--- FOR A THRILL-TIME EXPERIENCE YOU'LL REMEMBER FOREVER! IT'S ALL IN---
"ADVENTURES INTO THE UNKNOWN!"
Now PUBLISHED MONTHLY.
10¢ ON ALL STANDS

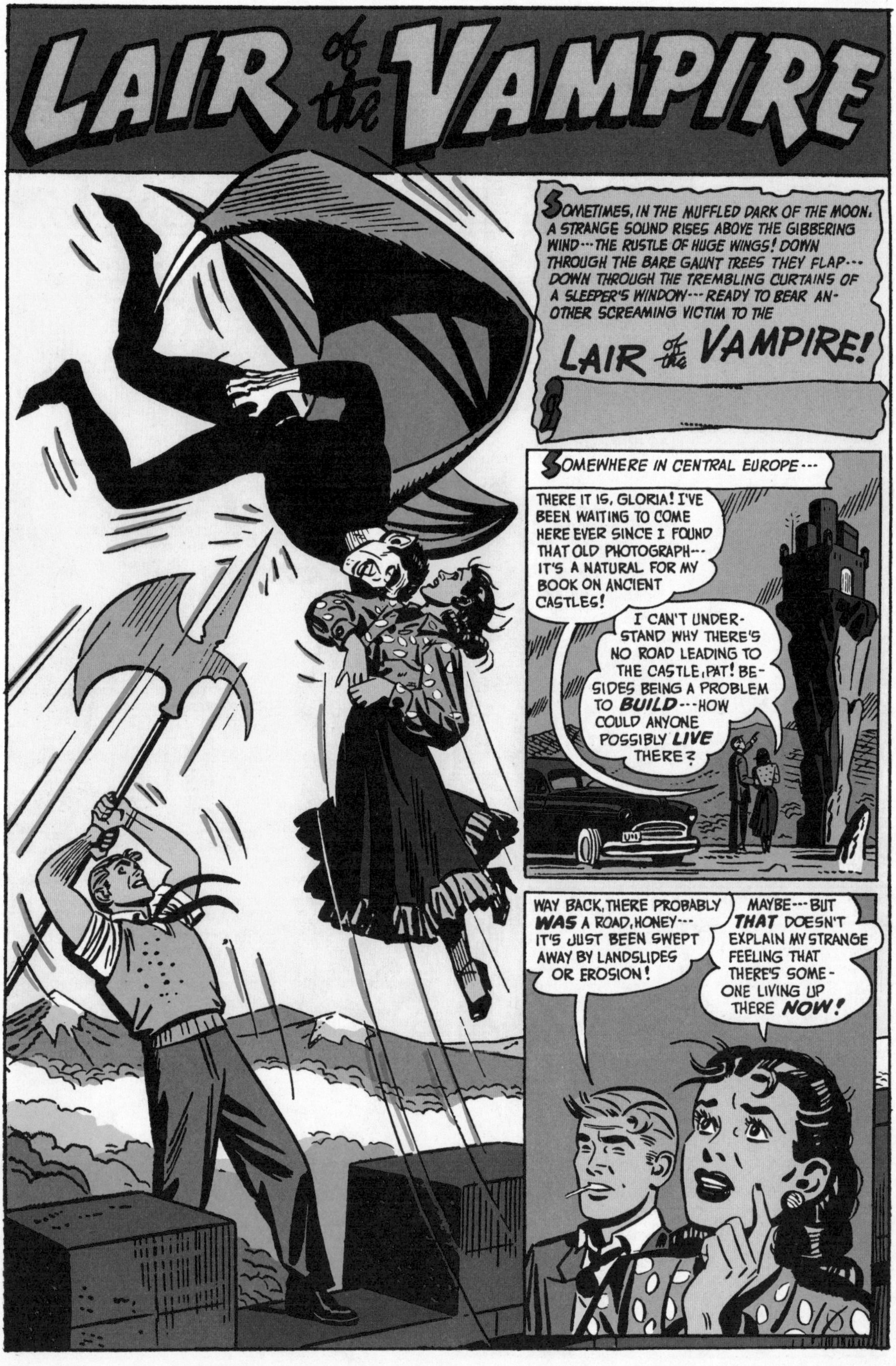
LAIR of the VAMPIRE
SOMETIMES, IN THE MUFFLED DARK OF THE MOON, A STRANGE SOUND RISES ABOVE THE GIBBERING WIND--- THE RUSTLE OF HUGE WINGS! DOWN THROUGH THE BARE GAUNT TREES THEY FLAP--- DOWN THROUGH THE TREMBLING CURTAINS OF A SLEEPER'S WINDOW--- READY TO BEAR ANOTHER SCREAMING VICTIM TO THE
LAIR of the VAMPIRE!
SOMEWHERE IN CENTRAL EUROPE---
THERE IT IS, GLORIA! I'VE BEEN WAITING TO COME HERE EVER SINCE I FOUND THAT OLD PHOTOGRAPH--- IT'S A NATURAL FOR MY BOOK ON ANCIENT CASTLES!
I CAN'T UNDERSTAND WHY THERE'S NO ROAD LEADING TO THE CASTLE, PAT! BESIDES BEING A PROBLEM TO BUILD---HOW COULD ANYONE POSSIBLY LIVE THERE?
WAY BACK, THERE PROBABLY WAS A ROAD, HONEY--- IT'S JUST BEEN SWEPT AWAY BY LANDSLIDES OR EROSION!
MAYBE--- BUT THAT DOESN'T EXPLAIN MY STRANGE FEELING THAT THERE'S SOMEONE LIVING UP THERE NOW!

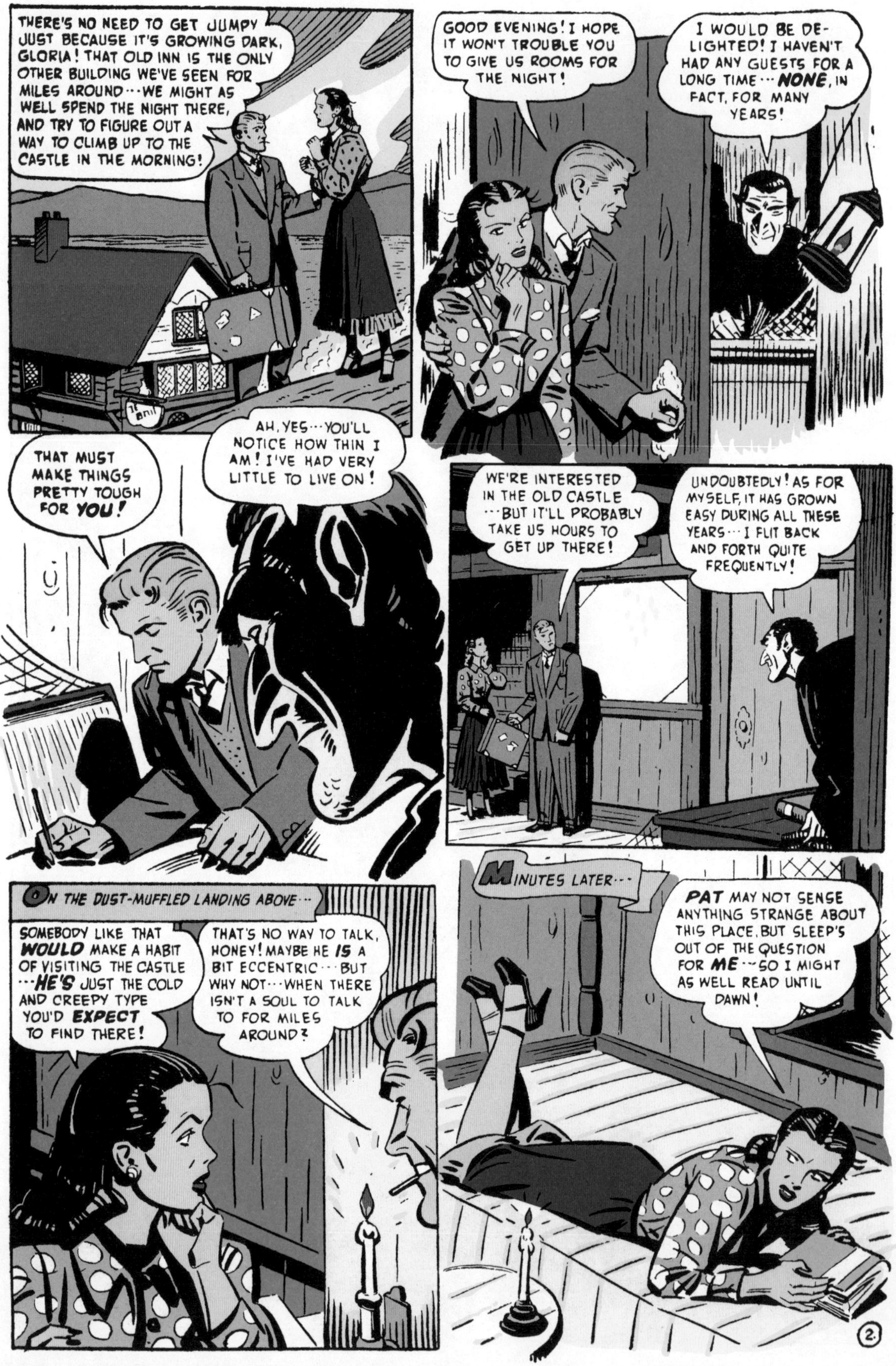
THERE'S NO NEED TO GET JUMPY JUST BECAUSE IT'S GROWING DARK, GLORIA! THAT OLD INN IS THE ONLY OTHER BUILDING WE'VE SEEN FOR MILES AROUND··· WE MIGHT AS WELL SPEND THE NIGHT THERE, AND TRY TO FIGURE OUT A WAY TO CLIMB UP TO THE CASTLE IN THE MORNING!
GOOD EVENING! I HOPE IT WON'T TROUBLE YOU TO GIVE US ROOMS FOR THE NIGHT!
I WOULD BE DE-LIGHTED! I HAVEN'T HAD ANY GUESTS FOR A LONG TIME··· NONE, IN FACT, FOR MANY YEARS!
THAT MUST MAKE THINGS PRETTY TOUGH FOR YOU!
AH, YES··· YOU'LL NOTICE HOW THIN I AM! I'VE HAD VERY LITTLE TO LIVE ON!
WE'RE INTERESTED IN THE OLD CASTLE ··· BUT IT'LL PROBABLY TAKE US HOURS TO GET UP THERE!
UNDOUBTEDLY! AS FOR MYSELF, IT HAS GROWN EASY DURING ALL THESE YEARS··· I FLIT BACK AND FORTH QUITE FREQUENTLY!
ON THE DUST-MUFFLED LANDING ABOVE···
SOMEBODY LIKE THAT WOULD MAKE A HABIT OF VISITING THE CASTLE ···HE'S JUST THE COLD AND CREEPY TYPE YOU'D EXPECT TO FIND THERE!
THAT'S NO WAY TO TALK, HONEY! MAYBE HE IS A BIT ECCENTRIC··· BUT WHY NOT··· WHEN THERE ISN'T A SOUL TO TALK TO FOR MILES AROUND?
MINUTES LATER···
PAT MAY NOT SENSE ANYTHING STRANGE ABOUT THIS PLACE, BUT SLEEP'S OUT OF THE QUESTION FOR ME··· SO I MIGHT AS WELL READ UNTIL DAWN!
2

LONG PAST MIDNIGHT, AS A CHILL CREEPS THROUGH THE ROOM...FURTIVE AS THE PANTING BREATH OF EVIL...

THAT'S QUEER...I WAS *SURE* THIS OLD BED DIDN'T HAVE A CANOPY!

THEN...WITH THE FAINT HINT OF A WHITE AND STARING FACE ABOVE HER...

THE INNKEEPER! BUT HE'S CHANGED...*HE'S GOT HORRIBLE BLACK WINGS!*

NO...*NO!* FOR HEAVEN'S SAKE...*DON'T TOUCH ME!*

HAA! WHY WAIT UNTIL MORNING TO SEE THE CASTLE, WHEN YOU CAN GO *NOW*...WITH *ME?*

IN THE NEXT SECOND...

THIS'LL TEACH YOU TO KEEP YOUR SLIMY HANDS TO YOURSELF, BUD!

POW

GREAT GUNS...HE DIDN'T EVEN BAT AN EYELASH!

DO YOU THINK AN ORDINARY BLOW CAN HARM *ME?* TRY AGAIN... *WHILE YOU HAVE A CHANCE!*

AS PAT LUNGES FORWARD...

A *CHANCE* IS ALL I ASK, RAT!

HAA HA HA!

117

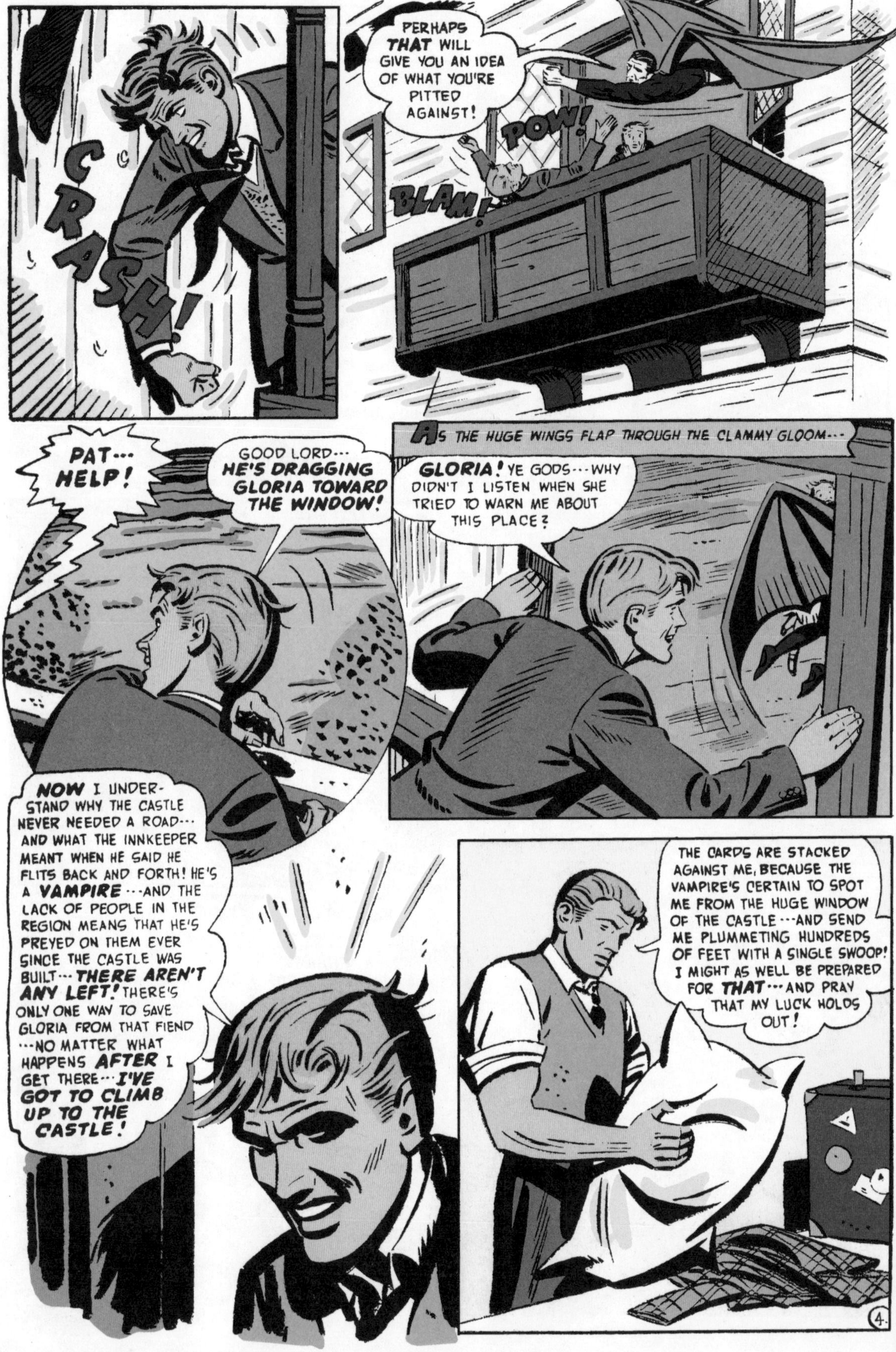
CRASH!
PERHAPS THAT WILL GIVE YOU AN IDEA OF WHAT YOU'RE PITTED AGAINST!
POW!
BLAM!
PAT... HELP!
GOOD LORD... HE'S DRAGGING GLORIA TOWARD THE WINDOW!
AS THE HUGE WINGS FLAP THROUGH THE CLAMMY GLOOM...
GLORIA! YE GODS... WHY DIDN'T I LISTEN WHEN SHE TRIED TO WARN ME ABOUT THIS PLACE?
NOW I UNDERSTAND WHY THE CASTLE NEVER NEEDED A ROAD... AND WHAT THE INNKEEPER MEANT WHEN HE SAID HE FLITS BACK AND FORTH! HE'S A VAMPIRE... AND THE LACK OF PEOPLE IN THE REGION MEANS THAT HE'S PREYED ON THEM EVER SINCE THE CASTLE WAS BUILT... THERE AREN'T ANY LEFT! THERE'S ONLY ONE WAY TO SAVE GLORIA FROM THAT FIEND ...NO MATTER WHAT HAPPENS AFTER I GET THERE... I'VE GOT TO CLIMB UP TO THE CASTLE!
THE CARDS ARE STACKED AGAINST ME, BECAUSE THE VAMPIRE'S CERTAIN TO SPOT ME FROM THE HUGE WINDOW OF THE CASTLE... AND SEND ME PLUMMETING HUNDREDS OF FEET WITH A SINGLE SWOOP! I MIGHT AS WELL BE PREPARED FOR THAT... AND PRAY THAT MY LUCK HOLDS OUT!
4.

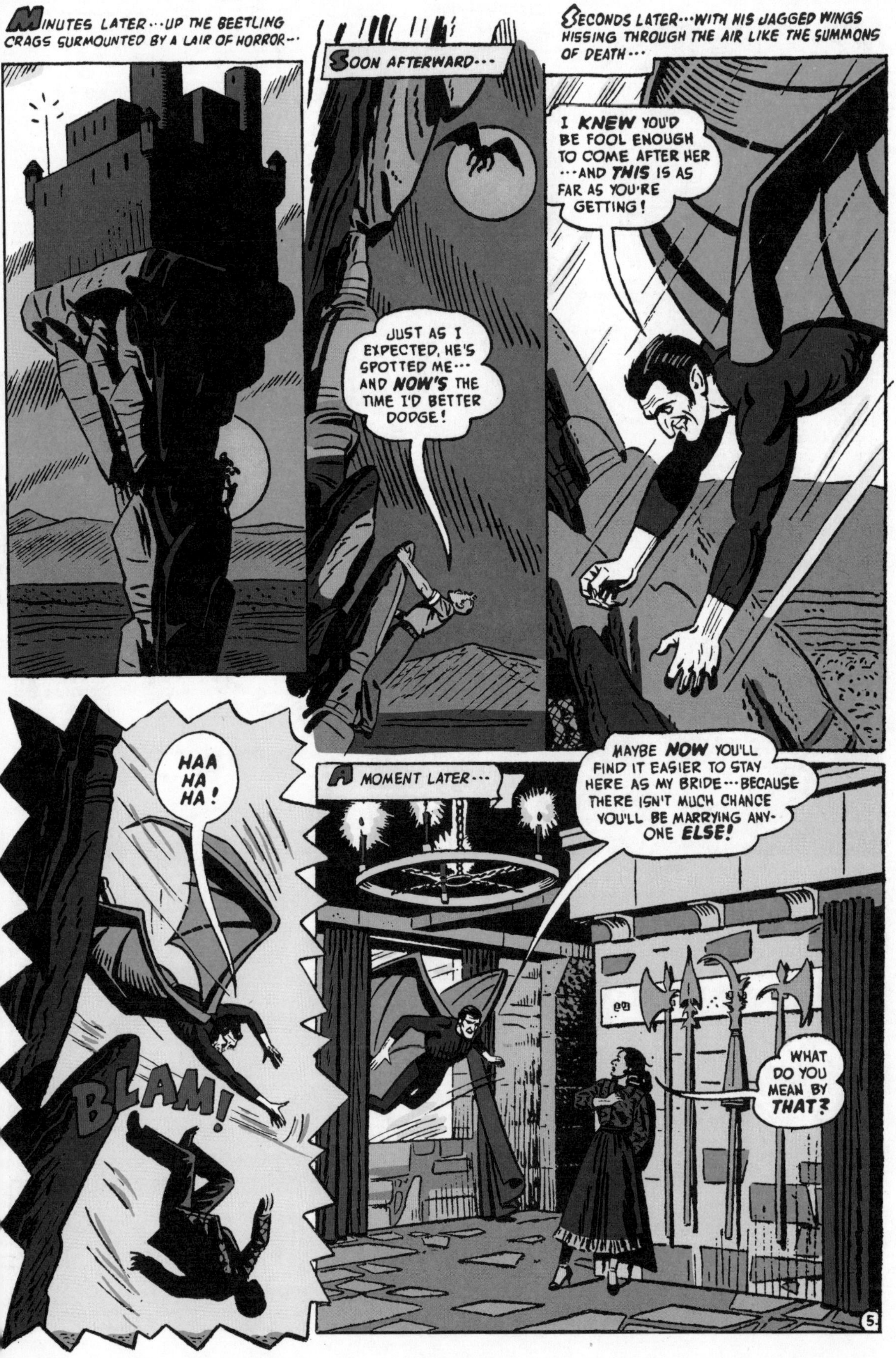
MINUTES LATER···UP THE BEETLING CRAGS SURMOUNTED BY A LAIR OF HORROR···
SOON AFTERWARD···
JUST AS I EXPECTED, HE'S SPOTTED ME··· AND NOW'S THE TIME I'D BETTER DODGE!
SECONDS LATER···WITH HIS JAGGED WINGS HISSING THROUGH THE AIR LIKE THE SUMMONS OF DEATH···
I KNEW YOU'D BE FOOL ENOUGH TO COME AFTER HER ···AND THIS IS AS FAR AS YOU'RE GETTING!
HAA HA HA!
BLAM!
A MOMENT LATER···
MAYBE NOW YOU'LL FIND IT EASIER TO STAY HERE AS MY BRIDE···BECAUSE THERE ISN'T MUCH CHANCE YOU'LL BE MARRYING ANY-ONE ELSE!
WHAT DO YOU MEAN BY THAT?
5.

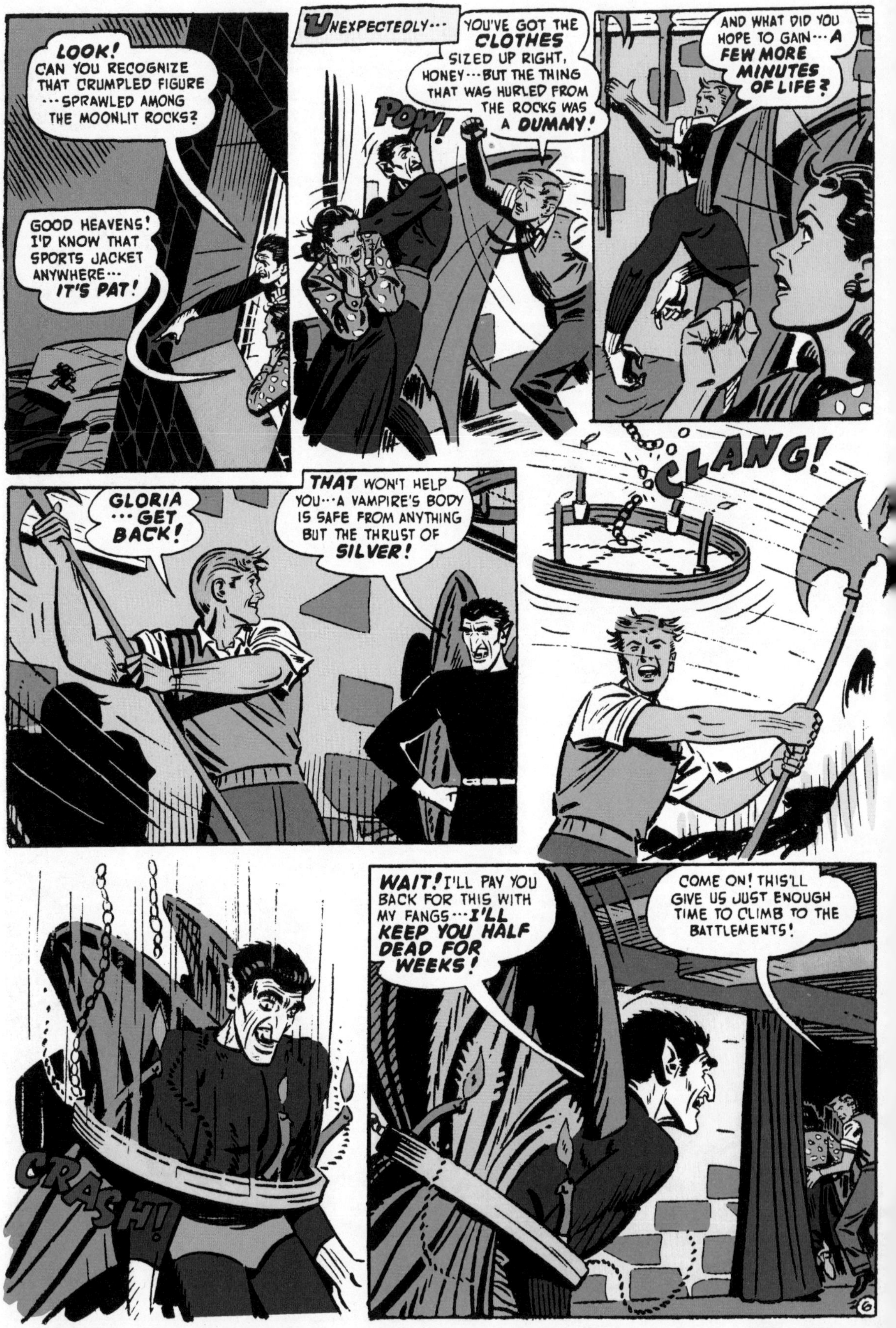

LOOK! CAN YOU RECOGNIZE THAT CRUMPLED FIGURE ···SPRAWLED AMONG THE MOONLIT ROCKS?
GOOD HEAVENS! I'D KNOW THAT SPORTS JACKET ANYWHERE··· IT'S PAT!
UNEXPECTEDLY···
YOU'VE GOT THE CLOTHES SIZED UP RIGHT, HONEY···BUT THE THING THAT WAS HURLED FROM THE ROCKS WAS A DUMMY!
POW!
AND WHAT DID YOU HOPE TO GAIN··· A FEW MORE MINUTES OF LIFE?
GLORIA ···GET BACK!
THAT WON'T HELP YOU···A VAMPIRE'S BODY IS SAFE FROM ANYTHING BUT THE THRUST OF SILVER!
CLANG!
CRASH!
WAIT! I'LL PAY YOU BACK FOR THIS WITH MY FANGS···I'LL KEEP YOU HALF DEAD FOR WEEKS!
COME ON! THIS'LL GIVE US JUST ENOUGH TIME TO CLIMB TO THE BATTLEMENTS!
6

WE'RE JUST GETTING OURSELVES IN A WORSE TRAP THAN EVER, PAT... WE'LL **NEVER** ESCAPE FROM THE CASTLE ROOF!

THERE'S NO USE **TRYING** TO ESCAPE WHILE THE VAMPIRE'S STILL ALIVE! I TRICKED HIM ONCE, AND MAYBE I CAN DO IT **AGAIN** IN AN ATTEMPT TO FINISH HIM OFF... BECAUSE TRYING TO **FIGHT** HIM OFF WILL BE SHEER SUICIDE!

A MOMENT LATER ...ON THE WIND-SWEPT HEIGHTS...

HE'S COMING, PAT! WHAT IN HEAVEN WILL WE DO?

KEEP YOUR HEAD... **AND HIDE!** THIS WHOLE IDEA WILL BE WORTHLESS IF THE VAMPIRE CATCHES SIGHT OF YOU!

HAA! IS **THIS** THE WAY YOU EXPECTED TO ESCAPE?

THERE'S NO USE LOOKING FOR GLORIA ...**SHE'S** JUST BEEN PICKED UP BY THE HELICOPTER I ARRANGED FOR! IT'LL BE BACK TO GET **ME** IN A FEW MINUTES ...AND UNTIL THEN, I'LL BE SAFE RIGHT HERE!

SAFE! FOOL ...DO YOU THINK THAT PERCH IS ANY OBSTACLE TO **ME**?

SUPPOSE YOU TRY TO CLIMB UP...AND FIND OUT? COME ON, CREEP...**GET ME!** I'M ITCHING FOR A CHANCE TO KICK YOUR UGLY FACE IN... WHILE YOU'RE CLINGING TO THE POLE!

YOU FORGET I CAN **FLY!** ALL I HAVE TO DO IS DIVE LIKE A HAWK...AND **THIS** TIME I'LL BE SURE IT **IS** YOU WHO HURTLES TO THE ROCKS BELOW!

AS THE EVIL SHAPE FLAPS HIGHER IN THE MOONLIGHT...

HE'S READY TO DIVE! ONE WAY OR ANOTHER... **THIS'LL BE THE PAYOFF!**

7.

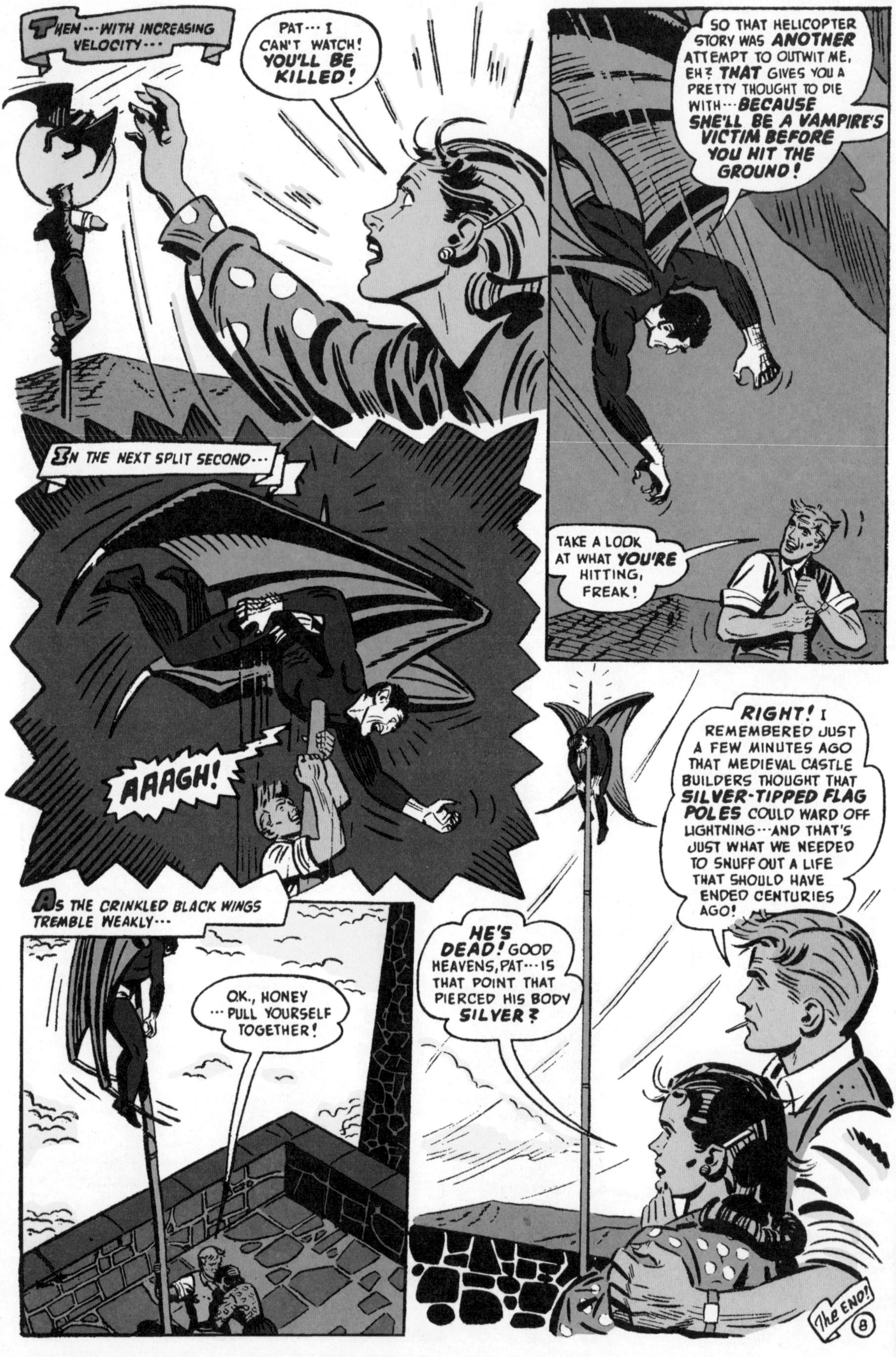
THEN ··· WITH INCREASING VELOCITY ···
PAT··· I CAN'T WATCH! YOU'LL BE KILLED!
SO THAT HELICOPTER STORY WAS ANOTHER ATTEMPT TO OUTWIT ME, EH? THAT GIVES YOU A PRETTY THOUGHT TO DIE WITH··· BECAUSE SHE'LL BE A VAMPIRE'S VICTIM BEFORE YOU HIT THE GROUND!
TAKE A LOOK AT WHAT YOU'RE HITTING, FREAK!
IN THE NEXT SPLIT SECOND···
AAAGH!
AS THE CRINKLED BLACK WINGS TREMBLE WEAKLY···
O.K., HONEY ··· PULL YOURSELF TOGETHER!
HE'S DEAD! GOOD HEAVENS, PAT··· IS THAT POINT THAT PIERCED HIS BODY SILVER?
RIGHT! I REMEMBERED JUST A FEW MINUTES AGO THAT MEDIEVAL CASTLE BUILDERS THOUGHT THAT SILVER-TIPPED FLAG POLES COULD WARD OFF LIGHTNING···AND THAT'S JUST WHAT WE NEEDED TO SNUFF OUT A LIFE THAT SHOULD HAVE ENDED CENTURIES AGO!
The END!
8

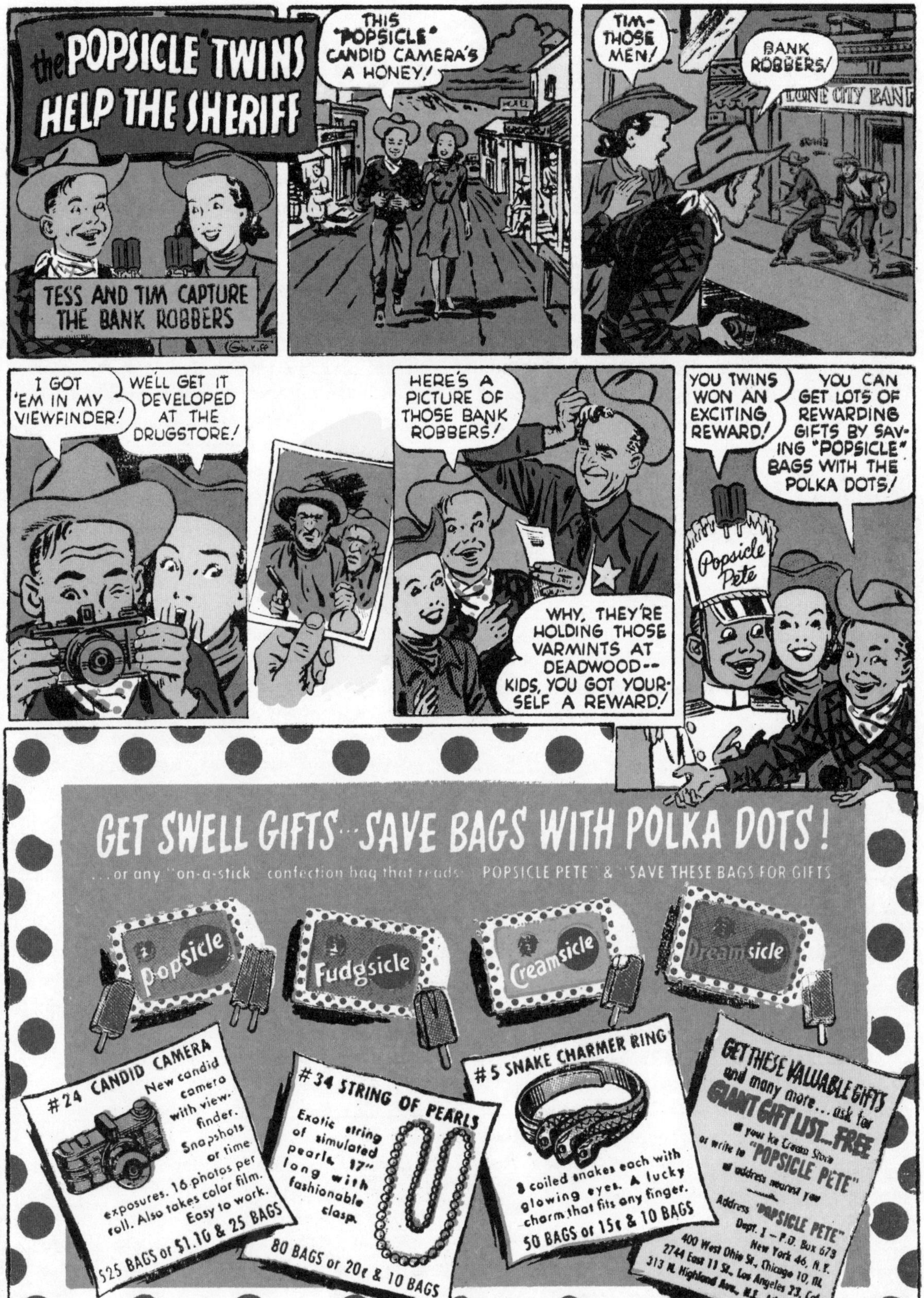
the "POPSICLE" TWINS HELP THE SHERIFF
TESS AND TIM CAPTURE THE BANK ROBBERS
THIS "POPSICLE" CANDID CAMERA'S A HONEY!
HOTEL
TIM- THOSE MEN!
BANK ROBBERS!
LONE CITY BANK
I GOT 'EM IN MY VIEWFINDER!
WE'LL GET IT DEVELOPED AT THE DRUGSTORE!
HERE'S A PICTURE OF THOSE BANK ROBBERS!
WHY, THEY'RE HOLDING THOSE VARMINTS AT DEADWOOD-- KIDS, YOU GOT YOURSELF A REWARD!
YOU TWINS WON AN EXCITING REWARD!
YOU CAN GET LOTS OF REWARDING GIFTS BY SAVING "POPSICLE" BAGS WITH THE POLKA DOTS!
Popsicle Pete
GET SWELL GIFTS...SAVE BAGS WITH POLKA DOTS!
...or any "on-a-stick" confection bag that reads: "POPSICLE PETE" & "SAVE THESE BAGS FOR GIFTS"
popsicle
Fudgsicle
Creamsicle
Dreamsicle
#24 CANDID CAMERA
New candid camera with view-finder. Snapshots or time exposures. 16 photos per roll. Also takes color film. Easy to work.
525 BAGS or $1.10 & 25 BAGS
#34 STRING OF PEARLS
Exotic string of simulated pearls 17" long with fashionable clasp.
80 BAGS or 20¢ & 10 BAGS
#5 SNAKE CHARMER RING
2 coiled snakes each with glowing eyes. A lucky charm that fits any finger.
50 BAGS or 15¢ & 10 BAGS
GET THESE VALUABLE GIFTS and many more... ask for GIANT GIFT LIST...FREE at your Ice Cream Store or write to "POPSICLE PETE" at address nearest you
Address "POPSICLE PETE" Dept. I – P.O. Box 673 New York 46, N.Y.
400 West Ohio St., Chicago 10, Ill.
2744 East 11 St., Los Angeles 23, Cal.
313 N. Highland Ave., N.E., Atlanta, Ga.

The RETURN

THE THIRD DAY after Mrs. Peabody had settled into her new summer cottage on Lake Owasco, she decided to pay a visit to her nearest neighbor a few hundred yards down the path that skirted the shore. But before she had even gotten within sight of her neighbor's house in the tree-fringed cove, Mrs. Peabody's attention was drawn to the woebegone figure of a little girl crouching at the water's edge, staring soulfully into the blue depths.

As Mrs. Peabody approached, she was startled to see that the girl's clothes and hair were dripping wet, and that her skin had the awful white pallor of a shroud.

She's probably just recovered from a long illness, Mrs. Peabody thought. That would explain her ghastly whiteness. This might be her very first day out-of-doors, but she'll probably be having a relapse after that wetting she apparently just got.

"How did you get so wet, child?" Mrs. Peabody asked with concern. "Did you fall into the lake?"

The girl looked up at her with eyes of cloudy blue. "Oh, yes," she said gravely. "And it was cold. So cold...for so long."

"Well, why don't you go on home and get dry and warm? You'll catch your death sitting there like that!"

The girl smiled slowly, sadly. "You don't catch death. Death catches you. But it isn't so bad. He looks very terrible, but he's very gentle with little girls. It didn't hurt much."

The poor thing's delirious, Mrs. Peabody thought in alarm. "Where do you live, child? I'll have to take you home right away!"

"Oh, you're coming into the lake with me?" the girl exclaimed, standing up with a pleased expression on her face. "That'll be fun! There's no one else down there

except some grouchy old fisherman. Come on...take my hand and I'll show you how easy it is. All you have to do is step right into the lake and..."

Mrs. Peabody drew back in horror as she felt the icy clamminess of the girl's hand touching hers. The child's temperature must be terribly low due to shock and exposure, she thought wildly; *that was the only explanation for the deathly iciness of that touch.* And as for what the girl had said...well, that was merely the raving of a sick mind.

Realizing that the delirious girl probably wouldn't obey any orders from a stranger to return to her home, Mrs. Peabody said, "What's your name, child?"

"Alice Hanscombe. But aren't you coming into the lake with me...?"

Hanscombe. The renting agent had told Mrs. Peabody that her nearest neighbor's name was Hanscombe. "No, dear," Mrs. Peabody said as she began to hurry away. "Now you stay right there and I'll be right back."

As Mrs. Peabody rounded the edge of the cove and saw the Hanscombe house ahead, she thought she heard a splash coming from behind her...and that only made her quicken her steps into a run. When she burst into the kitchen of the house, she said breathlessly to the woman standing at the stove, "Mrs. Hanscombe...I...I'm your new neighbor...and I just saw your daughter Alice standing dripping wet at the edge of the lake! You...you'd better go out there and bring her back, before she..."

"Oh, again?" Mrs. Hanscombe gasped. "This is the...the third year she's come back...on *the anniversary of the day she drowned in the lake!*"

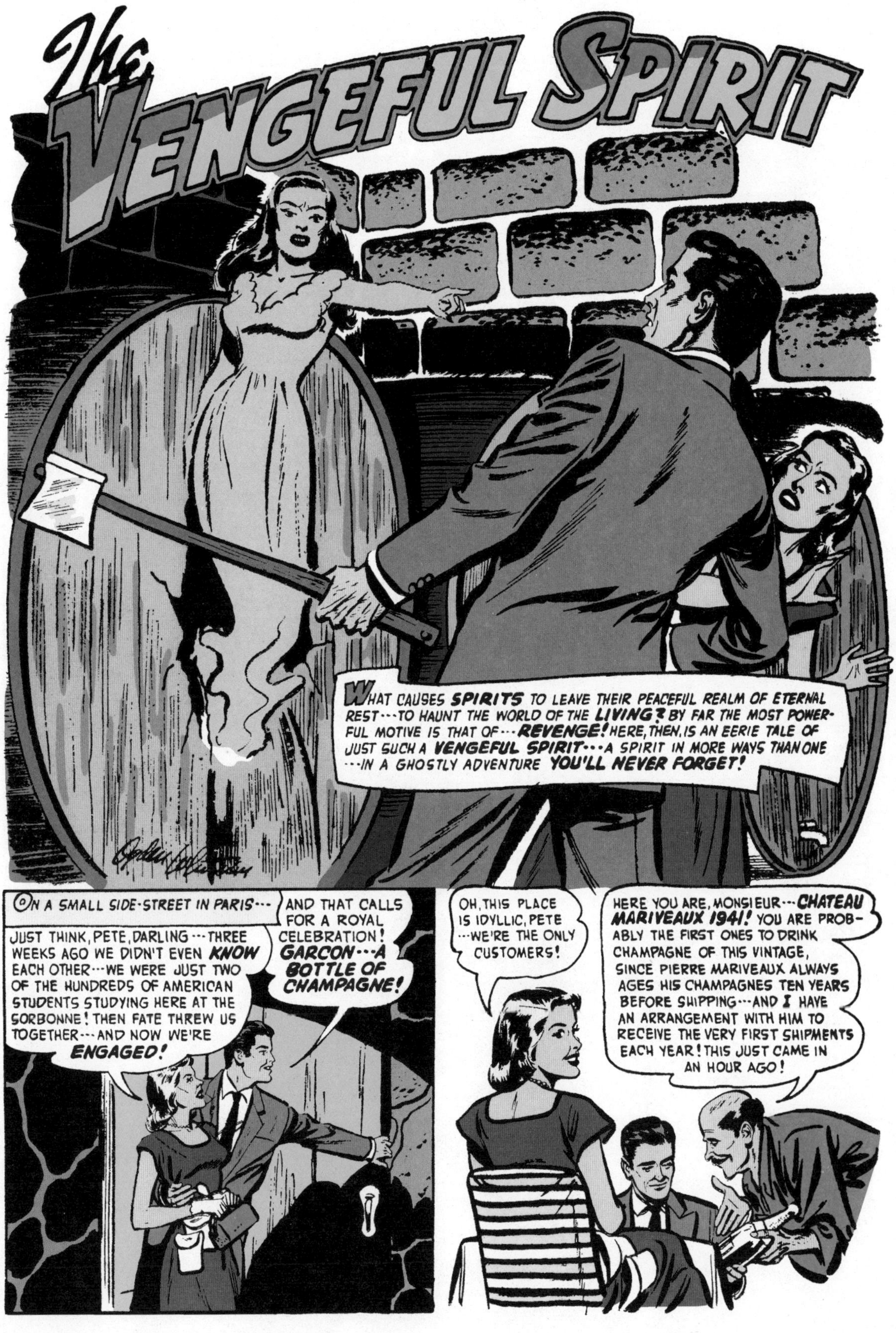
The Vengeful Spirit
WHAT CAUSES SPIRITS TO LEAVE THEIR PEACEFUL REALM OF ETERNAL REST---TO HAUNT THE WORLD OF THE LIVING? BY FAR THE MOST POWERFUL MOTIVE IS THAT OF---REVENGE! HERE, THEN, IS AN EERIE TALE OF JUST SUCH A VENGEFUL SPIRIT---A SPIRIT IN MORE WAYS THAN ONE ---IN A GHOSTLY ADVENTURE YOU'LL NEVER FORGET!
ON A SMALL SIDE-STREET IN PARIS---
JUST THINK, PETE, DARLING --- THREE WEEKS AGO WE DIDN'T EVEN KNOW EACH OTHER---WE WERE JUST TWO OF THE HUNDREDS OF AMERICAN STUDENTS STUDYING HERE AT THE SORBONNE! THEN FATE THREW US TOGETHER---AND NOW WE'RE ENGAGED!
AND THAT CALLS FOR A ROYAL CELEBRATION! GARCON---A BOTTLE OF CHAMPAGNE!
OH, THIS PLACE IS IDYLLIC, PETE ---WE'RE THE ONLY CUSTOMERS!
HERE YOU ARE, MONSIEUR---CHATEAU MARIVEAUX 1941! YOU ARE PROBABLY THE FIRST ONES TO DRINK CHAMPAGNE OF THIS VINTAGE, SINCE PIERRE MARIVEAUX ALWAYS AGES HIS CHAMPAGNES TEN YEARS BEFORE SHIPPING---AND I HAVE AN ARRANGEMENT WITH HIM TO RECEIVE THE VERY FIRST SHIPMENTS EACH YEAR! THIS JUST CAME IN AN HOUR AGO!

TALKATIVE, WASN'T HE? I'M GLAD HE WENT BACK INTO THE KITCHEN---NOW WE CAN CELEBRATE IN PRIVACY!

YEAH---IF I CAN EVER GET THIS BOTTLE *OPEN!*

FROM THE BOTTLE---A WEIRD VISION!

WHAT THE---!

EDNA---DID--- DID *YOU* SEE WHAT *I* SAW?

YOU---YOU MEAN THAT WRAITH- LIKE FIGURE OF A GIRL? I---I THOUGHT IT WAS JUST MY IMAGINATION---BUT IF *YOU* SAW IT TOO---

BUT IT'S---*CRAZY!* THIS VINTAGE IS PROBABLY HEAVILY CARBONATED--- AND WHEN I OPENED THE BOTTLE, THE ESCAPING GAS JUST ASSUMED AN ODD SHAPE THAT *RESEMBLED* A GIRL! COME ON, LET'S DRINK UP--- TO *US!*

N---NO, THANKS, PETE---I...I DON'T SEEM TO WANT TO DRINK ANY MORE OF *THAT* WINE! AND I WISH *YOU* WOULDN'T, EITHER!

DON'T BE SILLY---! I'LL SHOW YOU IT'S HARMLESS--- *ULP!*

GO---GO TO THE CHATEAU MARIVEAUX!

I---I *HEARD* IT---SHE *SPOKE* TO ME!

I DIDN'T HEAR ANY- THING, BUT I *SAW* HER, ALL RIGHT! PETE---LET---LET'S GET AWAY FROM HERE---*FAST!*

CRAK!

NO---THIS IS THE FIRST TIME I'VE HEARD OF AN ALCOHOLIC SPIRIT THAT *IS* A SPIRIT---AND I'VE *GOT* TO FIND OUT IF IT *REALLY HAPPENED!* I'LL TEST IT AGAIN---

2.

ONCE AGAIN···THAT EERIE SPECTACLE···BUT *THIS TIME*···

GO···GO TO THE CHATEAU MARIVEAUX ···THERE YOU WILL FIND *ME*!

I···I SAW THAT···SHE *KISSED* YOU! AND YOU LOOKED AS IF YOU *LIKED* IT!

THE···THE TOUCH OF HER HANDS···HER LIPS···THAT WAS *REAL*!···I···I'VE *GOT* TO DO AS SHE SAYS ···SEE IF I CAN FIND HER, *HELP* HER!

THE CHATEAU MARIVEAUX AT EPERNAY···THAT'S WHERE I'M GOING!

YOU MEAN THAT'S WHERE *WE'RE* GOING! THAT GIRL WAS TOO BEAUTIFUL, EVEN IF SHE *IS* ONLY A BODILESS SPECTER!

NEXT DAY···

WE'VE PASSED NOTHING BUT VINEYARDS FOR HOURS ···THIS IS THE HEART OF THE GRAPE-GROWING DISTRICT!

YES, AND ALL THESE LANDS MUST BELONG TO THE CHATEAU MARIVEAUX··· BECAUSE THERE'S THE CHATEAU ITSELF UP AHEAD!

I AM SORRY··· MY MASTER, MONSIEUR MARIVEAUX, REFUSES TO SEE VISITORS!

I'LL HAVE TO TRY A SHOT IN THE DARK···!

TELL YOUR MASTER WE'VE COME TO SEE HIM ABOUT THE *SPIRIT OF THE 1941 VINTAGE*!

LET··· *LET THEM IN*!

I AM *PIERRE MARIVEAUX!* COME INTO MY LIBRARY AND TELL ME WHAT YOU MEANT ABOUT THE *SPIRIT OF THE 1941 VINTAGE!* DID···DID *YOU* SEE HER TOO···DID SHE *TELL* YOU ANYTHING?

THEN YOU KNOW ABOUT HER, EH? YES, I SAW HER WHEN I DRANK FROM A BOTTLE OF YOUR '41 CHAMPAGNE···BUT ALL SHE SAID WAS THAT I'D *FIND HER HERE*!

OUI, SHE IS HERE! HER SATANICAL SPIRIT IS IMPRISONED IN EVERY BOTTLE OF THE '41 VINTAGE···AS WELL AS IN THE HUGE WINE CASKS IN MY CELLAR VAULTS! I BEGAN SENDING OUT THAT YEAR'S VINTAGE BEFORE I KNEW OF *HER* PRESENCE WITH IT···AND NOW THAT CHAMPAGNE IS ON ITS WAY ALL OVER THE WORLD! I···I *MUST* EXORCISE HER SPIRIT BE- FORE SHE DOES ANY *HARM*!

3.

BUT WHO···WHO *IS* THAT SPIRIT?

MY SISTER, ODETTE···AN EVIL *WITCH,* CURSED BE HER NAME! I THOUGHT I WAS RID OF HER WHEN SHE DIED IN 1941··· *BUT HER DEMON'S SOUL LIVES ON!* I···I STILL REMEMBER WHAT HAPPENED WHEN I FIRST SAMPLED THE '41 VINTAGE FROM THE CELLAR CASKS···HOW HER FIENDISH FINGERS REACHED FOR MY THROAT! THE ONLY WAY I CAN FORGET HER IS IN DRINK···

···ANYTHING BUT THE '41 CHAMPAGNE!

HE···HE'S GOING TO DRINK HIMSELF INTO A STUPOR! LET'S GET OUT OF HERE, PETE··· FORGET THIS CRAZY BUSINESS!

NO! I'VE GOT TO GET TO THE BOTTOM OF THIS···I CAN'T *BELIEVE* THAT GIRL WAS AN EVIL WITCH! I'VE GOT A PLAN···WE'LL JUST WAIT UNTIL HE DRINKS HIMSELF INTO UNCONSCIOUSNESS···

*T*WENTY MINUTES LATER···

BEFORE YOUR MASTER···ER, RETIRED, HE SAID THAT WE WERE TO SPEND THE NIGHT HERE! COULD YOU SHOW US TO OUR ROOMS, PLEASE?

MAIS OUI··· *AFTER* I HAVE PUT MY MASTER TO BED!

AND HERE IS *YOUR* ROOM, MONSIEUR!

PETE···I···I'M SCARED! WON'T YOU CHANGE YOUR MIND AND LEAVE··· *PLEASE?*

THERE'S NOTHING TO BE AFRAID OF, DARLING! JUST LOCK YOUR DOOR···AND I'LL SEE YOU IN THE MORNING!

*A*S MIDNIGHT TOLLS LIKE THE KNELL OF DOOM···

THEY'RE ALL ASLEEP···NO ONE WILL KNOW THAT I'VE STOLEN DOWN TO THE WINE CELLAR! IF THE ANSWER TO THIS MYSTERY IS ANYWHERE IN THIS HOUSE, *IT'S DOWN THERE!*

*D*OWN···DOWN INTO THE SUBTERRANEAN VAULTS, WHERE THE SMELL OF FERMENTING WINE HANGS LIKE THE FETID BREATH OF SOME MONSTROUS SPIRIT···

AH, HERE ARE THE '41 CASKS! I'LL JUST OPEN THE SPIGOT AND DRAW A CUPFUL···

OH-OH ··· *HER* AGAIN!

TAKE-- THAT AXE ---BREAK OPEN THE CASK!

I---I CAN'T! IT'S VALUABLE---AND IT'S NOT MY PROPERTY---

YES, BUT IT WOULD GIVE FREE REIN FOR MY SPIRIT TO ESCAPE! I HAVE NOT THE STRENGTH TO SPEAK LONG--- *HURRY!*

YOUR---YOUR LIPS---I---I CAN'T RESIST YOU!

CRASH!

THEN--- YOU---YOU'RE MUCH CLEARER NOW---AND THAT GHOSTLY LIGHT AROUND YOU IS STRONGER!

YES---ALL THESE CASKS CONTAIN *MORE* THAN ALCOHOLIC SPIRITS---THEY CONTAIN ALSO *MY* SPIRIT! AND ENOUGH OF MY SPIRIT ESSENCE IS ESCAPING FROM THIS CASK NOW TO SUSTAIN ME FOR A WHILE AND GIVE ME THE STRENGTH TO *TELL YOU MY STORY!*

I AND MY BROTHER PIERRE WERE THE LAST OF THE MARIVEAUX FAMILY---THE LAST ONES TO INHERIT THE FABULOUS FAMILY VINEYARDS! BUT PIERRE WAS NEVER A TRUE MARIVEAUX, OR A TRUE FRENCHMAN---FOR WHEN THE NAZIS CONQUERED FRANCE IN 1940, HE BECAME A COLLABORATOR IN ORDER TO RETAIN HIS FORTUNE---WHILE *I* JOINED THE MAQUIS OF THE FREE FRENCH UNDERGROUND!

"*I* MADE NO ATTEMPT TO CONCEAL MY IDENTITY--- AND THE NAZIS SOON PLACED A PRICE ON MY HEAD!"

MAYBE *NOW* YOU BOCHE WILL RAISE THE REWARD FOR MY CAPTURE!

ODETTE MARIVEAUX 50,000 FRANCS

RAT-TAT-TAT!

"*B*UT WHEN THE GESTAPO DRAGNET TIGHTENED AROUND MY BAND OF MAQUIS, I TURNED IN DESPERATION TO PIERRE, FOOL-ISHLY BELIEVING THAT HE WOULDN'T BETRAY HIS OWN SISTER!"

THE NAZIS TRUST YOU--- THEY WOULD NEVER THINK OF SEARCHING YOUR WINE CELLARS FOR MAQUIS! IT WOULD MAKE A PER-FECT HIDEOUT FOR US---

NO! I AM IN TOO WELL WITH THE NAZIS NOW---I CANNOT AFFORD TO RISK MY LIFE AND FORTUNE BY HELP-ING YOU! BUT *YOU* CAN HELP *ME* SOLIDIFY MY POSITION WITH THE NAZIS---

5.

OHHHHH!

···WHEN THE NAZIS LEARN THAT I KILLED MY OWN SISTER FOR THEM, THEN I WILL **REALLY** BE IN WITH THEM!

BANG!

"*The* NAZIS PAID EVEN HIGHER PRICES FOR PIERRE'S WINES AND CHAMPAGNES AFTER HE HAD THUS PROVEN HIS LOYALTY TO THEM ···AND PIERRE GREEDILY PLANTED EVERY SQUARE FOOT OF HIS LAND WITH GRAPE VINES, EAGER FOR THE MONEY THAT EACH ADDITIONAL BOTTLE WOULD BRING HIM! BUT HE MADE HIS FATAL MISTAKE WHEN HE PLANTED VINES ON **MY GRAVE!**"

HA··· YOU SERVE MY PURPOSE EVEN AFTER YOUR DEATH, MY SISTER! THE WINE THAT I WILL EXTRACT FROM THIS 1941 CROP WILL CONTAIN YOUR VERY HEART'S BLOOD!

BUT THE VINES CONTAINED **MORE**··· THEY ALSO IMPRISONED MY **SPIRIT!** AND SINCE CHAMPAGNE IS ALWAYS A **BLENDED** MIXTURE, MY SPIRIT WAS DIFFUSED THROUGHOUT THE ENTIRE 1941 VINTAGE··· AND EXISTED IN EACH CASK, IN EVERY BOTTLE! BUT I CAN APPEAR ONLY WHEN THE CARBONIC GAS ESCAPES, FOR I USE THE GAS TO FORM MY SPECTRAL SHAPE···

I GET IT NOW··· THE MORE GAS THAT ESCAPES, THE CLEARER AND STRONGER YOUR SPIRIT IS!

EXACTLY···AND THAT WAS WHY I COULD ONLY APPEAR MOMENTARILY TO YOU IN THAT PARIS CAFE! THERE IS ONLY ENOUGH OF MY SPIRIT IN EACH BOTTLE TO WHISPER A FEW WORDS···WHILE THERE WAS ENOUGH IN THIS CASK TO ALLOW ME TO TELL YOU MY STORY! AND THAT IS ALSO WHY I DID NOT HAVE THE STRENGTH TO WREAK MY REVENGE ON PIERRE WHEN HE OPENED HIS FIRST BOTTLE! BUT NOW, I AM BECOMING WEAKER, MORE TRANSPARENT··· THE GAS IS ALMOST COMPLETELY EVAPORATED FROM THE CASK···

IT···IT IS UP TO **YOU**··· TO AVENGE MY MURDER! YOU HAVE THE STRENGTH··· TO **KILL** MY BROTHER! AVENGE ME··· AND ALLOW ME TO RETURN TO ETERNAL REST! REMEMBER···

···KILL MY BROTHER··· KILL MY BROTH···

SHE···SHE'S EVAPORATED···VANISHED! BUT I··· I CAN'T DO WHAT SHE ASKED ···I CAN'T COMMIT **MURDER!** I'D BETTER GET OUT OF HERE, OUT INTO THE FRESH AIR···WHERE I CAN THINK THIS OUT!

BUT OUTSIDE---

ARE YOU---MONSIEUR MARIVEAUX? I··· I WAS TOLD TO COME HERE···BY A···A LOVELY VISION···A GIRL! SHE SAID I WOULD FIND HER HERE···

OH-OH, HE MUST HAVE HAD A BOTTLE OF CHATEAU MARIVEAUX CHAMPAGNE···VINTAGE 1941! I'VE GOT TO DISCOURAGE HIM···BEFORE *HE* GETS ENTANGLED IN THIS!

I AM FROM THE MINISTRY OF HEALTH, MONSIEUR---AND I CAN TELL YOU THAT YOUR VISION WAS MERELY AN HALLUCINATORY EFFECT, CAUSED BY A DRUG IN THE CHATEAU MARIVEAUX CHAMPAGNE! MANY OTHERS HAVE IMAGINED THAT SAME GIRL---BUT SHE EXISTS ONLY IN THE IMAGINATION! WE HAVE CONFISCATED ALL THE CONTAMINATED CHAMPAGNE HERE---SO I ADVISE YOU TO GO HOME AND FORGET THE VISION YOU HAD!

FORGET---*HER?* NEVER, MONSIEUR! I WILL GO HOME---BUT I WILL NEVER FORGET HER CARESSING HANDS---HER LIPS---

HUNDREDS, PERHAPS THOUSANDS, WILL BE COMING HERE IN THE DAYS AND WEEKS TO COME···SEARCHING FOR A VISION THEY SAW IN A CHAMPAGNE BOTTLE! AND IT'LL *KEEP* ON HAPPENING···UNLESS *I* PUT THAT SPIRIT TO REST! I CAN'T KILL PIERRE···BUT I THINK I KNOW *HOW TO GIVE ODETTE'S SPIRIT ENOUGH STRENGTH TO WREAK HER OWN REVENGE ON HIM!*

NEXT MORNING ---

EH? ARE YOU TWO *STILL* HERE? GET OUT···OUT OF MY HOUSE!

ARE YOU *SURE* YOU WANT US TO LEAVE---WHEN WE KNOW THAT *YOU* MURDERED YOUR SISTER?

SO···YOU SPOKE TO ODETTE'S SPIRIT AGAIN! SHE TOLD YOU ALL ABOUT IT, EH? WELL, *YOU* WON'T LIVE LONG ENOUGH TO TELL ANYONE *ELSE* ABOUT IT!

IT WON'T DO YOU ANY GOOD TO KILL *ME!* YOUR '41 CHAMPAGNES ARE GOING ALL OVER THE WORLD---HUNDREDS OF PEOPLE WILL SOON BE BEATING A TRAIL TO YOUR DOOR, URGED ON BY ODETTE'S SPIRIT! YOUR ONLY CHANCE IS TO LISTEN TO *ME*···BECAUSE I ALONE KNOW HOW TO DOWN HER AVENGING SPIRIT!

ODETTE TOLD ME HER STRENGTH WOULD DISAPPEAR AS SOON AS ALL THE FERMENTING GAS ESCAPED FROM THE CASKS IN YOUR CELLAR VAULTS! SO ALL YOU HAVE TO DO IS BLOW UP THE CASKS ---AND BLOW HER SPIRIT TO SMITHEREENS!

AH, YOU WILL BE WELL REWARDED FOR THAT INFORMATION! I CAN SAFELY DYNAMITE THE '41 CASKS, BECAUSE THE STONE WALLS OF THE VAULT WILL WITHSTAND THE EXPLOSION---AND I'LL DO IT *RIGHT NOW!*

THE STRENGTH OF ODETTE'S SPIRIT DEPENDS ON HOW MUCH OF THE FERMENTING GAS ESCAPES FROM THE CHAMPAGNE···SO IF ALL THE CASKS ARE BLOWN UP AT THE SAME TIME, ENOUGH GAS OUGHT TO ESCAPE TO GIVE HER *ENORMOUS* POWER! THEN IT'LL BE UP TO *HER* TO *WREAK HER REVENGE!*

AH, THE DYNAMITE IS ALL SET NOW!

DIE, ODETTE ··· DIE *AGAIN!*

BOOM!

*A*S THE CHAMPAGNE AND FERMENTING GAS POUR OUT OF THE WRECKED CASKS···

ODETTE ···NO··· *NO* ···!

TRAITOR··· MURDERER ···NOW *YOU* DIE!

YAAAGHH!

AT LAST I AM REVENGED ···THANKS TO *YOU!* AND NOW CAN MY SPIRIT FADE AWAY···AND FIND ETERNAL REST! FAREWELL···!

PETE···SHE ···SHE'S *DISAPPEARING!*

YES ···FOR *GOOD!*

*W*EEKS LATER···

SAY···CAN'T YOU NEWLYWEDS POSTPONE YOUR HONEYMOON LONG ENOUGH TO DRINK A *CHAMPAGNE TOAST?*

NOT *US!* WE'RE NEVER GOING TO TOUCH ALCOHOLIC SPIRITS AGAIN···NOT AFTER HAVING SEEN A *REAL* ONE!

THE END!

8.

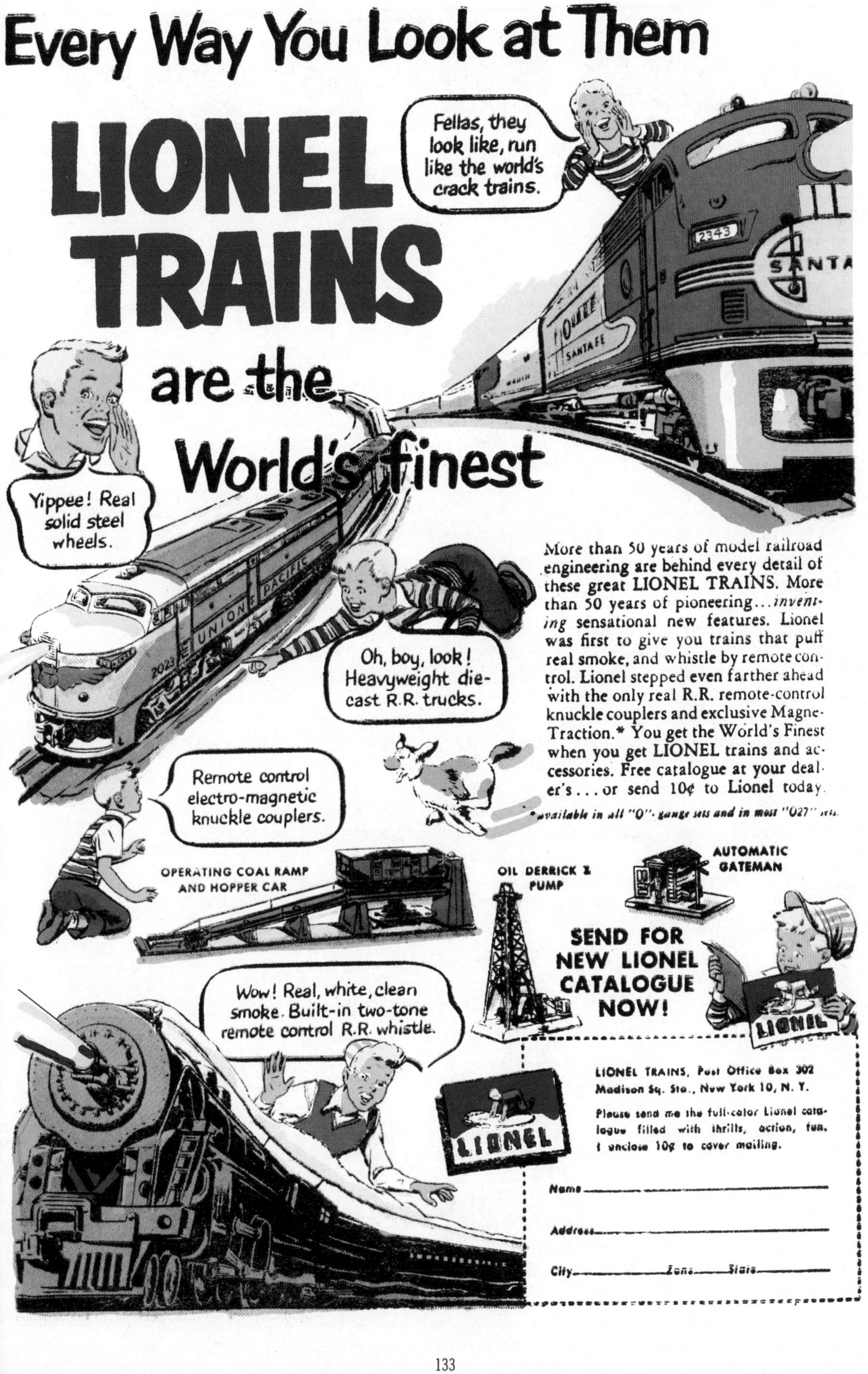

Every Way You Look at Them
LIONEL TRAINS are the World's finest
Fellas, they look like, run like the world's crack trains.
Yippee! Real solid steel wheels.
Oh, boy, look! Heavyweight die-cast R.R. trucks.
More than 50 years of model railroad engineering are behind every detail of these great LIONEL TRAINS. More than 50 years of pioneering... *inventing* sensational new features. Lionel was first to give you trains that puff real smoke, and whistle by remote control. Lionel stepped even farther ahead with the only real R.R. remote-control knuckle couplers and exclusive Magne-Traction.* You get the World's Finest when you get LIONEL trains and accessories. Free catalogue at your dealer's... or send 10¢ to Lionel today.
*available in all "O"-gauge sets and in most "027" sets.
Remote control electro-magnetic knuckle couplers.
OPERATING COAL RAMP AND HOPPER CAR
OIL DERRICK & PUMP
AUTOMATIC GATEMAN
SEND FOR NEW LIONEL CATALOGUE NOW!
LIONEL
Wow! Real, white, clean smoke. Built-in two-tone remote control R.R. whistle.
LIONEL
LIONEL TRAINS, Post Office Box 302
Madison Sq. Sta., New York 10, N. Y.
Please send me the full-color Lionel catalogue filled with thrills, action, fun. I enclose 10¢ to cover mailing.
Name
Address
City Zone State

From YOUR EDITOR—to YOU!

THREE RAPS OF a ghostly gavel---and the meeting is called to order! Greetings, all you wonderful people who are doing so much to make "Forbidden Worlds" a sellout! You've given us your wholehearted support, greeting our new magazine with an enthusiasm which is fast making publishing history. All of the loyal fans of our companion publication, "Adventures Into The Unknown", have leaped onto the bandwagon of our new book---and we've added hosts of new readers. All of which guarantees the fact that "Forbidden Worlds" will continue to thrill and entertain its vast and growing public for many years to come!

It's no simple job to thrill and entertain readers who know and demand the best. It calls for constant research on the parts of experienced delvers into the occult---for searching out the strange, eerie and little-known facts that lie hidden deep within the menacing realm of the supernatural. It calls for the skilful efforts of able and imaginative writers geared to turn out the type of story material calculated to leave you breathless and gasping. And it demands the talent of ace artists who can translate weird story material into spine-tingling life. All of this we are bringing you---and shall continue to do so. You'll see the gripping results in this current issue. For we've assembled a galaxy of fast-paced yarns which should be right up the alley of you experienced fans! There's "Lair of the Vampire", presenting a weird menace from out of the Unknown. There's "The Vengeful Spirit", one of the most imaginative and novel ghost stories you've ever read. And "Domain of the Doomed", a gasp-laden adventure into truly forbidden worlds! "Skull of the Sorcerer" is a Hallowe'en story which should make you bar the door comes All Hallow's Eve---and "The Witch's Apprentice" packs an out-of-this-world punch you'll long remember!

Please---write us about how you like this issue. Tell us which stories you like, and why! And tell us what you'd like to see in future issues, because this is your magazine! Address your letters to The Editor, Forbidden Worlds, 45 West 45th Street, New York 19, N. Y. And in case you'd like to know what other readers think. here goes!

"Dear Editor:-

    I have just read your newest book, 'Forbidden Worlds'. I find this magazine most interesting and exciting, and hope that I will see many more copies of it. I liked all the stories in it, especially that titled 'The Way of The Werewolf'. I hope you continue this book and keep up the exciting stories that you put into this last issue. I have also read 'Adventures Into The Unknown', and find it completely thrilling and absorbing. Keep up your swell work on both of them!
                                  --June Mueller, Cleveland, O."

"Dear Editor:-

    My favorite comic up to now has been 'Adventures Into The Unknown', but at last I've found one which I like equally---'Forbidden Worlds'! Yes, I think that 'Forbidden Worlds' has done a great job in living up to your earlier magazine in every respect---even though I would have thought it impossible! I especially liked the stories, 'Demon of Destruction' and 'The Monster Doll'. I'd like to see you try some good robot stories---also zombies.
                                --Michael R. Elliott, Portland, Ore."

"Dear Editor:-

    I have just finished reading your new book called 'Forbidden Worlds', and I think it is the best book I have ever read. I can also say the same thing about your 'Adventures Into The Unknown'---so take your pick! I am crippled with arthritis and cannot walk, and wonderful books like these help me to pass my time thrillingly. The stories I like best are about vampires and werewolves---but any stories of the Unknown and supernatural send me. Keep up the good work---and keep these books rolling!

                                --Frances E. LeJeune, Fremont, O."

The DOMAIN of the DOOMED

M ANKIND HAS ALWAYS CONSIDERED THE REMOTE REACHES OF THE UNIVERSE AS A LAST OUTPOST OF MYSTERY···LITTLE REALIZING THAT IT HARBORS AN EVIL FAR MORE GRISLY THAN ANY EARTHBOUND MENACE! ONLY ONE THING CAN ACTIVATE THE MONSTROUS CREATURES WHO SYMBOLIZE THIS EVIL···AND IT HAPPENS WHEN ATOMIC SCIENCE REACHES *THE DOMAIN OF THE DOOMED!*

I'VE GOT ONE VISITOR, CORPORAL! SHE'S BEEN CLEARED WITH HEADQUARTERS!

OK., DR. NORTON! GUESS ANYONE *YOU* BRING IS A GOOD SECURITY RISK!

U.S. ARMY ATOMIC BOMB PROJECT

I'M AWFULLY PROUD THAT YOUR RECORD AS A PHYSICIST MADE THE ARMY CHOOSE YOU TO HEAD THIS STRATOSPHERE EXPERIMENT, BRUCE···BUT I'VE *STILL* GOT ONLY A VAGUE IDEA OF WHAT IT'S ALL ABOUT!

THAT'LL CHANGE IN JUST A MINUTE, BETTY··· BECAUSE YOU'RE GOING TOO *SEE* EXACTLY WHAT WE'VE GOT IN MIND!

GOOD HEAVENS ---THAT BALLOON IS *IMMENSE!*

IT *HAS* TO BE, SWEETHEART--- *IT'S CARRYING AN ATOMIC BOMB TWENTY MILES UP INTO THE STRATOSPHERE!*

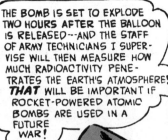

THE BOMB IS SET TO EXPLODE TWO HOURS AFTER THE BALLOON IS RELEASED---AND THE STAFF OF ARMY TECHNICIANS I SUPERVISE WILL THEN MEASURE HOW MUCH RADIOACTIVITY PENETRATES THE EARTH'S ATMOSPHERE! *THAT* WILL BE IMPORTANT IF ROCKET-POWERED ATOMIC BOMBS ARE USED IN A FUTURE WAR!

JEEPERS BRUCE ---I'M NOT SURE I WANT TO GET TOO CLOSE TO AN A-BOMB--- EVEN AROUND *YOU!*

THERE'S NOTHING TO BE AFRAID OF! COME ON --- I WANT TO EXPLAIN A FEW OF THE INSTRUMENTS WE'VE INSTALLED IN THE TOP OF THE CYLINDER!

A MOMENT LATER---

ONE WAY OR ANOTHER ---THIS SABOTAGE ATTEMPT WILL MEAN CERTAIN DEATH FOR *US!*

THAT DOESN'T MATTER---AS LONG AS WE CARRY OUT OUR ASSIGNMENT TO *LEVEL THE AREA WITH AN ATOMIC BLAST!*

THEY ZIPPED RIGHT PAST THE SENTRY! *HEY, DOWN THERE ---STOP THAT CAR!*

TECHNICAL STA

RAT-TAT-TAT!

SCREEECH!

*I*N THE NEXT SECOND---

CRASH!

2.

WITH A SUDDEN LURCH...

OH! THE MOORING CABLES... *THEY'VE SNAPPED!*

CRAK!

SNAP!

DR. NORTON AND HIS FIANCÉE ARE UP THERE IN THE INSTRUMENT COMPARTMENT! WE'VE GOT TO BRING THEM DOWN ...*EVEN IF IT MEANS FIRING AT THE BALLOON!*

IMPOSSIBLE... THE IMPACT WOULD BE SURE TO EXPLODE THE BOMB! NORTON AND THE GIRL WOULD DIE ANYWAY...*AND SO WOULD EVERYONE WITHIN FIVE MILES OF THE BLAST!*

MINUTES LATER...AS THE HUGE SPHERE SOARS THROUGH THE ICY LEVEL OF THE UPPER CLOUDS...

BRUCE! I CAN'T REVIVE HIM...AND IT'S GETTING HARDER AND HARDER TO BREATHE! A FEW MORE HUNDRED FEET...AND WE'LL *BOTH* DIE FROM THE LACK OF OXYGEN!

MILE AFTER MILE, THE BALLOON RISES THROUGH THE LIFELESS REACHES OF THE STRATOSPHERE...CARRYING TWO MOTIONLESS FIGURES INTO THE VOID NO HUMAN HAS EVER ENTERED!

Then...WITH THE EARTH OUT OF SIGHT IN THE BLACK CHASM THAT REELS BELOW...

OHH!

BETTY! IT'S A MIRACLE... BUT WE'RE *ALIVE!*

I NEVER DARED HOPE WE *WOULD* BE, BRUCE! HOW DID IT HAPPEN?

MY GUESS IS THAT WE'VE ABSORBED ENOUGH ATOMIC RAYS FROM THE FISSIONABLE MATERIAL *INSIDE THE BOMB* TO ENABLE US TO WITHSTAND THE EXTREME COLD AND LACK OF OXYGEN!

LOOK... ARE THOSE *CLOUDS?*

THERE *AREN'T* ANY CLOUDS IN THE STRATOSPHERE... BUT *WHATEVER* THEY ARE...THEY'RE *CHANGING SHAPE!*

3

THEN---IN AN ENGULFING WAVE OF HORROR---

BRUCE--- THEY'RE CLOSING IN!

DEEP IN THE MUFFLED DARKNESS---

THE BALLOON'S MOVING IN A *NEW* DIRECTION, BRUCE---WE'RE BEING *TAKEN* SOMEWHERE!

YOU'RE RIGHT! WE'RE ENTERING A DEFINITE ATMOSPHERE ---AND IT'S CHARGED WITH EVIL!

MINUTES LATER---A LURID FLASH BREAKS AROUND THE BALLOON--- COUPLED WITH A DIZZY PLUNGE THROUGH SPACE!

AS THE BALLOON AND ITS DEADLY BURDEN SETTLE ON A WEIRD SUBWORLD...

I CAN'T GUESS WHERE WE ARE, BETTY---BUT IT MUST BE ONE OF THE SMALL, NAMELESS PLANETS THAT SOMETIMES ENTER THE SOLAR SYSTEM FROM THE OUTER LIMITS OF SPACE!

BRUCE! GOOD HEAVENS ---WHAT ARE THEY?

HUMANS!

THE DARK POWERS ABOVE HAVE SENT THEM HERE--- *TO* US!

BETTY---*HIDE!* THE ROCKS ARE *CRAWLING* WITH THESE THINGS!

IN A SCUTTLING RUSH---

HAA HA! WHO CAN HIDE---*HERE*?

THAT IS WHAT WE HAVE BEEN WAITING FOR---THE ONE THING THAT CAN HELP US IN THE DOMAIN OF THE DOOMED!

YOU MEAN YOU KNOW WHAT WE'VE CARRIED INTO THE STRATOSPHERE?

WE WERE ONCE HUMAN---WE WERE THE EVIL-DOERS WHO PLAGUED OUR FELLOW MEN---UNTIL DEATH SENT US INTO AN EXILED AFTER-LIFE HERE! WE HAVE BEEN BANNED FROM THE EARTH, BUT NEWCOMERS TO THE DOMAIN OF THE DOOMED BRING US NEWS OF IMPORT-ANT EVENTS THERE--- LIKE THE ATOMIC BOMB!

AN ATOMIC EXPLOSION WILL HAVE ONLY ONE EFFECT ON THE DOMAIN OF THE DOOMED---IT WILL EXERT A CREATIVE FORCE THAT CAN CHANGE US INTO MORTAL BEINGS! WE'LL KEEP OUR HIDEOUS SHAPES, BUT OUR RETURN TO LIFE WILL MEAN WE CAN ESCAPE FROM THE DOMAIN OF THE DOOMED ---AND MAKE OUR WAY BACK TO THE EARTH!

WE'VE HAD NO CHANCE TO WREAK TERROR AND DESTRUCTION HERE---BUT ONCE WE REACH THE WORLD OF THE LIVING, WE'LL BE ABLE TO FULFILL OUR EVIL DESTINIES WITHOUT LIMIT!

GOOD LORD, BRUCE! WHATEVER ELSE HAPPENS ---WE CAN'T LET THESE THINGS CARRY OUT AN IN-VASION OF HORROR!

HA HA HA! SHE THINKS WE CAN BE STOPPED ---BY HUMANS!

AS IF WE DIDN'T KNOW HOW HELPLESS THEY ARE--- AND THAT THE BOMB WILL EXPLODE WITHIN A FEW MINUTES!

UNEXPECTEDLY---

PLENTY CAN HAPPEN WITHIN A FEW MINUTES, CREEPS!

POW!

BRM!

GET TO THE BALLOON, BETTY--- FAST!

5.

THEY'RE RIGHT BEHIND US, BRUCE ··· BUT WE'RE CERTAINLY NOT GOING TO BE SAFE AROUND THE *BOMB!*

I CAN'T PREVENT IT FROM EXPLODING, AND RESTORING THOSE FIENDS TO LIFE ··· BUT I'M GOING TO MAKE SURE *WE* AREN'T CAUGHT IN THE BLAST! HURRY ··· CLIMB UP ON THAT CABLE!

THEN···

GOOD THING THE CONTROLS ARE WORKING! THE BALLOON'S UNCOUPLED FROM THE BOMB ··· *IT'S STARTING TO RISE!*

IN THE NEXT SECOND···

BRUCE! FOR HEAVEN'S SAKE ··· *DON'T LET THEM GET YOU!*

THE BALLOON'S MOUNTING FAST ··· *THIS IS MY LAST CHANCE!*

POW!

WITH A DESPERATE LEAP···

THE CABLE! GRAB IT··· THEY'RE ESCAPING!

A THOUSAND FEET ABOVE THE DOMAIN OF THE DOOMED ···

BRUCE IS JUST MANAGING TO HOLD ON! AND IF HE LOSES HIS GRIP ··· HE'LL BE DISINTEGRATED BY THE BOMB BLAST AFTER HE HITS!

6.

I MAY BE PITTED AGAINST SOMETHING STRONGER THAN BLOOD AND MUSCLE... BUT I'M NOT BEATEN YET!

JUST WAIT! IN A MATTER OF SECONDS... WE'LL HAVE YOU BOTH!

SOK!

I'LL CLIMB THE CABLE AND RELEASE ENOUGH HYDROGEN TO BRING THE BALLOON BACK TO THE DOMAIN OF THE DEAD... AND EVEN IF SHE ESCAPES THE EXPLOSION, WE'LL CAPTURE HER RIGHT AFTER WE'VE GAINED A NEW HOLD ON LIFE!

CRAK!

AAAGH!

A SECOND LATER...

BOOM!

As THE TOWERING ATOMIC CLOUD CLEARS---

SEE THEM? THE EXPLOSION DID JUST WHAT THE FIENDS EXPECTED... THEY'RE NOW MORTAL CREATURES... ABLE TO RETURN TO EARTH!

WAIT, BRUCE... CAN YOU MAKE OUT THAT WEIRD JUMBLE OF ROCKS THROWN UP BY THE BLAST?

IT'S NOT ONLY THAT THEY LOOK STRANGE--- THEY'RE ACTUALLY MOVING!

YE GODS... REMEMBER WHAT THE FIENDS SAID ABOUT THE CREATIVE FORCE OF THE ATOMIC BLAST? THERE'S NO TELLING WHAT WE CAN EXPECT FROM THIS NEW BATCH OF MONSTERS... BUT I'M GOING TO LET OUT ENOUGH HYDROGEN TO BRING US DOWN FOR A CLOSER LOOK!

7.

BLACK AND BRUTISH---AS PRIMITIVE AS THE ROCK FROM WHICH THEY WERE FORMED---

WELCOME! WE HAVE **BOTH** GAINED LIFE IN THE SAME SINGLE SECOND!

THAT MAKES US **ALLIES**---UNITED IN A COMMON CAUSE FOR EVIL!

EVIL! FOR A MOMENT, IT SEEMS AS IF THE WORD HAS NO MEANING TO THESE MUTE AND GROPING MINDS---

AND THEN---UNEXPECTEDLY---

CR-RAK!

WITH A FURIOUS BATTLE RAGING BELOW---

I HATE TO SAY THIS, BRUCE---BUT THE MONSTERS SEEM TO BE GETTING THE UPPER HAND!

YOU'RE RIGHT! THE ATOMIC CREATURES NEED HELP, AND THERE'S ONLY ONE WAY THEY CAN GET IT--- **THE BALLOON!**

O.K., BETTY--- HOLD ON TIGHT--- **AND BRACE YOURSELF FOR A JOLT!**

BUT HEAVENS, BRUCE--- YOU **CAN'T!** THE BALLOON IS SOMETHING **WE** NEED---IF WE'RE EVER GOING TO GET BACK TO EARTH AGAIN!

IT'S A TOUGH THING TO ASK, HONEY---BUT WE'VE GOT TO MAKE A CHOICE! MAYBE WE **WON'T** REACH THE EARTH---BUT NEITHER WILL THOSE FIENDS---AND **THAT'S** THE IMPORTANT THING!

8

As the flames mount in a seething flash---

WOOOSH!

UGH!

PON!

BRUCE---ARE YOU ALL RIGHT?

NEVER MIND *ME!* THE ATOMIC CREATURES WON'T BE HARMED BY WHAT'S GOING TO HAPPEN---BUT NOW THAT THE FIENDS ARE *LIVING* ---THEY'RE WITHIN A SPLIT SECOND OF EXTERMINATION!

Then ---IN A SPOUTING, WHITE-HOT INFERNO---

WOOOSH

BRUCE---IT WAS HORRIBLE! THOSE JETS OF FLAMING GAS WERE LIKE A VOLCANIC ERUPTION!

IT'S THE ONLY THING THAT COULD WORK, HONEY! ASIDE FROM A HAZE OF SMOKE AND A FEW CRINKLED ASHES---*THE FIENDS ARE FINISHED!*

BUT WHAT ABOUT *THEM?* THEY'RE HIDEOUS---*WORSE THAN THE FIENDS!*

MAYBE---BUT DON'T JUDGE THEM BY APPEARANCES! THEY MAY NOT HAVE MINDS OR SOULS, BUT THEY SPRANG FROM THE BASIC MATTER OF THE UNIVERSE---*THE VERY SOURCE OF LIFE!* THAT MEANS THEY'RE *GOOD*---AND IF I CAN GET THEM TO UNDERSTAND ME---*I'M SURE THEY'LL HELP US!*

9.

SLOWLY, WITH REPEATED GESTURES, BRUCE SPEAKS TO THE WEIRD CREATURES ···AND BIT BY BIT···A DIM IDEA FORMS IN THEIR GROPING CONSCIOUSNESS!

THEY'RE GROUPING TOGETHER, BRUCE! THEY SEEM TO HAVE UNDERSTOOD YOU··· BUT **CAN** THEY HELP?

DON'T **YOU** FEEL SOME KIND OF STRANGE FORCE AROUND US? YOU'D BETTER BRACE YOURSELF ···**IT'S GROWING STRONGER EVERY SECOND!**

THEN···WITH A BLINDING GLARE BREAKING ABOVE THE ATOMIC CREATURES···

OHH!

CRRKAK!

BRUCE ···WHAT'S HAPPENING?

WE'RE BEING PROJECTED ALONG A MOLECULAR BEAM GIVEN OFF BY THE ATOMIC CREATURES···**AND IT'S STRONG ENOUGH TO CARRY US THROUGH SPACE** TO THE EARTH'S ATMOSPHERE!

EARTHWARD···AT A SPEED THAT BRIDGES THE BLACK GULF OF THE UNIVERSE!

DO YOU THINK WE'LL **EVER** BE ABLE TO EXPLAIN WHAT WE'VE BEEN THROUGH, BRUCE?

I'M NOT EVEN GOING TO **TRY**, HONEY! WE CAN ALWAYS PRETEND THERE WERE A COUPLE OF PARACHUTES IN THE INSTRUMENT COMPARTMENT··· BECAUSE **THAT** WILL BE A LOT EASIER TO BE- LIEVE THAN THE **DOMAIN OF THE DOOMED!**

SECONDS LATER, AN INVISIBLE FORCE CHECKS THE HURTLING FLIGHT···AND SUDDENLY···

YOU CAN OPEN YOUR EYES, BETTY··· **WE'RE BACK!**

The END!

10.

GIANTS ON THE EARTH

NOT ALL THE **FORBIDDEN WORLDS** ARE ON OTHER PLANETS OR IN THE REALMS OF THE SUPERNATURAL---FOR SOME ARE RIGHT HERE ON THE EARTH! ONE SUCH PLACE IS A MYSTERIOUS WORLD ALL TO ITSELF--- THE FORBIDDEN LAND OF **TIBET**--WHERE **GIGANTIC SNOWMEN** STALK THE UNWARY TRAVELER!

FOR MANY YEARS, ARCHAEOLOGISTS AND EXPLORERS WHO HAVE PENETRATED INTO THE INTERIOR OF TIBET HAVE BEEN BRINGING BACK STRANGE TALES OF THE "**ABOMINABLE SNOWMEN**" ---GIGANTIC, SILVERY-FURRED APEMEN WHO FEED UPON YAKS AND HUMANS ALIKE!

MIRKA! BAD MANSHI!

HMM--**MIRKA** MEANS THAT GIANT BIPED THE NATIVES ARE SO TERRIFIED ABOUT! IT SEEMS AS IF ALMOST EVERY TIBETAN MONASTERY IN THE HIMA-LAYAS HAS A LURID DRAWING OR CARVING OF ONE OF THOSE BEASTS!

BUT THERE HAVE BEEN MORE THAN MERE LEGENDS ABOUT THE GIGANTIC SNOWMEN-- FOR NATIVES HAVE LED EXPLORERS TO MONSTROUS HUMAN TRACKS ON MANY OC-CASIONS! THE FIRST AUTHENTIC REPORT OF SUCH FOOTPRINTS CAME FROM THE JALPAIGURI DISTRICT IN 1928...

MI-GO--- MIRKA!

GREAT SCOTT--THE LEG-ENDS ABOUT THE GIGANT-IC SNOWMEN ARE *TRUE!*

THROUGH THE YEARS, OTHER TRACKS WERE FOUND AS FAR SOUTH AS BELAKOBA IN THE PROVINCE OF BENGAL---AND SOME WERE MEASURED BY A BRIT-ISH REPORTER FROM REUTER'S NEWS AGENCY ON JUNE 20, 1938, NEAR JALPAIGURI...

BY GEORGE--THESE PRINTS ARE 24 INCHES LONG AND 11 INCHES WIDE! THE MONSTER THAT LEFT THEM MUST HAVE BEEN AT LEAST 18 FEET TALL!

PERHAPS THE MOST ENORMOUS FOOTPRINTS OF ALL WERE THOSE FOUND BY WING COMMANDER E.B. BEAUMAN AND ERIC SHIPTON, THE EVEREST CLIMBER, IN THE GARHWAL AND KUMAON DISTRICTS! NO TAPE MEASURES WERE AVAILABLE AT THAT TIME--- BUT SOME OF THE PRINTS WERE FOUR TIMES LARGER THAN THOSE OF THE EXPLORERS!

IF THEIR FEET ARE FOUR TIMES LARGER THAN OURS, THEN THOSE MONSTERS MUST BE FOUR TIMES TALLER THAN US--- OR OVER 24 FEET TALL!

1.

MONG OTHERS WHO SAW THE GIGANTIC TRACKS WERE FRANK S. SMYTHE, THE ENGLISH EXPLORER AND MOUNTAINEER, AND H.W. TILMAN, LEADER OF THE 1938 MT. EVEREST EXPEDITION! BUT DURING THE LAST WAR, A GROUP OF U.S. FLIERS FORCED DOWN ON THE FAMOUS "HUMP" ROUTE OVER THE HIMALAYAS ACTUALLY *SAW* THE INCREDIBLE MONSTERS THEMSELVES!

HOLY COW--- THOSE...THOSE *THINGS* ARE OVER 20 FEET TALL!

THEY SEEM TO BE CURIOUS ABOUT OUR PLANE---LET'S GET OUT OF HERE BEFORE THEY TURN THEIR ATTENTION TO *US!*

CCORDING TO THE TIBETAN LEGENDS, THE GIANT SNOWMEN SOMETIMES WANDER AWAY FROM THEIR MOUNTAIN FASTNESSES AND DESCEND INTO THE SURROUNDING AREAS--AND SURE ENOUGH, THE REVEREND HAROLD YOUNG, A MISSIONARY, REPORTED THAT HE HAD ENCOUNTERED GIGANTIC, SILVER-HAIRED APE-MEN IN THE YUNNAN JUNGLES OF CHINA IN 1934!

BUT OTHERS WHO CAME INTO CONTACT WITH THE GIANTS DIDN'T GET OFF SO EASILY! THE SURVIVOR OF A POLISH EXPEDITION THAT HAD SET OUT TO INVESTIGATE THE GIGANTIC TRACKS SAID HIS PARTY HAD REACHED A HEIGHT OF 20,500 FEET ON THE SLOPE OF NANDA DEVI WHEN HE SAW SOME OF THE GIANTS HURL AN AVALANCHE DOWN ON THOSE WHO HAD LAGGED BEHIND!

OTHER PILGRIMS FROM THE HIMALAYAS HAVE TOLD OF DIRECT ATTACKS BY THE GIANT SNOWMEN UPON THEIR CARAVANS!

CCORDING TO JEAN MARQUES-RIVIERA, THE FRENCH EXPLORER, THE GIGANTIC CREATURES HAVE BEEN SEEN BEATING DRUMS AND ENGAGING IN SOME WILD, UNHOLY RITE!

HOW CAN WE EXPLAIN THE EXISTENCE OF SUCH MONSTROUS CREATURES? WELL, ACCORDING TO PALEONTOLOGISTS WHO HAVE UNEARTHED THE BONES OF *GIGANTOPITHECUS*, THE CHINA GIANT THAT LIVED IN EASTERN ASIA ABOUT HALF A MILLION YEARS AGO, SUCH CREATURES MAY HAVE SURVIVED TO THE PRESENT DAY IN THE INACCESSIBLE FASTNESSES OF TIBET, THE FORBIDDEN LAND!

PALEONTOLOGICAL EVIDENCE INDICATES THAT GIANTS ROAMED THE EARTH UNTOLD AEONS AGO, AND THAT MAN BECAME SMALLER AS HE EVOLVED! THAT WOULD ACCOUNT FOR THE WORLD-WIDE LEGENDS OF ANCIENT GIANTS-- AND FOR THE POSSIBILITY THAT THEIR ELUSIVE DESCENDANTS *EXIST TODAY!*

THE END...

SKULL of the SORCERER

AL WILLIAMSON

ALL HALLOWS' EVE-- HALLOWE'EN-- THE NIGHT WHEN WITCHES RIDE-- WHEN STRANGE SPECTERS RISE FROM THE CLAMMY VAULTS OF THE *UNKNOWN!* BUT OF ALL EERIE HALLOWE'EN TALES, THERE'S NONE MORE SPINE-TINGLING THAN THE STORY OF THE *SORCERER'S SKULL!*

SHUCKS, THIS AIN'T MUCH OF A HALLOWE'EN BONFIRE-- THERE'S NOTHIN' *SPOOKY* ABOUT IT!

WAIT-- I KNOW JUST THE THING TO MAKE IT *REALLY* SPOOKY-- THE *SKULL* IN MY DAD'S STUDY! COME ON!

GOSH, DAVEY-- WILL YOUR FATHER LET US BORROW IT?

HE WON'T EVEN KNOW I TOOK IT! HE AND MY MOM WENT TO A COSTUME BALL TONIGHT! SHH-- LET'S GO IN THE SIDE WAY, SO THE BUTLER WON'T SEE US!

DAD ALWAYS GAVE STRICT ORDERS THAT THE SKULL WAS NEVER TO BE TOUCHED-- BUT WE'RE NOT GONNA HURT THE OLD THING! WE'LL JUST PUT IT ON TOP OF A POLE IN THE MIDDLE OF THE BONFIRE-- AND THEN DANCE AROUND IT, PRETENDIN' WE'RE *WITCH-DOCTORS!* WE'LL BRING IT BACK BEFORE DAD EVEN COMES BACK FROM HIS PARTY!

1

AW--THE FIRE DIED DOWN WHILE WE WERE GETTIN' THE SKULL!

GOOD--IT'LL GIVE US A CHANCE TO SET THE POLE IN THE GROUND, WITH THE SKULL ON TOP OF IT! THEN WE'LL JUST BUILD THE FIRE UP AGAIN AROUND THE POLE!

THE INNOCENT MERRIMENT PROCEEDED! LITTLE DID THEY KNOW OF THE GHOSTLY WITNESS THAT WATCHED--

WOO-WOOOO! WE'RE WITCHDOCTORS AND SUMMONING SPECTERS!

SUDDENLY...

LOOK-- THE POLE'S CAUGHT FIRE!

IT'S FALLING DOWN! GOOD GOSH--THERE GOES THE SKULL!

DO YOU THINK IT'S THE SKULL MAKIN' THAT GHOSTLY LIGHT IN THE FLAMES? M--MAYBE WE'D BETTER BEAT IT!

GEE-- THERE MUSTA BEEN SOMETHIN' SPOOKY ABOUT IT! I'M GONNA HIDE IN THOSE BUSHES AND SEE WHAT HAPPENS NEXT-- MAYBE MY DAD WILL WANT TO KNOW!

AND BEFORE DAVEY KNOX'S HORRIFIED GAZE--

A-- A HEADLESS SPECTER DISAPPEARED IN THE FIRE-- AND NOW SOMETHIN' ELSE IS TAKIN' ITS PLACE!

A FEW MILES AWAY, AT A FASHIONABLE HALLOWE'EN MASQUERADE BALL --

ISN'T IT ABOUT TIME YOU DANCED WITH *ME?* AFTER ALL, WE OUGHT TO KEEP ON *PRETENDING* WE'RE A HAPPY COUPLE -- JUST FOR APPEARANCE'S SAKE!

I SEE-- YOU DON'T WANT PEOPLE TO KNOW I MARRIED YOU FOR YOUR *MONEY* -- IS THAT IT, ROBERT?

EXACTLY! BUT I'VE FIXED YOU -- I'VE CHANGED MY WILL TO LEAVE ALL MY MONEY TO DAVEY!

THAT DOESN'T BOTHER ME ONE BIT-- YOU'RE HEALTHY ENOUGH TO LIVE ANOTHER FIFTY YEARS! BUT NOW EXCUSE ME -- THERE'S SOMEONE NEW OVER THERE I *HAVEN'T* DANCED WITH YET!

MY, WHAT AN UNUSUAL COSTUME! AND THAT HOOD MAKES A WONDERFULLY EFFECTIVE MASK! I'D LIKE TO BE THE FIRST TO DANCE WITH THE MYSTERY MAN WHO'S SURE TO WIN THE PRIZE FOR THE BEST COSTUME-- LET'S HAVE YOUR HAND!

THAT-- THAT COSTUME-- THE SACRED ROBES OF THE DALAI RAMA!

OHNNHHH!

WHAT DID HE DO TO MAKE HER FAINT-- AND WHO IN BLAZES IS HE?

THERE-- THERE'S ONLY ONE WAY TO FIND OUT! IT'S NOT MIDNIGHT YET, BUT LET'S ALL *UNMASK* NOW!

ALL RIGHT, WHOEVER YOU ARE... OR *WHATEVER* YOU ARE! IF YOU BELONG TO THIS PARTY, YOU'LL DROP YOUR HOOD-- *NOW!*

OH, NO!

THOSE ELONGATED EYEHOLES-- IT'S THE SKULL OF AN ORIENTAL! BUT IT... IT MUST BE JUST A HALLUCINATION-- IT CAN'T BE THE SPIRIT OF THE DALAI RAMA! I'VE GOT TO GET BACK TO MY STUDY-- MAKE SURE THE SKULL IS STILL THERE-- INTACT!

THE SKULL-- IT'S GONE!

IT'S ALL MY FAULT, DAD-- I KNOW WHAT HAPPENED TO THE SKULL!

--AND AFTER THE SKULL FELL INTO THE BONFIRE, I SAW A--

ALL RIGHT, DAVEY-- I CAN IMAGINE WHAT HAPPENED NEXT! GO ON TO BED NOW AND TRY TO FORGET IT ALL! NO MATTER WHAT HAPPENS TO ME, AT LEAST I KNOW THAT YOU'RE WELL TAKEN CARE OF!

I SHOULD HAVE KNOWN THIS WOULD HAPPEN SOME DAY! I SHOULD HAVE KEPT THAT ACCURSED SKULL IN A FIREPROOF SAFETY VAULT-- BUT NO, I WANTED TO HAVE IT HERE, WHERE I COULD LOOK AT IT EACH DAY AND REASSURE MYSELF THAT I STILL HAD IT!

TAP! TAP!

IT--IT'S YOU-- YOU'VE COME FOR ME! I'LL HAVE TO KILL YOU AGAIN-- THE WAY I FINISHED YOU TEN YEARS AGO!

④

SHOTS-- FROM THE KNOX MANSION! LET'S GO!

YEAH, BUT FAST! KNOX IS THE ONE WHO PUT UP THE MONEY TO ELECT THE D.A.-- AND IF ANYTHING HAPPENS TO HIM-- THE D.A. WILL BUST US RIGHT OFF THE FORCE!

BANG!

BANG!

THE-- THE BULLETS WENT RIGHT THROUGH IT-- AS IF NOTHING WAS THERE-- AND YOU'VE GOT TO SAVE ME FROM IT! LOCK ME UP, ARREST ME-- I'M A MURDERER, A THIEF!

HE'S GONE OFF HIS NUT-- WE'D BETTER TAKE HIM TO THE D.A.!

BOB-- WHAT IN THE WORLD ARE YOU DOING HERE?

I--I'M GLAD YOUR MEN BROUGHT ME HERE, FRANK-- I WANT TO CONFESS TO A MURDER I COMMIT- TED! TELL YOUR MEN TO WAIT OUTSIDE WHILE I TELL YOU ABOUT IT! AND HAVE THEM KEEP EVERYONE, AND EVERYTHING, AWAY!

WHAT'S ALL THIS RIDICULOUS TALK ABOUT A MURDER! IS IT A HALLOWE'EN GAG OF SOME KIND?

NO, FRANK, IT'S ALL TRUE !-- I ONCE TOLD YOU THAT I WAS AN ANTHROPOLOGIST BEFORE I CAME INTO WEALTH-- BUT NO ONE ALIVE KNOWS THAT I GOT THAT WEALTH AS A RE- SULT OF MY PROFESSION! IT ALL BEGAN TEN YEARS AGO, WHEN I WAS DOING FIELD RESEARCH IN AN ISOLATED REGION OF THE HIMALAYAS, BETWEEN INDIA AND TIBET!

"...I WAS THE FIRST WHITE MAN EVER TO PENE- TRATE INTO THE FORBIDDEN WORLD OF KARAK, WHOSE RULER WAS THE DALAI RAMA-- THE HIGH PRIEST! I PROBABLY WOULD HAVE BEEN EXECU- TED IF NOT FOR THE FACT THAT THE DALAI RAMA'S SON WAS SUFFERING FROM TYPHOID-- AND WHEN MY VACCINES SAVED HIS LIFE, THE DALAI SPARED MINE..."

AS A REWARD, I SHALL LET YOU LOOK UPON THE SACRED RUBY OF KALI!

THE OUTSIDE WORLD HAS HEARD MANY LEGENDS ABOUT THE RUBY, O MIGHTY DALAI-- I AM INDEED HONORED TO BE THE FIRST WHITE MAN TO GAZE UPON IT!

"AND THERE, IN THE DIMNESS OF THE SACRED TEMPLE--"

GREAT SCOTT-- THAT GEM IN THE IDOL'S FOREHEAD! ALL THE LEGENDS ABOUT IT ARE TRUE-- IT'S THE LARGEST RUBY IN THE WORLD! I-- I'VE GOT TO HAVE IT!

SORRY, DALAI-- THAT RUBY IS GOING TO BE MINE!

BANG!

"MY SENSES REELED AT THE VISION OF ALL THE WEALTH THAT RUBY WOULD BRING ME-- AND BEFORE I KNEW WHAT I WAS DOING..."

I...I TRUSTED YOU-- AND YOU DEFILED THE SACRED TEMPLE OF KALI! I DIE-- BUT MY SPIRIT WILL NEVER REST-- UNTIL THE SACRILEGE IS REDEEMED BY *YOUR* DEATH! WHEN MY SKULL IS CONSUMED TO ASHES IN MY FUNERAL PYRE--*THEN* SHALL MY SPIRIT RISE UP IN WRATH -- TO SEEK *REVENGE!*

I...I REMEMBER NOW-- THE TIBETAN FOLK LEGENDS ALWAYS SPOKE OF THE DALAI RAMA OF KARAK AS A MIGHTY *SORCERER*-- WHOSE SPIRIT COULD ARISE FROM THE ASHES OF HIS SKULL! AND IF THE LEGEND ABOUT THE RUBY WAS TRUE, THEN *THIS* LEGEND MIGHT ALSO BE TRUE!

WITH MY DYING BREATH-- I CURSE YOU! MAY YOUR SON BETRAY YOU -- MAY-- OHH!

HE'S GONE -- BUT I CAN'T AFFORD TO TAKE ANY CHANCES ABOUT HIS SPIRIT! I'VE SEEN TOO MUCH OF THE ORIENT TO DOUBT THAT THERE *ARE* MYSTERIOUS, SUPERNATURAL FORCES THAT WE WESTERN-ERS KNOW NOTHING ABOUT! AND THE ONLY WAY TO MAKE SURE THAT THE DALAI'S SPIRIT DOES NOT RISE FROM THE ASHES OF HIS SKULL---

"I FLED-- CARRYING IN ONE HAND THE RUBY OF KALI, AND IN THE OTHER, THE HEAD OF THE DALAI RAMA OF KARAK-- "

--IS TO KEEP THAT SKULL ALWAYS IN MY POSSESSION!

I'VE GOT TO STOP THINKING ABOUT THE DALAI -- AND THINK ONLY OF THE FORTUNE THE RUBY WILL BRING ME! A MAHARAJAH WOULD PAY A COOL MILLION FOR IT-- BUT I'LL PROBABLY HAVE TO SETTLE FOR HALF THAT AMOUNT WHEN I SELL IT ON THE BLACK MARKET AT CALCUTTA!

...AND THAT'S HOW I CAME INTO MY WEALTH! BUT NOW THAT THE SKULL HAS BEEN BURNT TO ASHES, YOU'VE GOT TO SAVE ME FROM THE DALAI'S VENGEFUL SPIRIT! ARREST ME-- KEEP ME UNDER CONSTANT WATCH-- SO HE DOESN'T *GET* ME!

THERE IT IS -- FIVE HUNDRED THOUSAND DOLLARS IN AMERICAN MONEY! BUT TELL ME, MY FRIEND-- DO YOU HAVE SOMETHING *ELSE* IN THE *OTHER* BASKET THAT YOU WANT TO SELL?

NO... *NO!* WHAT-EVER I HAVE IN THERE ISN'T FOR SALE-- AT *ANY* PRICE!

DON'T WORRY ABOUT A THING, BOB! ER-- DON'T YOU THINK A LONG REST IN SOME -- AH -- *INSTITUTION* MIGHT HELP YOU?

NO... NO! I'M NOT CRAZY! THE DALAI'S SPIRIT WILL GET ME, UNLESS YOU PROTECT ME! IF YOU DON'T BELIEVE ME, I'LL--

MIKE... WALLY! CALL THE HOSPITAL-- AND TELL THEM TO BRING A STRAITJACKET!

YOU'VE GOT TO BELIEVE ME! LISTEN TO ME--

WOW! THIS ONE'S A REAL CASE!

THAT SEDATIVE WE GAVE HIM WILL MAKE HIM QUIET DOWN PRETTY SOON! AND MEANWHILE, HIS SHOUTS WON'T DISTURB THE OTHER PATIENTS-- BECAUSE THIS ROOM IS COMPLETELY SOUNDPROOF!

NO! DON'T LEAVE ME ALONE!

GETTING SLEEPY... SO SLEEPY-- CAN'T KEEP... MY EYES... OPEN--

NO... HELP-- HEL-- AARGHHHH!

I AM REVENGED-- NOW I CAN REST!

LATER-- IT... IT CAN'T BE A CASE OF SELF-STRANGULATION-- HE'S STILL IN HIS STRAITJACKET!

I GUESS THERE WAS SOMETHING TO THAT WILD STORY HE TOLD ME! WE'LL JUST HAVE TO SAY THAT ROBERT KNOX WAS KILLED BY FORCES UNKNOWN-- FROM OUT OF THE UNKNOWN!

The END

7

Pursuit into the Past

THE TWO MEN sat in a booth at the far end of the dimly-lighted tavern, drinking and talking. Or, rather one of them...the drunken one...was doing all the talking. They had met only a few minutes ago at the bar, and the inebriated one... obviously under a tremendous strain, obviously in need of someone to pour his troubles out to...had invited the second man over to the booth for a drink.

"I...I can't stand this waiting any longer," the first man said desperately. "Never knowing when they'll catch up with me, when they'll drag me back to the world I came from, *to the world of 2967 A. D.!*"

The man paused to drink from the glass in front of him, as if to give himself courage for what he felt he had to say. "I...I know you won't believe me," he continued after draining his glass and signaling the bartender for another. "But it's just as well that you think I'm raving in a drunken delirium, or that I'm a madman. I don't care *what* you think, as long as you listen to me...if...if I don't talk about this to someone, I...I *will* go crazy!"

The second man nodded sympathetically, as if he understood...and the first man continued: "You see, I originally came from the 30th century. You couldn't possibly have any idea what that world is like. The robots control all aspects of life...from the moment of birth, the human infant is assigned to his place in life, according to what the robot analyzers think he's best suited for. And from that moment on, the human's life becomes ordered and regimented down to the very last detail.

"There's no chance for the slightest expression of individualism, of freedom of will or choice. It all amounts to what you Americans would call a slave-state...where all humans are slaves to the all-powerful, eternal, heartless robots!

"In that world, I was an historian of the past. Mine was the job of using the time-machine to return to the dead ages of the past, investigate those ages, and then return to the 30th century to write up the history. It was expected that I return...it was unthinkable that I should not. And the thought never crossed my mind to remain in the Stone Ages, or in the era of the Roman Empire, for example...until I came to the United States in the year 1951.

"At first I was astonished at the democracy that you Americans take for granted. I was amazed at the freedom all of you had, at your ability to choose your own lives, to do pretty much what you pleased, as long as you hurt no one else. And as I lived among you day after day, studying your habits and customs, I slowly realized that *this* was the kind of life I wanted and longed for...that I could never go back to that despotic slave-state of the robots after once having tasted the freedom and democracy here.

"So I deserted my century and my masters. I destroyed the instrument that was necessary for my return to 2967 A. D. ... and became one of you! But I know it is impossible to keep a secret from my robot masters. I am long overdue, and I am sure that they have long since sent a detective to follow me into the past and force me to return...to my death! And since my pursuer must be a man who has been trained in the arts of detection since the moment of his birth, I know I cannot escape...no matter how well I cover my tracks and try to lose myself among you. Any day now my pursuer will find me, place a strong hand on my shoulder and say..."

The second man reached over, placed a hand on the first man's shoulder, and said, "I *have* found you, Rog Halith! But I, too, love this democracy I find myself in! We will *both* remain here...and persuade all those who come after *us* to do the same!"

The WITCH'S APPRENTICE

"This is my story··· a strange, unearthly story! I am writing it in a prison cell, where I face a charge of murder··· **SELF-CONFESSED MURDER!** Before it is too late, I want to tell everything··· how I met old Kate, the witch··· how I lived in her eerie cottage··· how she taught me the dread secrets of her **BLACK MAGIC!** and how, on that terrible night, I stalked a man through the rain-soaked woods until my hands fastened around his throat and I obeyed old Kate's final command as ——
The WITCH'S APPRENTICE!"

"It all began, I suppose, the day I ran away from the orphanage at the age of thirteen! I didn't care in what direction the freight train was going··· just as long as it took me away from the place where I had been so desperately unhappy!"

"It was October··· and cold! As evening approached, I was chilled to the bone! When the freight slowed to round a bend, I half-jumped, half-fell off!"

"It was hungry and scared as I picked myself up and struck out through the woods towards a town I'd seen in the distance! And then, abruptly, I came on a low cottage hidden deep in the trees! A light shone from a window···"

Maybe they'll give me something to eat! But I'll have to be careful··· if they get wise I've run away, the cops will send me back to the orphanage!

"I CREPT CLOSER, PEERED THROUGH THE WINDOW! THERE WAS A MAN···A STRANGE OLD WOMAN GAZING INTO A GLASS BALL! AND THE ROOM···IT WAS **SPOOKY-LOOKING!**"

GOOD··· GOOD GOLLY!

"SUDDENLY THE MAN JUMPED TO HIS FEET, GRASPED THE OLD WOMAN BY THE THROAT···STARTED TO CHOKE HER!"

HE'S·· HE'S GONNA KILL HER! I'VE GOT TO **DO** SOME- THING!

"I PICKED UP A ROCK AND THREW IT AT THE WINDOW, BREAKING THE GLASS! IT WAS THE ONLY THING I COULD THINK OF!"

CRASH!

"WHEN THE MAN HAD FLED···"

MAYBE···MAYBE SHE'S **DEAD!**

"BUT THE OLD WOMAN **STILL** LIVED! WHEN I REVIVED HER···"

YOU SAVED MY **LIFE**, LAD! HE WAS GOING TO **KILL** ME!

THAT'S···THAT'S WHY I BROKE THE WINDOW··· TO **SCARE** HIM!

"THE OLD WOMAN SEEMED TO RECOVER QUICKLY! WITHOUT A WORD, SHE BROUGHT ME FOOD! I WONDERED HOW SHE KNEW I WAS HUNGRY! I WAS TO WONDER ABOUT A **LOT** OF THINGS BEFORE I WAS THROUGH WITH **OLD KATE!**"

EAT, LAD! YOU MUST BE STARVED AFTER YOUR LONG TRIP ON THAT FREIGHT TRAIN!

HOW···HOW DID YOU KNOW ABOUT **THAT?**

AH, I HAVE MY WAYS! DON'T BE AFRAID···I WON'T TELL ANYONE THAT YOU RAN AWAY FROM THE ORPHANAGE!

THE **RADIO!** THEY BROADCAST OVER THE RADIO THAT I'D ESCAPED! **THAT'S** HOW YOU KNEW!

"THERE WAS SOMETHING FRIGHTENING ABOUT THE OLD WOMAN'S FACE AS SHE STARED AT ME! IT WAS AS IF SHE WERE READING MY VERY THOUGHTS! HER EYES WERE GREENISH-- AND GLOWED LIKE A CAT'S!"

I HAVE NO RADIO, LAD--- I NEED NONE! I HAVE THE POWER TO SEE INTO THE PAST AND INTO THE FUTURE! PEOPLE BELIEVE I AM JUST A FORTUNE TELLER---A CHARLATAN! THE FOOLS COME HERE FOR AMUSEMENT---LIKE THAT MAN! BUT I SAW IN THE CRYSTAL THAT HE HAD MURDERED SOMEONE AND HAD NEVER BEEN CAUGHT! THAT IS WHY HE ATTACKED ME---TO SILENCE ME! YOU SEE, I'M A *WITCH!*

ULP!

"I WAS PETRIFIED WITH FRIGHT! I WANTED TO GET AWAY FROM THIS PLACE---FROM HER! BUT I COULDN'T MOVE! I SEEMED TO BE HELD BY INVISIBLE BONDS!"

ALL THE ANCIENT SECRETS OF WITCHCRAFT ARE MINE---AND THEY SHALL BE *YOURS!* YOU HAVE BEEN SENT TO ME---YOU HAVE SAVED MY LIFE! FOR THAT I WILL TEACH YOU EVERYTHING I KNOW! I WILL MAKE YOU INTO A *WIZARD!*

NO! NO!

YOU WILL DO AS I SAY--- *NOW* IT IS TIME TO SLEEP! RESTFUL SLEEP! SLEEP--- *SLEEP---*

"I STAYED AT OLD KATE'S THAT NIGHT AND THE NEXT---AND THE NEXT! IT WAS AS IF I WERE MESMERIZED! I DIDN'T WANT TO STAY THERE ---YET, I'LL HAVE TO ADMIT OLD KATE WAS GOOD TO ME! SHE WAS THE ONLY PERSON I EVER REMEMBER WHO SEEMED TO CARE FOR ME! BUT I WAS *AFRAID* OF HER!"

THIS AFTERNOON ONE OF THE TOWN OFFICIALS ASKED ME ABOUT YOU, TIM! I TOLD HIM YOU WERE MY NEPHEW AND WERE STAYING WITH ME! BUT YOU WILL HAVE TO GO TO SCHOOL, LAD! THERE'S A LAW---

YES, I--- KNOW...

"OLD KATE WAS RIDICULED BY THE PEOPLE---BUT SHE WAS FEARED! AND MY SCHOOL MATES WEREN'T SLOW IN TAUNTING ME---PARTICULARLY NED RAWSON---"

TIM! TIM! THE WITCH'S BOY!

GET ON YOUR BROOMSTICK! WE DON'T WANT *YOUR* KIND AROUND HERE!

"I MADE THE MISTAKE OF TURNING ON MY TORMENTORS! THIS WAS JUST WHAT NED WANTED!"

STAY OUT OF MY WAY, OR YOU'LL GET WORSE THAN THAT!

GIVE IT TO HIM, NED!

"OLD KATE SAW MY TORN CLOTHES AND BLACK EYE, BUT DIDN'T ASK ME WHAT HAPPENED! SHE *KNEW!*"

SO YOU'VE HAD TROUBLE WITH THAT *NED RAWSON!*

I---I TRIED TO FIGHT HIM! BUT HE'S TOO BIG AND STRONG!

3.

YOU CAN BEAT HIM...*IF YOU DO AS I SAY!* GET SOMETHING BELONGING TO HIM... LIKE STRANDS OF HIS HAIR...

"*I* FOLLOWED OLD KATE'S INSTRUCTIONS...I ALWAYS DID WHAT SHE SAID! WHEN I SAW NED IN THE BARBER-SHOP NEXT DAY, I SLIPPED IN, GRABBED A HANDFUL OF HIS HAIR..."

GET THE *WITCH* TO CUT YOUR HAIR... THIS IS NO PLACE FOR *YOU!*...HEY! WHAT'RE YOU AFTER?

ER...DROPPED MY GLOVE, THAT'S ALL!

"*OLD* KATE HAD A HUGE CALDRON BUBBLING OVER THE FIRE! SHE DROPPED THE HAIR INTO A DARK, SEETHING LIQUID, THEN ADDED THE CONTENTS OF A NUMBER OF BOTTLES! AND ALL THE TIME ...SHE *CHANTED!*"

BOIL...BOIL...SIMMER AND BUBBLE ...MAGIC CHARM AGAINST ALL TROUBLE ...BOIL...BOIL...SIMMER AND BUBBLE...

DRINK IT! AND WHEN YOU MEET THAT BULLY, LOOK HIM IN THE EYE! YOU'LL HAVE NO MORE TROUBLE FROM HIM... *OR ANYONE!*

"*NEXT* MORNING WHEN I WENT TO THE GROCERY STORE FOR OLD KATE, I KNEW THAT THE TEST HAD COME! FOR THERE AHEAD, WAITING FOR ME, WAS NED AND HIS GANG!"

GET OFF THE SIDEWALK, WITCH'S BOY! THE ROAD IS THE PLACE FOR *YOU!*

I'VE HAD ENOUGH FROM *YOU,* NED RAWSON!

"*I* WAS BARELY CONSCIOUS OF MY OWN FIST COMING UP...UNTIL IT CONNECTED WITH NED'S JAW!"

HERE'S SOMETHING TO *REMEMBER* ME BY!

WOW! WHAT A WALLOP!

YOU--- YOU WIN! ONLY DON'T LOOK AT ME LIKE THAT ...PLEASE!

"OLD KATE WAS RIGHT! I NEVER HAD ANY MORE TROUBLE FROM NED! IT WAS ALMOST AS IF I HAD SOME POWER OVER HIM AND THE OTHERS, TOO! FROM THAT MOMENT ON, MY LIFE WAS CHANGED! I HAD FELT AN OUTCAST AT SCHOOL, BUT NOW, SUDDENLY, I WAS INCLUDED!"

"I BECAME POPULAR---WENT TO THE SCHOOL DANCES AND WAS ASKED TO PARTIES AT THE HOMES OF THE BEST PEOPLE IN TOWN! NOBODY CALLED ME 'WITCH'S BOY' ANY MORE!"

OH, TIM, YOU'RE A WONDERFUL DANCER!

"ALL THE TIME, OLD KATE WAS TEACHING ME MANY THINGS--- DARK AND MYSTERIOUS THINGS--- HOW TO BUILD CHARMS! HOW TO USE SECOND-SIGHT AND MENTAL TELEPATHY! SHE EVEN HELPED ME WITH MY SCHOOL WORK..."

LOOK THROUGH THAT PIECE OF GROUND GLASS, LAD, AND THE KNOWLEDGE IN THOSE PAGES WILL BE YOURS FOREVER!

"I BECAME BRILLIANT IN SCHOOL! NOTHING WAS TOO DIFFICULT! MY TEACHERS WERE STARTLED---FOR FREQUENTLY I KNEW MORE THAN THEY DID!"

IT'S UNCANNY! HE SEEMS TO ANTICIPATE EACH QUESTION I ASK AND HAS THE ANSWER INSTANTLY!

BRIGHTEST PUPIL WE'VE EVER HAD! ALMOST TOO BRIGHT!

"IT WASN'T JUST IN THE SCHOOL ROOM THAT I SHONE! I BECAME THE STAR HITTER OF THE BALL TEAM! I FOUND IT EASY TO OUTGUESS THE PITCHERS! MY BATTING AVERAGE WAS IMPRESSIVE---"

THAT KID TIM IS BIG LEAGUE STUFF!

ANOTHER HOMER!

"THE PRETTIEST AND MOST POPULAR GIRL IN TOWN WAS THELMA STARR, BANKER'S DAUGHTER! PRACTICALLY EVERY BOY TRIED TO DATE HER! BUT WHEN I DECIDED THAT SHE WOULD BE MY GIRL--- SHE WAS!"

I'M TAKING YOU TO THE PROM, THELMA!

I'D PROMISED SAM--- BUT I'LL GO WITH YOU, TIM!

5.

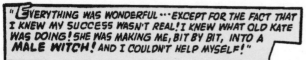

"EVERYTHING WAS WONDERFUL...EXCEPT FOR THE FACT THAT I KNEW MY SUCCESS WASN'T REAL! I KNEW WHAT OLD KATE WAS DOING! SHE WAS MAKING ME, BIT BY BIT, INTO A MALE WITCH! AND I COULDN'T HELP MYSELF!"

YOU MUST LISTEN AND LEARN! FOR SOONER OR LATER, MY LIFE MUST END---AND WHEN IT DOES, YOU WILL HAVE THE SECRETS TO GO ON WITH!

"THE YEARS PASSED! I GRADUATED FROM HIGH SCHOOL WITH THE HIGHEST HONORS, WENT TO A SMALL COLLEGE IN A NEIGHBORING CITY! THEN ONE DAY, WHEN I RETURNED HOME..."

KATE! WHAT'S HAPPENED?

I'M---DYING, LAD! HE CAME BACK--- THE ONE WHO WAS HERE BEFORE! I KNEW HE WOULD---BUT MY POWERS HAVE BEEN DIMMING! I SHOULD HAVE KNOWN THE MOMENT HE WAS COMING---BUT I---I FAILED! HE SHOT ME---FIND HIM, TIM! REVENGE ME!

WHO IS HE? WHERE WILL I FIND HIM?

LOOK IN THE---CRYSTAL BALL! IT WILL TELL YOU ---AHHHHHHHH!

"SHE LAPSED INTO UNCONSCIOUSNESS, AND BY THE TIME I GOT A DOCTOR, OLD KATE WAS DEAD! I BURIED HER BENEATH THE OAK TREES---"

YOU WERE---GOOD TO ME, KATE! I'LL FIND THE MAN WHO KILLED YOU---AND THEN---

"FROM A SECRET COMPARTMENT I TOOK THE CRYSTAL BALL AND THE ANCIENT BOOK---THE BOOK WHICH OLD KATE HAD NEVER ALLOWED ME TO READ MYSELF! IT CONTAINED ALL THE MYSTIC RITES OF SORCERY--- STRANGE AND WEIRD RITES---"

"THEN, WITHIN THE CRYSTAL BALL---"

THERE HE IS--- OLD KATE'S MURDERER!

"I HAD NO IDEA WHAT THE MAN'S NAME WAS OR WHERE HE LIVED! BUT THE NEXT MORNING I FELT AN IMPELLING URGE TO GO TO A DISTANT CITY---"

TIM, DARLING, WHAT'S WRONG? YOU LOOK SO STRANGE! WHEN WILL YOU BE BACK?

I DON'T KNOW, THELMA! PER- HAPS NEVER!

"WHEN I ARRIVED IN THE CITY, I SET OUT IMMEDIATELY FOR A RESIDENTIAL SECTION! I WENT NOT KNOWING WHY, ONLY GUIDED BY SOME MYSTERIOUS FORCE! I CAME TO A HANDSOME HOUSE, AND AS I STOOD THERE, A CAR TURNED INTO THE DRIVE!"

THE MAN IN THE CRYSTAL! THE MAN WHO KILLED HER!

"FOR A SPLIT SECOND, THE MAN'S EYES LOCKED WITH MINE! THEN A CURIOUS THING HAPPENED! THE CAR SUDDENLY SPURTED FORWARD AND CRASHED HEADLONG INTO A TREE!"

CR-RASH!

"AND IN THAT EVENING'S PAPER···"

DAILY O WORLD
HENRY SYMON INJURED IN FREAK ACCIDENT. CANDIDATE FOR STATE SENATE IN HOSPITAL.

"HENRY SYMON'S INJURY WASN'T SERIOUS··· HE WAS SOON BACK AT HIS OFFICE! I WATCHED HIM CONSTANTLY, EVERYWHERE HE WENT, IN NIGHT CLUBS, AS HE MADE HIS CAMPAIGN SPEECHES FOR STATE SENATOR···"

SYMON FOR SENATOR

"A CHAIN OF MISFORTUNE SEEMED TO WRAP ITSELF AROUND SYMON! HIS BUSINESS FAILED···HE WAS BADLY BEATEN IN THE ELECTION···"

"THEN, FOLLOWING THE MYSTERIOUS URGE WHICH MOTIVATED ALL MY ACTIONS, I WENT BACK TO THE COTTAGE! TWO NIGHTS LATER, I HEARD MUFFLED SOUNDS COMING FROM THE WOODS···"

SOMEONE IS AT OLD KATE'S GRAVE! IT'S···SYMON! HE'S COME TO BURN OLD KATE'S BODY TO RID HIMSELF OF HER CURSE!

WE HAVE BEEN EXPECTING YOU, MR. SYMON!

7.

161

"HE TURNED ON ME, SPADE UPRAISED TO STRIKE! I MOVED IN CLOSER---AND MY HANDS WENT INVOLUNTARILY TO HIS THROAT!"

NO--- NO--- ARGH!

"SYMON FELL---DEAD! I WENT TO THE POLICE, GAVE MYSELF UP!---THAT'S MY STORY! THAT'S HOW IT HAPPENED!"

I'VE NEWS FOR YOU, TIM!

AN AUTOPSY'S BEEN PERFORMED ON SYMON! HE DIDN'T DIE OF STRANGULATION---BUT FROM HEART FAILURE! YOU CAN GO HOME, TIM! YOU'RE FREE!

LATER---IN THE COTTAGE IN THE WOODS---

I'D BETTER BURN ALL OF KATE'S BOOKS---HER SECRETS! IT'S BETTER THAT WAY! MAYBE IT WILL HELP---TO BREAK HER GRIP ON ME---

BUT THE SECOND THE FLAME TOUCHED THE PAPERS---A BLINDING BLAZE OF UNHOLY FIRE---

IN A TWINKLING, THE COTTAGE IS A MASS OF FLAMES!

YOU HAVE DONE WHAT I WANTED, LAD---NOW YOU CAN GO! ALL THE RECORDS OF WITCHCRAFT ARE DESTROYED! YOU ARE RELEASED, TIM---RELEASED!

OLD KATE!

LATER---

IT'S GOOD TO HAVE YOU BACK, TIM---BUT YOU'VE CHANGED! THERE USED TO BE SOMETHING ABOUT YOU THAT MADE ME AFRAID! NOW--- IT'S GONE!

YES, THELMA, IT'S GONE---FOREVER! NOW I CAN LIVE A FREE, NORMAL LIFE! NOW I CAN ASK YOU TO ---MARRY ME!

The END!

8.

Draw me!

$1050.⁰⁰ in Valuable Prizes

30 Prizes! Scholarships and Cash to Amateur Artists

1st and 2nd prizes, Complete $280.00 Art Course; 3rd $100.00 cash; 4th, $75.00; 5th $50.00; 6th, $25.00; and 24 prizes of $10.00!

Here's your big chance, if you want to become a commercial artist, designer, or illustrator! An easy-to-try way to win FREE art training from one of the world's greatest art schools . . . the same home-study school that has taught many famous American artists during the past 36 years!

Whether you win or not we send you our comments on your work, if your drawing shows promise! Trained illustrators, artists and cartoonists now making big money. Find out now if YOU have profitable art talent. You've nothing to lose—*everything to gain.* Start your drawing now. Mail it today.

HOW TO FIX
ANY PART OF ANY CAR

USED BY U.S. ARMED FORCES

QUICKLY-- EASILY-- RIGHT!

IGNITION · STEERING GEAR · BODY WORK · REAR END · OIL FILTER · GENERATOR · CARBURETOR · DISTRIBUTOR · SHOCK ABSORBERS · WHEEL ALIGNMENT · UNIVERSAL · AUTOMATIC TRANSMISSION · BRAKES · CLUTCH

NOW—Whether You're a Beginner or an Expert Mechanic —You Can "Breeze Through" ANY AUTO REPAIR JOB! MOTOR'S BRAND-NEW 1951 AUTO REPAIR MANUAL Shows You HOW—With 2300 PICTURES AND SIMPLE STEP-BY-STEP INSTRUCTIONS.

Free 7-DAY TRIAL Return and Pay Nothing If Not Satisfied!

COVERS EVERY JOB ON EVERY CAR BUILT FROM 1935 THRU 1951

YES, it's easy as A-B-C to do any "fix-it" job on any car whether it's a simple carburetor adjustment or a complete overhaul. Just look up the job in the index of MOTOR'S New AUTO REPAIR MANUAL. Turn to pages covering job. Follow the clear, illustrated step-by-step instructions. Presto—the job is done!

No guesswork! MOTOR'S Manual takes nothing for granted. Tells you where to start. What tools to use. Then it leads you easily and quickly through the entire operation!

Over TWO THOUSAND Pictures! So Complete, So Simple, You CAN'T Go Wrong!

NEW REVISED 1951 Edition covers everything you need to know to repair 800 car models. 771 giant pages, 2300 "This-Is-How" pictures. Over 200 "Quick-Check" charts—more than 38,000 essential repair specifications. Over 225,000 service and repair facts. Instructions and pictures are so clear you can't go wrong!

Even a green beginner mechanic can do a good job with this giant manual before him. And if you're a top-notch

mechanic, you'll find short-cuts that will amaze you. No wonder this guide is used by the U. S. Army and Navy! No wonder hundreds of thousands of men call it the "Auto Repair Mans' Bible"!

Meat of Over 150 Official Shop Manuals

Engineers from every automobile plant in America worked out these time-saving procedures for their own motor car line. Now the editors of MOTOR have gathered together this wealth of "Know-How" from over 150 Official Factory Shop Manuals, "boiled it down" into crystal-clear terms in one handy indexed book!

Try Book FREE 7 Days

SEND NO MONEY! Just mail coupon! When the postman brings book, pay him nothing. First, make it show you what it's got! Unless you agree this is the greatest time-saver and work-saver you've ever seen — return book in 7 days and pay nothing. Mail coupon today! Address: *MOTOR Book Dept., Desk 9011B, 250 West 55th St., N. Y. 19, N. Y.*

Same FREE Offer On MOTOR'S Truck and Tractor Manual

Covers EVERY job on EVERY popular make gasoline truck, tractor made from 1936 thru 1949. FREE 7-Day Trial. Check proper box in coupon.

Many Letters of Praise from Users

"MOTOR'S Manual paid for itself on the first 2 jobs, and saved me valuable time by eliminating guesswork."
—W. SCHROP, Ohio.

He Does Job in 30 Min.—Fixed motor another mechanic had worked on half a day. With your Manual I did it in 30 minutes."
—C. AUBERRY, Tenn.

FORBIDDEN WORLDS #4 | January–February 1952

166

A QUEEN for the VOODOO CHIEF

"THIS GAL'S TERRIFIC!"

"SHE'LL BE A STAR OVERNIGHT!"

PAUL COOPER

A MODERN TELEVISION STUDIO--A BEAUTIFUL SINGING STAR--WHAT POSSIBLE CONNECTION COULD THESE HAVE WITH A TERROR-RIDDEN JUNGLE FAR ACROSS THE SEA--WITH A PRIMITIVE TRIBE OF VOODOO WORSHIPPERS WHO SUMMONED THE EVIL FORCES OF BLACK MAGIC TO MAKE DEAD MEN WALK?--HOLD ONTO YOUR NERVES, READER--AND FIND OUT!

OUR STORY REALLY BEGINS ON THE NIGHT JERI ADAMS MADE HER SENSATIONAL DEBUT BEFORE THE TELEVISION CAMERAS --A NIGHT THAT GAVE NO HINT OF IMPENDING TERROR!

"I'M DANNY KELLER, MISS ADAMS-- MY PAPER SENT ME TO INTER-VIEW YOU!"

"ALL RIGHT--BUT I'M AFRAID YOU WON'T FIND MY LIFE STORY VERY GLAMOROUS!"

TO DANNY'S SURPRISE, JERI REVEALED NOTHING BUT A PROSAIC, UNEVENTFUL PAST-- EVEN HER ANCESTORS WERE COMPLETELY ORDINARY PEOPLE--

"SO YOU SEE, THERE'S NOTHING INTERESTING AT ALL IN MY BACK-GROUND! IN FACT, IT WAS ONLY LUCK THAT GOT ME INTO TELEVISION!"

"YOU EXPECT ME TO WRITE THAT FOR MY READERS?"

"WHY, YOU HAVEN'T EVEN GOT THE IMAGINATION TO THINK UP A FEW GLAMOROUS DETAILS! NEVER MIND THE STORY, MISS ADAMS!"

"WELL, OF ALL THE--! ALL RIGHT, THEN-- TRY THIS ON YOUR READERS!"

"YOU ASKED FOR IT-- SO HERE IT IS! ACTUALLY, YOU MIGHT SAY MY LIFE STORY BEGAN CENTURIES AGO, IN THE FOR-BIDDEN JUNGLES OF HAITI! FAR FROM CIVILIZATION, THERE LIVED A WILD TRIBE OF VOODOO WORSHIPPERS, RULED BY A MYSTERIOUS WHITE QUEEN!"

1

"EVERY GENERATION SAW A NEW QUEEN, THE DAUGHTER OF THE OLD, AND EACH BORE THE CRESCENT-SHAPED MARK OF NAFARIS ON HER SHOULDER! UNDER THEIR WISE AND GENTLE RULE, THE TRIBE GREW POWERFUL AND PROSPEROUS--UNTIL ONE DAY..."

O GREAT NAFARIS--WHAT WICKED MEN ARE THESE WHO KILL OUR PEOPLE WITH THEIR STRANGE THUNDERSTICKS?

I DO NOT KNOW-- BUT WE ARE HELPLESS AGAINST THEM!

"SLAVERS!--THE SCOURGE OF THE JUNGLE-- WHO HUNT MEN DOWN LIKE BEASTS!"

A GOOD HAUL THIS TIME, EH, CAPTAIN?

COME WITH ME-- I'LL SHOW YOU SOMETHING EVEN BETTER!

WHAT THE--! A WHITE GAL!

YEAH-- SHE'S THEIR QUEEN! OUGHTA FETCH A HANDSOME PRICE IN THE STATES!

HOW DARE YOU LAY HANDS ON NAFARIS?

"AND SO NAFARIS WAS BROUGHT TO AMERICA TO BE SOLD AS A SLAVE! THE BIDDING FOR THE BEAUTIFUL GIRL WAS HIGH--"

COME, GENTLEMEN--WHAT MORE AM I BID FOR THIS PROUD BEAUTY WHO ONCE RULED AN ISLAND EMPIRE? GOING--GOING--

SIR, I WILL TOP ALL BIDS FOR THE GIRL!

"MONTHS LATER--THE WEALTHY YOUNG PLANTER WHO HAD BOUGHT NAFARIS FOUND HIMSELF UNABLE TO RESIST HER BEAUTY--"

NAFARIS-- BE MY QUEEN! I LOVE YOU!

AT LAST--NAFARIS HAS A KING!

AS JERI FINISHED HER STORY--

THAT HAPPENED A HUNDRED YEARS AGO! NOW--WHAT DO YOU THINK OF THIS?--I AM A DESCENDANT OF THE LAST QUEEN NAFARIS! HERE'S THE CRESCENT-SHAPED MARK TO PROVE IT!

SAY, YOU DO HAVE AN IMAGINATION, AFTER ALL! THAT'S THE MOST OUTLANDISH YARN I'VE EVER HEARD!

2.

YOU-- YOU'RE LIKE ALL THE REST! I TOLD THAT FIRST STORY BECAUSE I KNEW YOU WOULDN'T BELIEVE THE *TRUTH!*

HEY!

SMACK!

OKAY-- YOU WIN! I'LL PRINT IT, EVEN IF IT *IS* HOKUM! BUT I'LL EXACT MY *PRICE* FIRST!

OH! I DON'T KNOW WHETHER TO HATE YOU, OR--!

...SO JERI'S STORY WAS PRINTED -- LAUGHED AT -- AND THUS BEGAN A CHAIN OF EVENTS SO LADEN WITH HORROR AS TO CHILL THE VERY IMAGINATION!

HA! WHAT SOME PEOPLE WON'T DO FOR PUBLICITY! I'LL BET THIS ADAMS GIRL'S NEVER BEEN SOUTH OF CONEY ISLAND!

TV QUEEN ONCE RULED JUNGLE!

A FEW DAYS LATER -- A SWIFT, SLEEK PASSENGER PLANE, HIGH ABOVE THE DARK JUNGLES OF HAITI, SPUTTERS, PLUMMETS EARTHWARD--

CRASH!

OVERCOMING THEIR SUPERSTITIOUS FEAR OF THE WRECKED PLANE, THE NATIVES BEGAN LOOTING IT OF ITS PRECIOUS CARGO! SUDDENLY--

LOOK-- ALL OF YOU!

TV QUEEN ONCE RULED JUNGLE!

IT IS NAFARIS -- NAFARIS! THE GREAT WHITE QUEEN WHOSE IMAGE WE HAVE WORSHIPPED SINCE SHE WAS TORN FROM OUR MIDST A HUNDRED YEARS AGO! *SHE STILL LIVES!*

TV QUEEN ONCE RULED JUNGLE!

3

169

THAT NIGHT, THE TRIBE HELD A COUNCIL TO DISCUSS THE MOMENTOUS TURN OF EVENTS! KUFIR, THE WITCH DOCTOR, SPOKE--

O CHIEF--WE ALL KNOW THAT SINCE OUR GREAT WHITE QUEEN, NAFARIS, WAS DRAGGED AWAY FROM THE JUNGLE, OUR TRIBE HAS FALLEN UPON HARD TIMES! IF, HOWEVER, WE COULD GET NAFARIS BACK--

IF WE COULD-- AND HOW DO YOU PROPOSE TO ACCOMPLISH THIS, KUFIR?

I HAVE BEEN AMONGST WHITE MEN BEFORE-- I KNOW THEIR CUSTOMS! I WILL GO TO AMERICA--TO NAFARIS-- AND TELL OUR QUEEN WE NEED HER!

BY THIS TIME, JERI AND DANNY HAD FORGOTTEN THEIR QUARREL! ONE EVENING--

GOSH, DANNY-- I WAS WRONG ABOUT YOU-- YOU'VE HELPED ME A LOT!

FORGET IT-- I HAD REASONS!

NAFARIS!-- AT LAST I'VE FOUND YOU!

O GREAT QUEEN NAFARIS-- YOUR PEOPLE AWAIT YOU! RETURN WITH ME NOW-- TO THE LAND OF YOUR BIRTH!

HA! A CHARACTER!

WELL, IT LOOKS LIKE SOMEONE BELIEVED THAT STORY YOU PRINTED!

BUT-- WHAT SEEMED TO BE AN INNOCENT JOKE TURNED OUT TO BE DEADLY SERIOUS--

WHAT--! STOP! YOU'RE HURTING MY ARM!-- DANNY!

YOU FORGET YOUR DUTY TO YOUR PEOPLE, NAFARIS-- YOU MUST COME WITH ME!

WHY, YOU--

POW!

LATER-- IN KUFIR'S HOTEL ROOM--

TIME HAS DULLED NAFARIS' MEMORY-- SHE HAS FORGOTTEN THE DAYS OF HER GLORY-- AND OURS! WELL, SHE WILL FIND THAT **WE** HAVE NOT FORGOTTEN THE ANCIENT **BLACK MAGIC** OF THE GODS! IT WILL **RESTORE HER MEMORY!**

OH, NAFARIS--HEAR ME, WHEREVER YOU ARE! -- COME TO ME, NAFARIS!

MEANWHILE-- IN HER APARTMENT--JERI AND DANNY LAUGHED AT THE EVENING'S INCIDENT-- LITTLE DREAMING OF THE AWFUL CONSEQUENCES TO COME--

HAH! AS IF YOU COULD EVER HAVE BEEN A QUEEN! GO ON, HONEY-- ACT QUEENLY FOR KING DANNY!

THINK I CAN'T, EH? HOW'S THIS-- I-- AM-- NAFARIS--

SUDDENLY--

NAFARIS--HEAR ME! COME TO ME, O GREAT QUEEN! --COME TO ME!

I HEAR, KUFIR, AND I COME!

OKAY, BABY.. THAT'S ENOUGH! YOU NEEDN'T BE THAT CONVINCING! I-- JERI!

BUT WITH A NEW-FOUND SUPERNATURAL STRENGTH, JERI TURNED UPON THE HELPLESS MAN-- HER EYES EMOTIONLESS.. EMPTY--

FOOL! HOW **DARE** YOU LAY HANDS ON NAFARIS?

STOP, JERI-- YOU DON'T KNOW WHAT YOU'RE DOING --YOU-- UGH!

HOURS LATER--

JERI! -- WHAT WAS THE IDEA OF--? SHE'S GONE!

5

REALIZING NOW THAT HE WAS UP AGAINST SOMETHING SINISTER -- SOMETHING UNNATURAL -- DANNY SOUGHT OUT THE ONE MAN IN THE WORLD WHO COULD HELP HIM -- DR. JOHN MARBERRY, RESEARCHER IN PSYCHIC PHENOMENA --

WHAT CAN I DO FOR YOU, DANNY?

IT MAY SOUND SCREWY, DOCTOR-- BUT HERE GOES--

AFTER DANNY HAD UNFOLDED HIS FANTASTIC TALE--

IT MAY COME AS A SURPRISE TO YOU-- BUT JERI TOLD THE TRUTH! THERE WAS A WHITE QUEEN CALLED NAFARIS-- AND JERI COULD BE HER DESCENDANT! LOOK HERE--

FOLK-LORE OF HAITI

ACCORDING TO THIS BOOK, NAFARIS' OLD TRIBE STILL EXISTS! THE MAN YOU MET IN THE NIGHT CLUB WAS DOUBTLESS SENT BY THEM TO TAKE NAFARIS-- OR JERI-- BACK TO HAITI! APPARENTLY, HE PUT HER UNDER A VOODOO SPELL, AND--

BUT-- THAT MEANS JERI IS--

EXACTLY! JERI HAS BEEN FORCIBLY ABDUCTED INTO THE MIDST OF ONE OF THE WILDEST JUNGLE TRIBES IN THE WORLD-- A TRIBE WHOSE CHIEF WEAPON IS BLACK MAGIC!

IT'S-- UNBELIEVABLE! WHAT DO YOU SUGGEST I DO, DOCTOR?

THERE'S ONLY ONE THING YOU CAN DO, MY BOY-- GO AFTER HER!

OF COURSE I'LL GO-- BUT WHAT CAN I DO ALONE-- AGAINST THAT WHOLE TRIBE OF-- SORCERERS?

ALL MY LIFE I'VE WANTED TO PIT MY BOOK KNOWLEDGE AGAINST THE LIVING FORCES OF THE SUPERNATURAL! NOW YOU'VE GIVEN ME THE CHANCE! I'M GOING WITH YOU!

FEVERISH PREPARATIONS WERE QUICKLY MADE-- AND A FEW DAYS LATER--

IT'S A CINCH THEIR WITCHCRAFT WON'T WORK AGAINST THESE!

THERE IT IS, DANNY-- HAITI! LAND OF VOODOO AND BLACK MAGIC!

6

AT THAT VERY MOMENT-- FAR BELOW IN THE DENSE JUNGLE -- JERI AWOKE FROM HER VOODOO SPELL -- AWOKE TO TERROR!

WHERE AM I? HOW DID I GET HERE? OH-- MY HEAD!

KUFIR! COME QUICKLY-- THE WHITE QUEEN HAS ARISEN!

HORRIFIED-- JERI RECOGNIZED THE STRANGE MAN OF THE NIGHT CLUB INCIDENT--

O MIGHTY NAFARIS-- WELCOME BACK TO YOUR PEOPLE! UNDER YOUR RULE, WE SHALL ONCE AGAIN WAX RICH AND POWERFUL!

YOU! THIS IS RIDICULOUS! I'M JERI ADAMS-- AND I DEMAND TO BE SET FREE!

BUT PROTESTS AVAILED HER LITTLE! INSTEAD, SHE WAS CONDUCTED TO A WILD, PAGAN SCENE! AND THERE, ENTHRONED NEXT TO THE FIERCE CHIEF, SHE SAW A STRANGE AND ANCIENT REPLICA -- OF HERSELF!

HERE, NAFARIS, IS THE STATUE WE HAVE BEEN WORSHIPPING FOR A CENTURY! NOW, HAVING RETURNED, YOU WILL TAKE ITS PLACE -- ON THE THRONE OF THE WHITE QUEEN -- BESIDE YOUR KING!

YOU MEAN, HE'S TO BE MY KING? NEVER!

IT WAS THEN THAT HYSTERIA OVERTOOK JERI! SEIZING A MACHETE, SHE RUSHED FORWARD, AND--

IF THIS IS THE TIE THAT BINDS ME TO YOU, I'LL BREAK IT, NOW!

CRAK!

BUT THE AMERICAN GIRL DID NOT RECKON ON THE SLAVISH SUPERSTITION OF THESE VOODOO WORSHIPPERS! HER BLOOD RAN COLD AS KUFIR SPOKE--

FOR SUCH BLASPHEMY, YOU MUST DIE TONIGHT-- BEFORE THE VOODOO FIRES!

OH-- NO!

7

173

A FEW HOURS LATER -- IN THE NEARBY JUNGLE --

ACCORDING TO THE MAP -- WE'RE NEAR NAFARIS' COUNTRY!

LISTEN, DOC -- WHAT'S THAT BOOMING NOISE?

JUNGLE DRUMS! -- THE MOST TERRIFYING SOUND EVER HEARD BY HUMAN EARS! DR. MARBERRY'S FACE WHITENED AS HE LISTENED TO THEIR HIDEOUS MESSAGE --

GREAT SCOTT! THE NATIVES HAVE TURNED AGAINST NAFARIS! SHE'S TO BE SACRIFICED -- WITHIN THE HOUR!

JERI! C'MON, DOC -- HURRY!

A MAD RACE -- AGAINST DEATH!

THESE VINES -- LIKE STRANGLING SNAKES -- HOLDING US BACK!

NOT MUCH -- TIME, DANNY!

EVEN AT THAT VERY MOMENT, JERI ADAMS, TELEVISION STAR, WAS ABOUT TO DIE HORRIBLY ON A PAGAN ALTAR OF SACRIFICE --

O GREAT NAFARIS -- WE OFFER YOU THE BLOOD OF THIS TRAITOR! MAY YOUR WRATH BE APPEASED! LET THE KNIFE FALL!

BUT THE EVIL WITCH DOCTOR HAD NOT COUNTED ON AMERICAN COURAGE AND ENDURANCE! EVEN AS THE GREAT SWORD FELL --

DANNY!

ARGH!

BANG!

WHILE THE DOCTOR HELD THE ENRAGED TRIBESMEN AT BAY, DANNY CUT JERI FREE! NOW BUT ONE THOUGHT FILLED THEIR MINDS -- ESCAPE!

WE'LL HAVE TO MOVE FAST -- OR WE'RE DONE FOR!

I -- I FEEL SO WEAK!

RAT-TAT-TAT

8

SLOWED DOWN BY THE WEAKENED JERI, THE FUGITIVES FROM TERROR WERE IN DANGER OF BEING SURROUNDED BY THEIR VICIOUS PURSUERS--

LEAVE ME, DANNY!-- SAVE YOURSELVES!

SAVE YOUR BREATH-- YOU'LL NEED IT!

LOOK-- A CAVE! WE CAN TAKE REFUGE THERE--HURRY!

A NATURAL FORT! NOW THEY COMMANDED A VIEW OF ALL APPROACHES-- AND THERE WAS PLENTY OF AMMUNITION--

AS SOON AS JERI REGAINS HER STRENGTH, WE'LL FIGHT OUR WAY TO SAFETY-- THE PLANE IS ONLY A FEW MILES AWAY!

LOOKS LIKE WE HAVE A CHANCE, AFTER ALL!

BUT THEIR OPTIMISM WOULD HAVE BEEN SHORT LIVED HAD THEY BUT KNOWN OF THE AWFUL PLAN BEING LAID IN A NEARBY CLEARING--

THE FOOLS GLOAT, LITTLE REALIZING THEIR VICTORY IS BUT A TEMPORARY ONE! WE SHALL SEE WHAT THEIR FIRE-SPITTING WEAPONS CAN DO AGAINST THE INVINCIBLE POWER OF VOODOO!

ALONE, KUFIR RETURNED TO THE VILLAGE AND THE BODIES OF THE SLAIN TRIBESMEN! THERE, IN THE SILENT JUNGLE, A GRISLY RITUAL TOOK PLACE--

O GODS OF THE VOODOO-- I IMPLORE YOU-- HELP YOUR CHILDREN VANQUISH THE HATED FOREIGNERS!

THEN-- THE IMPOSSIBLE! SLOWLY, THE DEAD MEN STIRRED, GAINED THEIR FEET, STARING WITH SIGHTLESS EYES-- AWAITING THE COMMAND OF THEIR MASTER! ZOMBIES!

RISE, RISE, CHILDREN OF THE DARKNESS! YOUR HOUR OF VENGEANCE IS AT HAND!

STIFFLY, MECHANICALLY, THE TERRIFYING PROCESSION MOVED THROUGH THE JUNGLE ON THEIR UNSPEAKABLE ERRAND-- A LEGION OF THE LIVING DEAD!

9

SHORTLY AFTERWARD--

LOOK-- ANOTHER ATTACK! BUT THEY HAVE NO WEAPONS! THERE'S SOMETHING STRANGE ABOUT THIS!

WELL, IF IT'S A SUICIDE ATTACK--THEY CAME TO THE RIGHT PLACE!

A BURST OF DEATH-DEALING MACHINE-GUN FIRE-- AND NOW DANNY AND HIS FRIENDS WERE SEIZED BY A NAMELESS HORROR--

DOC! THEY--THEY KEEP COMING! I CAN SEE THE BULLETS STRIKE BUT--

GREAT SCOTT! ZOMBIES! THE FIENDS HAVE RESORTED TO BLACK MAGIC!

HA! SEE-- OUR ENEMIES ARE HELPLESS AGAINST THE UNKNOWN! VICTORY IS OURS! -- KILL! KILL!

AT THE CAVE, THE SITUATION LOOKED HOPELESS FOR THE DEFENDERS--

WE'VE GOT ONLY ONE CHANCE-- MY KNOWLEDGE OF THE SUPERNATURAL! THIS CLAY-- DANNY, CAN YOU HOLD THEM OFF FOR 5 MINUTES? YOU MUST!

THIS IS IT, DOC-- HERE THEY COME!

WE'RE GOING TO FIGHT THEM ON THEIR OWN TERMS--WITH BLACK MAGIC THAT MY ANCIENT BOOKS TAUGHT ME!

RUSH IT! BULLETS WON'T WORK-- I'M DOWN TO USING ROCKS NOW!

THE DOCTOR LABORED WITH FRANTIC HASTE-- AND IN HIS SKILLED HANDS, THE WET CLAY TOOK ON THE SHAPE OF -- KUFIR!

WE'RE FRESH OUT OF ROCKS, DOC-- AND THESE LIFELESS CREEPS ARE CREEPING BACK FAST!

I NEED ONE MORE MINUTE!

YOU'VE GOT YOUR MINUTE, DOC-- THAT'S HOW LONG IT'LL TAKE THESE DEVILS TO TEAR ME APART!

OH, NO! DANNY!

OH, PLEASE HURRY, DOCTOR-- THEY'VE GOT DANNY!

HOLD ON-- IT'S FINISHED!

10

WHAT MAN, HOWEVER BRAVE, CAN HOPE TO WITHSTAND AN ONSLAUGHT OF SUPERSTRONG ZOMBIES? IT SEEMED THAT DANNY HAD SACRIFICED HIS LIFE IN VAIN--

IT--IT'S TOO LATE!

AT THAT MOMENT-- WITH THREE LIVES AT STAKE--

SWISH!

AND EVEN AS THE DOLL'S HEART IS PIERCED-- DEATH CLAIMS ITS HUMAN COUNTERPART!

ARGH!

UNCONTROLLED-- THE ZOMBIES FALTERED, FELL --

WE'VE WON-- AND EVIL HAS DEFEATED ITSELF!

DANNY-- ARE YOU ALL RIGHT?

STILL LIVING, HONEY-- AND THAT'S ALL THAT COUNTS!

THUS ONCE AGAIN DID CIVILIZED MAN PROVE HIS SUPERIORITY OVER THE EVIL OF A DEAD PAST! ... SOME DAYS LATER, WE FIND OUR HEROINE BACK IN THE TELEVISION LIMELIGHT--

GREAT SHOW, MISS ADAMS! IT'S HOLLY-WOOD FOR YOU, NEXT!

A RE-PORTER'S WAITING, MISS-- SAID HE WANTS A STORY!

ANOTHER ONE? I'LL GET RID OF HIM, BUT FAST!

DANNY! YOU KNOW WHAT HAPPENED THE LAST TIME I GAVE YOU A STORY! BETTER FORGET IT!

AH, BUT THIS IS A DIFFERENT KIND OF STORY-- AND I CAN'T PRINT IT WITHOUT YOUR OKAY! THE HEAD-LINE WILL BE, "TELEVISION QUEEN MARRIES REPORTER!" -- HOW ABOUT IT?

HERE'S MY ANSWER-- YOUR MAJESTY!

11

The End

Devil-doomed SANDMAN

JOAN'S EYES WERE bitter with self-reproach. What a fool she'd been to quarrel with her husband on a night of storm and shipwreck! Surely only a woman bereft of her senses would seek the loneliness of a gale-lashed beach when the cottages on the bluff blazed with so much light and warmth! Gathering up her skirts, she started back across the sandbar.

She was wading through the backswell which surged in angry ripples between the bar and the beach' when a tall figure loomed out of the spray. The figure did not advance to meet Joan, but stood as though waiting for her to join him at the edge of the beach, his right arm upraised.

"Donald!" Joan cried, and plunged on recklessly, not caring how deeply her feet sank in the treacherous sand, her body suddenly buoyant with an eagerness she could not conceal. But it was not her husband who stood waiting for her at the edge of the rising tide. The man was heavily bearded and hollow-eyed, and a soaring fire of driftwood blazed at his back, bringing the harsh cruelty of his features into sharp relief.

In his right arm the stranger held a coil of rope, and as Joan turned in wild terror, he flung a long curving strand straight at her, his laughter ringing out in brutal exultation above the roar of the sea. The rope whipped around Joan's waist and tightened in swift, relentless coils. She struggled desperately, but felt herself being dragged forward, her feet slipping out from under her, her breath coming in choking gasps. And e-

ven as the tall figure drew her toward the beach, the flesh of his face seemed to wither and fall away, until Joan found herself looking for one awful instant into the eyes of a grinning skull!

Then Joan heard another voice screaming in the night. "It's the Devil-doomed Sandman! Fight it...or you'll be destroyed!" She saw her husband then, standing on the tip of the breakwater, a wild entreaty in his stare. Pulling back, she straightened as she faced the ghastly apparition.

"I know you for what you are!" she cried, her voice rising in sudden, sharp defiance. "Your rope is sand and you are a wrecker of ships, a stealer of cargoes! Long ago you built fires on this beach to lure mariners to their doom! For your crimes you were condemned to be chained to the bar...condemned to coil a cable of sand everlastingly! *A cable that can never hold!*"

There was a sudden, furious swirling at Joan's waist. Looking down, she saw a weaving spiral of sand slipping downward from her waist into the shining black tide. When the sand rope struck the water, it vanished with a hiss. A shriek of baffled rage came from the gaunt apparition before the fire. The next instant the fire flamed redly, dwindled and was gone, carrying the figure with it.

A moment later Joan had crossed the bar to the breakwater and was clinging to her husband and sobbing as he gently stroked her sea-drenched hair.

The bike that has EVERYTHING!

STYLED LIKE A MODERN AUTOMOBILE. Smart as the new convertibles, and almost as beautiful and easy riding. Smoothes out the roughest roads.

GRACEFUL AS A PLANE. Super streamlined air-flow design, with the sweeping curves and graceful lines of a speedy jet plane.

RUGGED AS A TANK. High frequency electronic welding and double-thick joints for extra strength, durability and safety.

Full 26-inch Size
Boys' and Girls' Models

Thrilling GENE AUTRY Models

Rich, Rodeo Brown finish . . . with life-like pony's head above front fork . . . "jewel" studded fenders, chain guard, saddle and front fork . . . pistol-type horn . . . genuine leather holster with red-handled, Gene Autry pistol . . . brown and white streamers on handlebar grips . . . fringed, two-tone "saddle blanket" with Gene Autry's famous "Flying A" insignia . . . and Gene Autry autograph on chain guard. 20 and 24 inch sizes. Boys' and girls' models. One year's fire and theft insurance included.

the Famous MONARK Super Deluxe

Double spring, rubber cushioned, shock absorbing front fork . . . "Strato-Liner" headlight with "Road Focus" beam and safety side lenses . . . "Protecto-Gard" tank rails, heavy duty luggage carrier and "Krome-gard" rear bumper . . . massive Motor-Bike fenders and jeweled, monogrammed pedals . . . "Air Wing" head shield, built-in auto-type tank and horn . . . and dozens of other Monark extras, including a full year's fire and theft insurance to protect you against loss. Tops in beauty, quality and performance.

See Them Today!

For the name of the nearest Monark dealer, pick up the phone and call Western Union by number. Ask for Operator 25. She'll tell you his name and address.

OPERATOR 25

MONARK SILVER KING, INC.

6501 West Grand Avenue, Chicago 35, Ill.

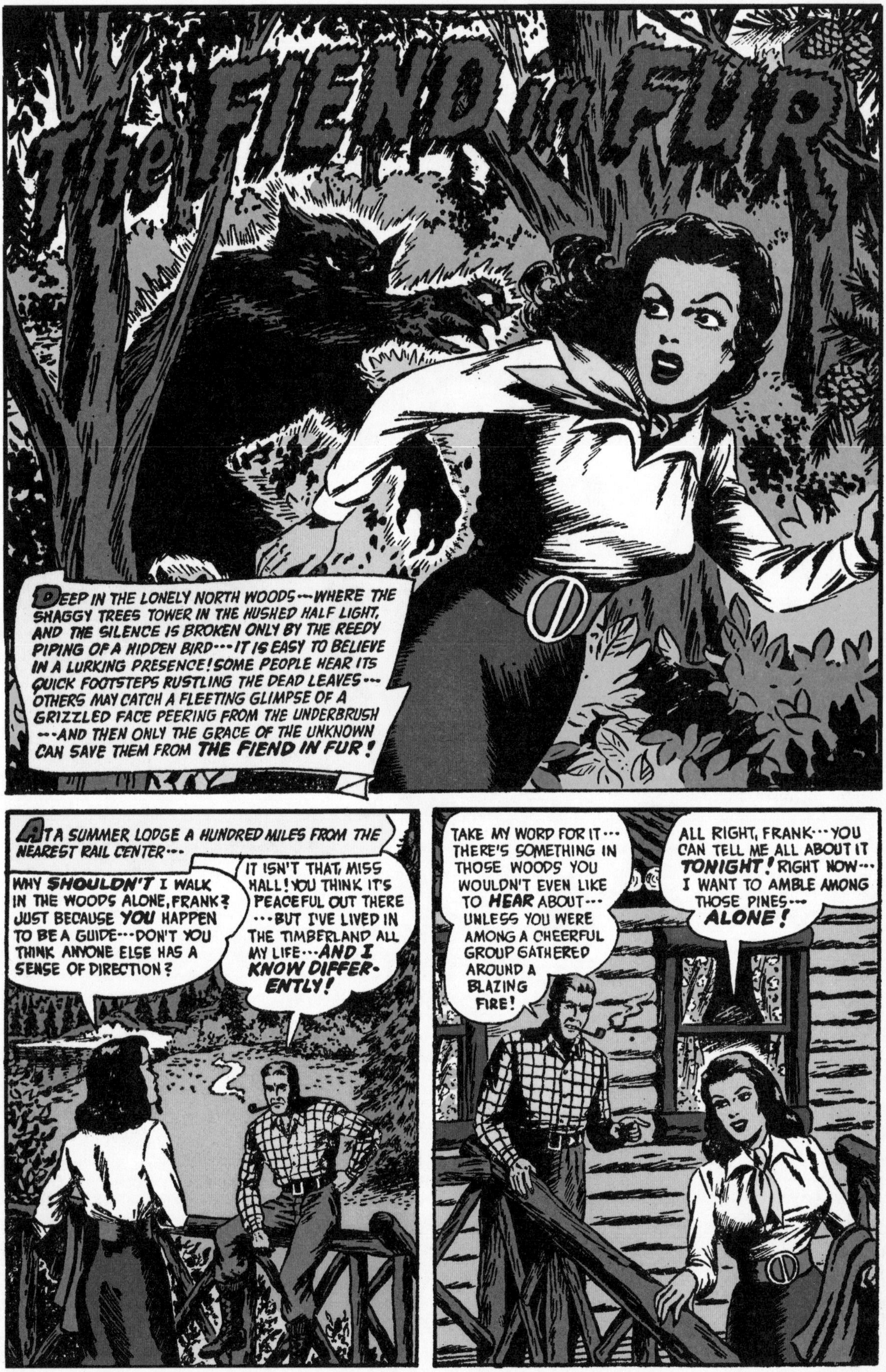
The FIEND in FUR
DEEP IN THE LONELY NORTH WOODS---WHERE THE SHAGGY TREES TOWER IN THE HUSHED HALF LIGHT, AND THE SILENCE IS BROKEN ONLY BY THE REEDY PIPING OF A HIDDEN BIRD---IT IS EASY TO BELIEVE IN A LURKING PRESENCE! SOME PEOPLE HEAR ITS QUICK FOOTSTEPS RUSTLING THE DEAD LEAVES--- OTHERS MAY CATCH A FLEETING GLIMPSE OF A GRIZZLED FACE PEERING FROM THE UNDERBRUSH ---AND THEN ONLY THE GRACE OF THE UNKNOWN CAN SAVE THEM FROM THE FIEND IN FUR!
AT A SUMMER LODGE A HUNDRED MILES FROM THE NEAREST RAIL CENTER---
WHY SHOULDN'T I WALK IN THE WOODS ALONE, FRANK? JUST BECAUSE YOU HAPPEN TO BE A GUIDE---DON'T YOU THINK ANYONE ELSE HAS A SENSE OF DIRECTION?
IT ISN'T THAT, MISS HALL! YOU THINK IT'S PEACEFUL OUT THERE ---BUT I'VE LIVED IN THE TIMBERLAND ALL MY LIFE---AND I KNOW DIFFERENTLY!
TAKE MY WORD FOR IT--- THERE'S SOMETHING IN THOSE WOODS YOU WOULDN'T EVEN LIKE TO HEAR ABOUT--- UNLESS YOU WERE AMONG A CHEERFUL GROUP GATHERED AROUND A BLAZING FIRE!
ALL RIGHT, FRANK---YOU CAN TELL ME ALL ABOUT IT TONIGHT! RIGHT NOW--- I WANT TO AMBLE AMONG THOSE PINES--- ALONE!

ALONE ··· IT WAS SEVERAL HOURS BEFORE PHYLLIS HALL REMEMBERED THE WORD ··· AND HARDLY REALIZING IT ··· BEGAN TO WONDER!

IT'S AN ATMOSPHERE I CAN'T DESCRIBE ··· BOTH QUIET AND MELANCHOLY ··· AND YET THERE'S SOMETHING *MORE* THAN THAT!

FRANK MENTIONED THAT THE INDIANS DON'T LIKE THE FOREST ··· AND ENTER IT ONLY ON RARE OCCASIONS! JUST THE SAME, I'VE GOT A FEELING THAT *SOMETHING'S* PADDING SILENTLY OVER THE PINE NEEDLES ··· ALWAYS MANAGING TO KEEP OUT OF SIGHT ··· *BUT FOLLOWING ME!*

HEAVENS ··· IT'S MUCH LATER THAN I THOUGHT! IT'LL BE DUSK WITHIN A FEW MINUTES ··· *I'LL NEVER BE ABLE TO FIND MY WAY BACK TO THE LODGE!*

SLOWLY ··· THE SHADOWS OF THE HULKING TREES ARE BLURRED BY THE SETTLING GLOOM!

I'VE GOT TO FORGET THAT NONSENSE OF FRANK'S ··· THERE'S NOTHING TO BE AFRAID OF JUST BECAUSE I'M BY MYSELF ··· *MILES FROM THE NEAREST PERSON!*

THEN ··· AS A BARELY-FELT BREEZE WHISPERS THROUGH THE UNDERBRUSH ···

OH!

THERE IT IS ··· THE PRESENCE I FELT ··· STALKING CLOSER NOW THAT DARKNESS HAS FALLEN!

MINUTES LATER ···

THIS WILL BE EASIER TO CLIMB THAN A TREE ··· I'VE GOT TO FIND SOME WAY TO HIDE FROM THAT THING!

2

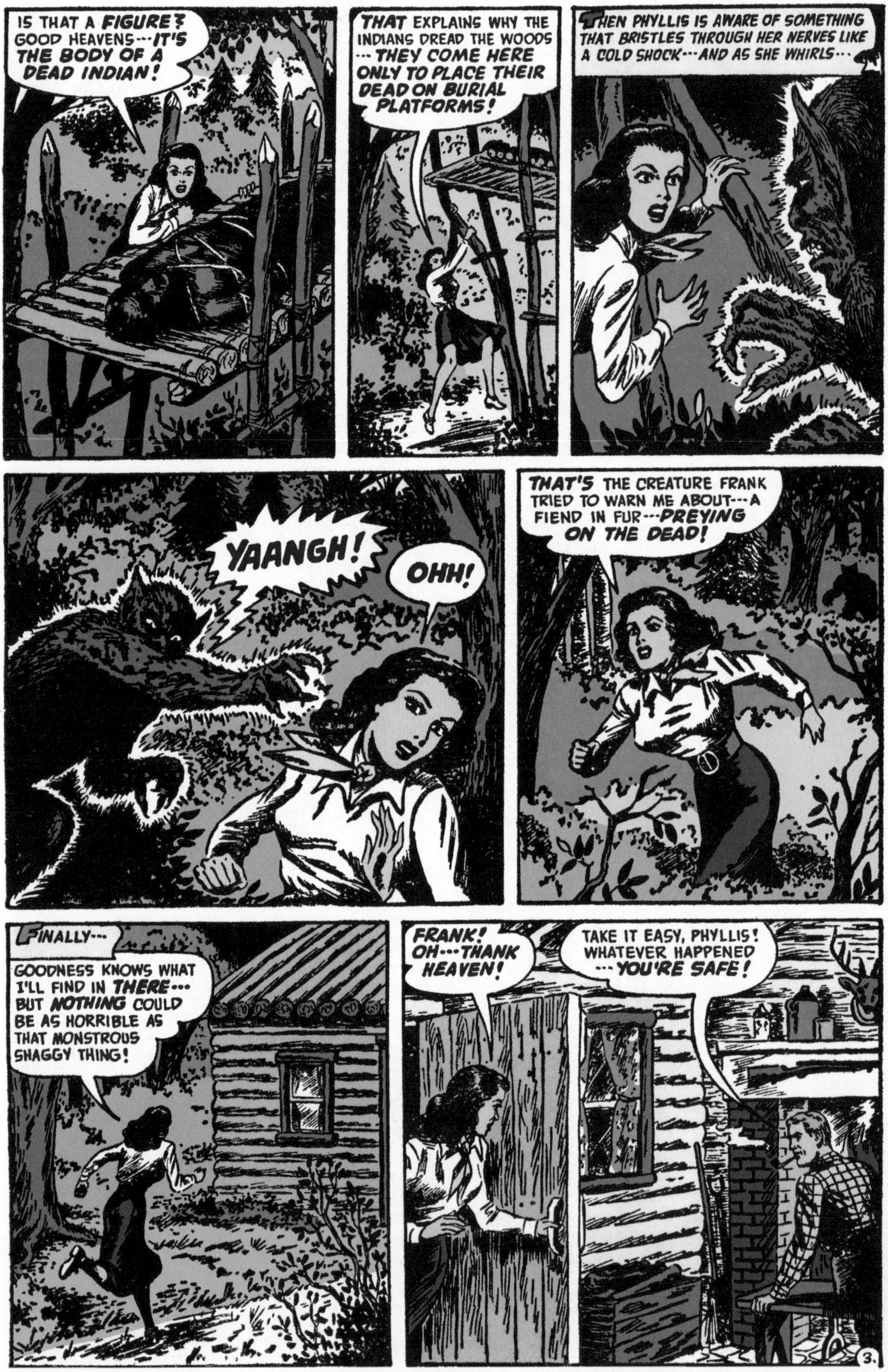
IS THAT A FIGURE? GOOD HEAVENS---IT'S THE BODY OF A DEAD INDIAN!
THAT EXPLAINS WHY THE INDIANS DREAD THE WOODS ---THEY COME HERE ONLY TO PLACE THEIR DEAD ON BURIAL PLATFORMS!
THEN PHYLLIS IS AWARE OF SOMETHING THAT BRISTLES THROUGH HER NERVES LIKE A COLD SHOCK---AND AS SHE WHIRLS---
YAANGH!
OHH!
THAT'S THE CREATURE FRANK TRIED TO WARN ME ABOUT---A FIEND IN FUR---PREYING ON THE DEAD!
FINALLY---
GOODNESS KNOWS WHAT I'LL FIND IN THERE---BUT NOTHING COULD BE AS HORRIBLE AS THAT MONSTROUS SHAGGY THING!
FRANK! OH---THANK HEAVEN!
TAKE IT EASY, PHYLLIS! WHATEVER HAPPENED ---YOU'RE SAFE!
3.

NOT FROM *THAT* THING FRANK... I'LL *NEVER* BE SAFE FROM WHAT I SAW IN THE WOODS! IT WASN'T A MAN... IT WASN'T A WOLF... IT WAS A HIDEOUS MIXTURE OF *BOTH!*

GREAT GUNS! IT'S A GOOD THING I SET OUT FROM THE LODGE *TONIGHT*... THINKING I'D START SEARCHING FOR YOU AT DAWN!

YOU KNOW SOMETHING ABOUT THAT CREATURE, FRANK! YOU DIDN'T WANT TO FRIGHTEN ME THIS AFTERNOON... *BUT NOW YOU'VE GOT TO TELL ME WHAT IT IS!*

ALL I'VE KNOWN ABOUT THE FIEND *UNTIL* NOW IS AN OLD INDIAN LEGEND, HONEY!

YOU MAY HAVE HEARD THAT THE INDIANS BIND THEIR DEAD TO PLATFORMS IN THE WOODS... BELIEVING THAT THE RAWHIDE THONGS WILL KEEP THEIR SPIRITS FROM ROAMING! WELL... THE FIEND IS SUPPOSED TO BE THE SPIRIT OF AN EVIL MEDICINE MAN... *WHO DIED CENTURIES AGO!* ACCORDING TO THE STORY... SOON AFTER THE MEDICINE MAN DIED, A FOREST FIRE RAGED THROUGH THIS AREA... *DESTROYING THE BURIAL PLATFORM AND RELEASING HIS SPIRIT!*

MAYBE ITS TERRIBLE APPEARANCE IS DUE TO THE FACT THAT *HUNDREDS OF WOLVES* PERISHED IN THE FIRE... BUT ANYWAY, IT HAS A LAIR SOMEWHERE DEEP IN THE WOODS... *A SPOT NO ONE HAS EVER DARED TRY TO FIND!*

THEN... LIKE AN ERUPTION OF TERROR...

CRASH!

FRANK... IT'S HERE!

GET OUT, PHYLLIS... HIDE IN THE BUSHES... ANYWHERE!

YAANGH!

THEN... WITH PHYLLIS PARALYZED BY TERROR...

WAM!

183

DIMLY...FRANK SEES THE PLODDING SHAPE REACH OUT!

NO...DON'T ...DON'T!

GOOD LORD ...MY HEAD'S SWIMMING... I CAN'T HELP HER!

A MOMENT LATER...AFTER THE LAST ECHO OF PHYLLIS'S TERRIFIED SCREAMS HAVE FADED OFF INTO THE TRACKLESS GLOOM...

A GUN WON'T DO ANY GOOD AGAINST THAT THING...BUT I'D BETTER TAKE ALONG A COMPASS! THE FIEND'S LAIR MAY BE MILES FROM HERE...AND WITH LUCK...I'LL REACH IT IN TIME TO SAVE PHYLLIS!

AN HOUR LATER...AS THE UNCLOUDED MOON FLOODS THE FOREST WITH ITS EERIE LIGHT...

A WISP OF GRIZZLED FUR... THAT MEANS I'M ON THE RIGHT TRACK! THE FIEND PASSED THIS WAY...AND ACCORDING TO THE COMPASS, IT'S MAKING A BEELINE THROUGH THE WOODS...TOWARD A DEFINITE DESTINATION!

THEN...AS FRANK TURNS...

BLAZES... THERE GOES MY COMPASS!

SPLANG!

FOR A SECOND, THE COMPASS NEEDLE SPINS ERRATICALLY...

...AND ABOVE...ON THE PLATFORM BURDENED WITH ITS LONELY CORPSE...

AAHH!

HOLY SMOKE! IT'S THE GHOST OF THAT DEAD INDIAN...AND SOMETHING'S RELEASED IT!

AS THE PHANTOM GLIDES SILENTLY THROUGH THE WOODS...

WHAT MADE IT RISE... AFTER LYING HERE THROUGH COUNTLESS SEASONS OF SNOW AND HEAT...HEMMED IN BY SOLITUDE? WHAT ELSE COULD IT BE...BUT THE SPINNING COMPASS NEEDLE?

5.

FEW MEN HAVE DELIBERATELY SOUGHT OUT HORROR LIKE *THIS*···BUT AGAIN···FRANK TAKES UP THE SEARCH!

YEP, WHEN A COMPASS NEEDLE POINTS TO ALL DIRECTIONS AT ONCE···IT'S INDICATING SOMETHING LIKE A NEW DIMENSION···*THE BOUNDLESS WORLD OF THE DEAD!* THAT MAY BE WORTH KNOWING···ONCE I'VE TRACKED DOWN THE FIEND!

HOURS LATER···IN A GRIM RETREAT HIDDEN IN THE BROODING WILDERNESS···

WHY DID THAT CREATURE BRING ME TO A GHOULISH PLACE LIKE *THIS* ? THERE'S NOTHING HERE BUT *WOLF SKELETONS*···*SCORES OF THEM!*

AS THE FIRST MURKY LIGHT OF DAWN HOVERS OVER THE FOG-SHROUDED TREES···

NOW I KNOW WHY IT HAS BEEN STARING TOWARD THE EAST···*WAITING FOR THE FIRST SIGN OF SUNRISE!* WHEN A WEREWOLF ATTACKS *THEN*···IT CAN CLAIM THE SPIRIT OF ITS VICTIM!

THEN, PANTING CLOSER···ITS UNHOLY FANGS GLISTENING IN THE SICKLY DAWN···

HUUH··· HUUH···

THAT THING KNOWS I CAN'T ESCAPE! I'M CAUGHT··· *IT'S GOING TO GET ME!*

UNEXPECTEDLY···

BABY···*THAT'S* SOMETHING I INTEND ARGUING ABOUT!

YAAANGH!

POW!

FRANK!

YOU SHOULDN'T HAVE COME HERE, FRANK! HOW WILL WE EVER MANAGE TO GET AWAY ?

THIS VALLEY WAS ONCE A LAKE···AND *HERE'S* WHERE THE WOLVES DROWNED WHEN THEY TRIED TO ESCAPE FROM THE FOREST FIRE! THE MEDICINE MAN'S EVIL SOUL TOOK POSSESSION OF THE WOLVES' SPIRITS···*BUT I'VE FOUND A WAY TO FREE THEM*··· AND DOOM THE FIEND!

6

FRANK...FOR HEAVEN'S SAKE, DON'T STOP *NOW!* IT'S COMING *CLOSER!*

GET A GRIP ON YOUR SELF, HONEY...BECAUSE *PLENTY'S* GOING TO HAPPEN WHEN I SPIN THIS COMPASS NEEDLE!

IN THE NEXT SECOND...THE ENTIRE VALLEY SWIRLS INTO MOTION!

GOOD HEAVENS! THEY'RE WOLF PHANTOMS ---RISING FROM THE SKELETONS!

AROOOO!

AROOOOO!

YARD BY YARD...IN A CLOSING CIRCLE...THE GHOSTLY CREATURES PAD TOWARD THE FIEND THAT HAD EN-SLAVED THEM!

YAANGH!

GARRRGH!

THEN...IN A WRITHING MASS OF FANGS AND FUR...

AAAGH!

FRANK---THEY'RE *TEARING IT APART!*

A MOMENT LATER...THE GHOSTLY PACK HOWLS OFF INTO THE LIMITLESS BYWAYS OF THE BEYOND!

THE FIEND'S GONE...BUT WHAT WILL THE WOODS BE LIKE WITH GHOSTLY WOLVES LURKING AMONG THE TREES?

THEY CAN'T HARM ANYTHING, PHYLLIS! IT TAKES SOMETHING *EVIL* TO MAKE A WEREWOLF ...*AND THE CURSE HAS BEEN LIFTED!*

AROOOO!

YOU *WERE* GOING TO TELL ME ABOUT THE FIEND IN FUR IN FRONT OF THE FIREPLACE TO-NIGHT, FRANK...BUT I KNOW ALL ABOUT IT NOW!

WE MIGHT AS WELL LET THE DATE STAND, HONEY.. BECAUSE THERE'S PLENTY YOU DON'T KNOW ABOUT *ME!*

The END!

2

"True" GHOSTS of HISTORY

The SPECTRAL SLEEPWALKER

IT WAS IN 1177 THAT YOUNG RICHARD THE LION-HEARTED, THEN TRAVELING IN HIS DUCHY OF AQUITAINE, FRANCE, FIRST SET EYES ON THE LOVELY FRENCH GIRL KNOWN AS JEANNE LA BLAZON---

SHE'S THE MOST BEAUTIFUL GIRL I'VE EVER SEEN---I WILL MAKE HER MY QUEEN!

PRINCE RICHARD BEGAN TO COURT JEANNE---BUT ONLY A FEW DAYS AFTER HE HAD FIRST MET HER---

I MUST LEAVE YOU, MY LOVE---TO DO BATTLE WITH KING HENRY OF ENGLAND FOR THE CROWN THAT IS RIGHTLY MINE! BUT I SHALL RETURN FOR YOU---WHEN I AM KING!

I WILL BE WAITING, RICHARD ---ALWAYS!

DAY IN AND DAY OUT, THE LOVELORN JEANNE WALKED THE TOWER D'OURLIAC OUTSIDE THE TOWN OF CARCASSONNE, WAITING FOR WORD FROM HER SWEETHEART---BUT ONE EVENING, A TREACHEROUS KNIGHT-AT-ARMS IN THE EMPLOY OF KING HENRY CREPT UP BEHIND THE GIRL IN AN ATTEMPT TO KIDNAP HER AND HOLD HER AS HOSTAGE---

IN THE ENSUING DESPERATE STRUGGLE---

OHHH!

JEANNE LA BLAZON'S EARTHLY BODY DIED FROM THE FALL---BUT HER SPIRIT STILL LIVES ON! SHE CAN STILL BE SEEN ON SUMMER EVENINGS WALKING ON THE TOWER D'OURLIAC, HER ARMS OUTSTRETCHED AS IF WALKING IN HER SLEEP---OR WAITING FOR HER SWEETHEART!

YES, JEANNE LA BLAZON HAD SAID SHE WOULD WAIT FOREVER---AND SHE STILL WAITS! BUT IF YOU SHOULD EVER VISIT CARCASSONNE AND TRY TO INTERRUPT HER NIGHTLY VIGIL, YOU'LL FIND THAT SHE WALKS RIGHT THROUGH YOU---AND THAT'S EXACTLY WHAT'S HAPPENED TO MANY A PROFESSOR AND EXPLORER OF THE SUPERNATURAL WHO CAME TO EXAMINE THE SPECTRAL SLEEPWALKER!

MON DIEU---IT---IT IS LIKE MIST PASSING---MIST WITH A FAINT ODOR OF MOLD AND DECAY!

From YOUR EDITOR- to YOU!

L F. / O. F. W.

An advertising slogan...a mystical incantation? No...just the initials of the fastest-growing club in the entire world... the organization known as *"Loyal Fans Of FORBIDDEN WORLDS"*!

Yes, with each issue, tens of thousands of enthusiastic new members join the club that's singing the praises of *"Forbidden Worlds"*.., America's magnificent new magazine of the supernatural. And issue No. 4 is just *for you!* You, our loyal readers, have written countless letters telling us the kind of spooky, spine-chilling stories you want us to print...and this issue gives you *just* what you've asked for!

For example, many have requested a tale of fiendish voodoo witchcraft...and *"A Queen for the Voodoo Chief"* is exactly that. Others have begged us for a blood-curdling story of a terrifying monster...and you're sure to get your fill of fear in *"Fiend in Fur"*. Then, for those of you who gloat shiveringly over adventures into the forbidden realm of the living dead, there's *"Whirlpool of Death"*... while those who crave an eerie setting that's literally out-of-this-world will be more than delighted with *"The Doom of the Moonlings"*, surely the weirdest story of this or any year. And last but not least, there's *"House of Horror"*...a ghoulish tale that was written by two members of L. F. / O. F. W. who dared to explore a forbidden world of their own!

But as exciting and suspenseful as this issue of *"Forbidden Worlds"* is, we can promise that each succeeding issue will bring you even *more* spine-tingling chills, hair-raising thrills and shuddery gasps! So, until the next shocking issue comes around, why not form a FORBIDDEN WORLDS CLUB in *your* neighborhood? And don't forget to write and let us know what *you* want to see in future issues. Just address your letters to The Editor, *Forbidden Worlds*, 45, West 45th Street, New York 19, N. Y. Here's what some *other* members of L. F. / O. F. W. have written us recently:

"Dear Editor:-

Wow! What a magazine! It's the best of its kind! Congratulations! I especially enjoyed the story, 'Love of a Vampire'. It combined heart-warming love with fingernail-chewing suspense. And let's hear more of 'Marzo', the Demon of Destruction. It was such a terrifying tale. And the illustrations were, as you might put it, 'out of this world'! But are we readers going to have the same trouble with you as we did with 'Adventures Into The Unknown'? Why, oh, why can't you publish this magazine every month, too?

—Helene Weiss, Manasquan, N. J."

P. S.—I'm overjoyed! 52 whole pages! Keep up the good work!"

"Dear Editor:-

The stories in 'Forbidden Worlds' are fascinating...because they give me the creeps! My favorite ones are those that are true...like 'True Witches of History' and 'The Boy Who Talked With Spirits'. All I can say is that your stories are super!

—Josephine Elias, Pacaima, Calif."

"Dear Editor:-

'Forbidden Worlds' is a spine-tingling magazine. It has thrills, chills, and all the things that accompany a really good magazine. 'Forbidden Worlds' is wonderful competition to your already great magazine, 'Adventures Into The Unknown'!

—Ken Jargowsky, Woodbine, N. J."

Don't YOU miss "Adventures Into The Unknown"!

WHIRLPOOL of DEATH

WHAT POWERS CAN BE RELEASED BY THE RAGING SEA--WHAT KIND OF EVIL STRONGHOLD LIES BEYOND THE FOG THAT SHROUDS THE BRISTLING WAVES? ONLY THOSE WHO HAVE PLUNGED DIZZILY TOWARD DEATH CAN KNOW THE ANSWER --WHEN SPECTRAL RIDERS LEAD THEM TO A WHIRLPOOL AT THE EDGE OF DARKNESS!

ONE NIGHT-- AS A HOWLING ATLANTIC STORM BATTERS THE NEW ENGLAND COAST--

YE GODS-- THE SAIL! WE'LL NEVER MAKE SHORE, NANCY!

THIS IS NO *ORDINARY* STORM-- IT'S AS IF THE SEA AND WIND ARE MERGING INTO A FIENDISH THING THAT HUNGERS FOR OUR LIVES!

I NEVER HEARD YOU TALK LIKE *THAT* BEFORE, REX! NOW I KNOW THERE'S NO HOPE -- *WE'RE GOING* TO DROWN!

1

I WON'T TRY TO KID YOU -- IT LOOKS BAD! BUT JUST THE SAME -- SOMETHING TELLS ME WE'LL COME OUT OF THIS *ALIVE!*

LISTEN TO THE WIND, REX! IT'S NOT HOWLING NOW -- IT'S *LAUGHING* -- JUST AS IF IT HEARD YOU!

LOUDER AND LOUDER RISES THE MOCKING CHORUS -- AND FOR A SPLIT SECOND -- THE BLACK CLOUDS PART BEFORE THE RUSH OF SPECTRAL RIDERS --

HO-HOOO!
HO-HOOO

THERE THEY ARE -- WHAT ARE THEY, REX? WHY ARE THEY APPEARING TO *US?*

GRAB SOMETHING -- WE'RE GOING OVER!

IN THE NEXT SECOND --

CRASH!

WITH THE SEA A FOAMING FURY AROUND THEM -- NUMBING AS LIQUID ICE --

YOU SAID WE'D COME OUT OF THIS ALIVE, REX -- BUT WE WON'T -- WE *CAN'T!*

AFRAID NOT, HONEY! IT'S HOPELESS -- I *CAN'T* KEEP US AFLOAT!

STRUGGLING WEAKLY -- REX AND NANCY SINK INTO THE CHILL GREEN DEPTHS --

THEN, WITH THEIR LUNGS BURSTING IN A FINAL STRUGGLE -- THE DROWNING PAIR ARE SWEPT INTO A HISSING VORTEX -- A CLAMMY WHIRLPOOL MIDWAY BETWEEN SEA AND AIR!

SECONDS OR CENTURIES MAY HAVE PASSED-- BEFORE THE EDDYING CLUTCH OF THE SEA GAVE WAY TO AN ENDLESS HAZE --

THE MIST IS ALL AROUND US, REX! I'VE NEVER FELT LIKE *THIS* BEFORE-- *DID* WE DROWN?

WE *COULDN'T* HAVE! LOOK-- THERE'S A SHIP COMING!

AS THE FOG-SHROUDED HULK DRIFTS CLOSER --

LOOKS LIKE A DERELICT-- BUT IT CERTAINLY IS A LIFESAVER TO *US!*

I DON'T KNOW WHAT TO THINK! IT SEEMS TO BE SUCH A *STRANGE* SHIP-- AND WHAT ABOUT THOSE HIDEOUS RIDERS WE SAW IN THE SKY?

I READ ABOUT THEM ONCE-- *THE WILD HUNTSMEN!* IT DOESN'T EXPLAIN WHY *WE* SAW THEM, THOUGH-- BECAUSE ACCORDING TO AN ANCIENT VIKING LEGEND-- *THEY'RE SUPPOSED TO ESCORT THE DEAD!*

SLOWLY, THE NIGHT SKY SCUDS BEFORE THE STORM--AND IN THE GREY, UNWORLDLY PALL --

REX-- DID YOU SAY VIKING?

GOOD LORD--IT'S A VIKING DRAGON SHIP.. *THE TYPE USED A THOUSAND YEARS AGO!*

THEN WE CAN STOP GUESSING, REX! IF IT'S A SHIP OF THE DEAD-- IT CAME FOR *US!*

BUT SUPPOSE IT'S CARRYING SOME- THING *ELSE?* THERE'S WHAT I MEAN -- *THAT GLOW AMIDSHIPS!*

GREAT GUNS--IT'S THE BODY OF A VIKING WARRIOR!

ANCIENT WARRIOR-- ANCIENT SHIP--GOOD HEAVENS-- *HOW LONG HAS HE BEEN DEAD?*

3

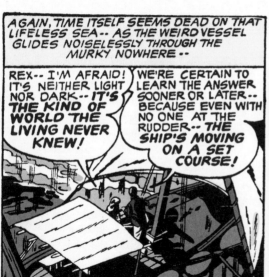

AGAIN, TIME ITSELF SEEMS DEAD ON THAT LIFELESS SEA -- AS THE WEIRD VESSEL GLIDES NOISELESSLY THROUGH THE MURKY NOWHERE --

REX -- I'M AFRAID! IT'S NEITHER LIGHT NOR DARK -- IT'S *THE KIND OF WORLD THE LIVING NEVER KNEW!*

WE'RE CERTAIN TO LEARN THE ANSWER SOONER OR LATER -- BECAUSE EVEN WITH NO ONE AT THE RUDDER -- *THE SHIP'S MOVING ON A SET COURSE!*

SUDDENLY, LOOMING FROM THE PEARLY EMPTINESS --

WE'RE NEARING LAND, NANCY -- *SEE IT?*

THE MIST SEEMS TO BE BRIGHTENING -- JUST LIKE SUNLIGHT COMING THROUGH STAINED GLASS! THERE'S *STILL* SOMETHING AWFULLY WEIRD ABOUT THIS, REX!

AS THE VESSEL HEADS SHOREWARD --

HEAVENS, REX -- *THEY'RE THE WILD HUNTSMEN!*

I DON'T KNOW WHO THE GIRL IS -- BUT WE'D BETTER KEEP OUT OF SIGHT UNTIL WE FIND OUT!

WANDERING SPIRIT OF EVIL -- *ARISE!* THIS IS YOUR LAST VOYAGE -- THIS IS YOUR LAST DARK HAVEN -- *THULE!*

A SECOND PASSES -- AND THEN, AS IRON ARMOR RINGS AGAINST THE WEATHERED DECK --

OH!

CLANG!

HOW CAN HE MOVE, REX -- WHEN HE'S *LIFELESS* -- WHEN HE'S BEEN THAT WAY FOR *CENTURIES?*

KEEP YOUR HEAD, SWEET-HEART -- I'M BEGINNING TO REALIZE WHAT IT'LL MEAN IF WE'RE DISCOVERED!

4

WHY DO YOU HESITATE? YOU WERE EVIL IN LIFE--WHAT MORE CAN YOU ASK THAN TO BE EVIL IN DEATH?

THERE ARE OTHER DEAD ABOARD THE DRAGON SHIP, HELA-- DEAD WHO DO NOT BELONG TO US!

DEAD! NO--NO-- WE CAN'T BE!

THIS WON'T BE GOOD, HONEY-- HE'S SPOTTED US!

THEN--MIDWAY IN A SAVAGE RUSH--

POW!

NOW I SEE WHAT THIS MEANS, NANCY! WE'RE IN A STRUGGLE BETWEEN LIFE AND DEATH-- WE'VE GOT TO ESCAPE!

NEVER--NEVER! SEIZE THEM, GRIM WARRIORS-- LET THEM LEARN WHAT IT MEANS TO VENTURE INTO THULE!

WAM!

FOR A MOMENT, REX WITHSTANDS THE BELLOWING RUSH-- BUT IN AN OVER- WHELMING ATTACK--

HO-HOO! HELA HAS SPOKEN-- HELA-- THE DAUGHTER OF DOOM!

5

193

A MOMENT LATER--

YOU HAVE MUCH MORE TO LEARN ABOUT HELA! I AM THE VERY PRIESTESS OF PERDITION-- RULER OF THE HIDDEN REACHES OF THULE-- **WHERE THE SPIRITS OF VIKINGS WHO GAVE THEMSELVES TO EVIL ARE HARBORED FOREVER!**

THERE'S NO USE ASKING WHO YOU ARE, HELA! YOU'RE BOUNDLESSLY EVIL-- AS ONLY A CREATURE BEYOND LIFE **CAN** BE!

MURDERERS--WIZARDS--TRAITORS-- NONE OF THEM COULD BE BURIED IN HALLOWED VIKING SOIL! THEIR BODIES WERE PLACED IN DRAGON SHIPS AND SET ADRIFT-- MOVED BY UNFELT WINDS AND UNSEEN CURRENTS-- UNTIL THEY REACHED THE UNCHARTED REALM **YOU** HAVE TRESSPASSED UPON!

YOU HAVEN'T ANY CLAIM ON **US!** WE MAY NOT BE ALIVE-- BUT WE DON'T BELONG **HERE!**

THAT IS TRUE OF **MANY** OF THE SPIRITS WHO WANDER TO THULE-- AND I WILL SHOW YOU WHAT IS FATED FOR **THEM!**

THEN-- AS IF THE GHOSTLY SEA WAS THE LAIR OF A MONSTER ROARING FOR PREY--

GREAT GUNS-- **WHAT'S THAT?**

ARRRGH!

BELOW--IN A HEAVING EXPANSE OF SPINNING FOAM--

THE WHIRLPOOL OF DEATH! THERE YOU WILL REMAIN FOREVER-- SPUN TO THE BOILING DEPTHS AND FLUNG UP AGAIN-- **OVER AND OVER AGAIN UNTIL THE END OF TIME!**

ARRGH!

FOR A SECOND, NANCY STARES DOWN AT THE SKIMMING FOAM-- AND THEN--

REX-- I'M GETTING DIZZY-- EVERYTHING'S TURNING BLACK!

WATCH OUT-- YOU'RE GOING TO FALL!

6

HAA! HA! HA!

SPLASH!

DEEPER AND DEEPER PLUNGE THE SWIRLING FIGURES SWEPT INTO THE BLACK AND GLISTENING VORTEX --

REX--WHERE ARE YOU? I'M CHOKING -- I'M FALLING -- *DON'T LEAVE ME ALONE!*

SUDDENLY-- A FLOOD OF LIGHT LIKE A SHATTERED RAINBOW --

REX -- REX! THAT HORRIBLE WHIRLPOOL WAS DRAWING ME UNDER!

EASY, SWEETHEART! I'M HERE-- *AND WE'RE SAFE!*

OF COURSE, THERE *AREN'T* ANY WHIRLPOOLS IN THESE WATERS-- BUT LOSING AND REGAINING CONSCIOUSNESS OFTEN PRODUCES A *SPINNING IMAGE* TO A DROWNING PERSON! I DIDN'T THINK YOU TWO WOULD SQUEAK THROUGH-- BUT WE MANAGED IT AFTER AN HOUR'S HARD WORK WITH A PULMOTOR!

IT'S THE CLOSEST THING TO A MIRACLE *I'LL* EVER EXPERIENCE! WE MUST HAVE BEEN MILES FROM SHORE-- HOW'D YOU HAPPEN TO FIND US?

YOU CAN THANK THE STORM FOR THAT! THE WAVES RIPPED UP THE BEACH AND UNCOVERED SOME KIND OF *OLD VESSEL* -- SWEEPING IT SEAWARD! WE WERE TRYING TO FIND IT WHEN WE SPOTTED YOUR BOAT SINKING-- AND LEFT OFF TO SEARCH FOR *YOU!*

AN OLD VESSEL-- *REALLY* OLD?

WELL-- OUR LOOKOUT SWEARS HE COULD MAKE OUT A DRAGON'S HEAD ON THE PROW! WHO KNOWS-- MAYBE IT *WAS* A VIKING SHIP THAT DRIFTED ACROSS THE ATLANTIC CENTURIES AGO-- AND GOT BURIED IN THE SAND!

The End

7

The UNDYING

GRAHAM WAS SURE that he had seen the last of his enemy! He stood staring at the bubbling quicksand, his breath coming in choking gasps, his face a rage-convulsed mask.

He had struggled furiously with young Evans, forcing him back into the bog. The quicksand had carried him down, and a deep hush had descended on the forest.

Evans was dead in the bog. He would never rise from the clinging mud. Only one arm remained above the quicksand, thrust up into the fog like a living grave marker. *Living?* Nonsense! The arm was as dead as the rest of Evans! How could Graham doubt it? So what did it matter that Evans seemed to be shaking his fist in *undying* hatred at the man who had robbed him of his life?

Graham turned and went stumbling back to his car through the dense undergrowth, driven by a sense of terror that made no sense at all. Surely he was in no danger! No one had seen him grappling with Evans. The bog was miles from the nearest farmhouse and if he kept his head and

drove swiftly away, the finger of suspicion would never point at him. The *finger* of suspicion! What a crazy thought!

The car stood in deep shadows at the edge of a narrow dirt road. The misty white fingers of the fog seemed to claw and pluck at the windshield as Graham bent above the wheel. Fingers again! Something primitive and menacing was at work in him, turning all of his thoughts back to the bog!

He didn't see the dead, white hand until the door of the car opened with a click, and a coldness swirled around his spine. Out of the fog it came, creeping straight toward him. And there was a terrible strength in the hand as it fastened on Graham's ankle and dragged him screaming from the car.

Straight back to the bog it dragged him, ignoring his babblings and wild pleadings. And the last thing Graham saw on earth was the quicksand bubbling up again, gurgling and churning around his own sinking shoulders. Then it settled to rest, and a deep hush descended on the forest.

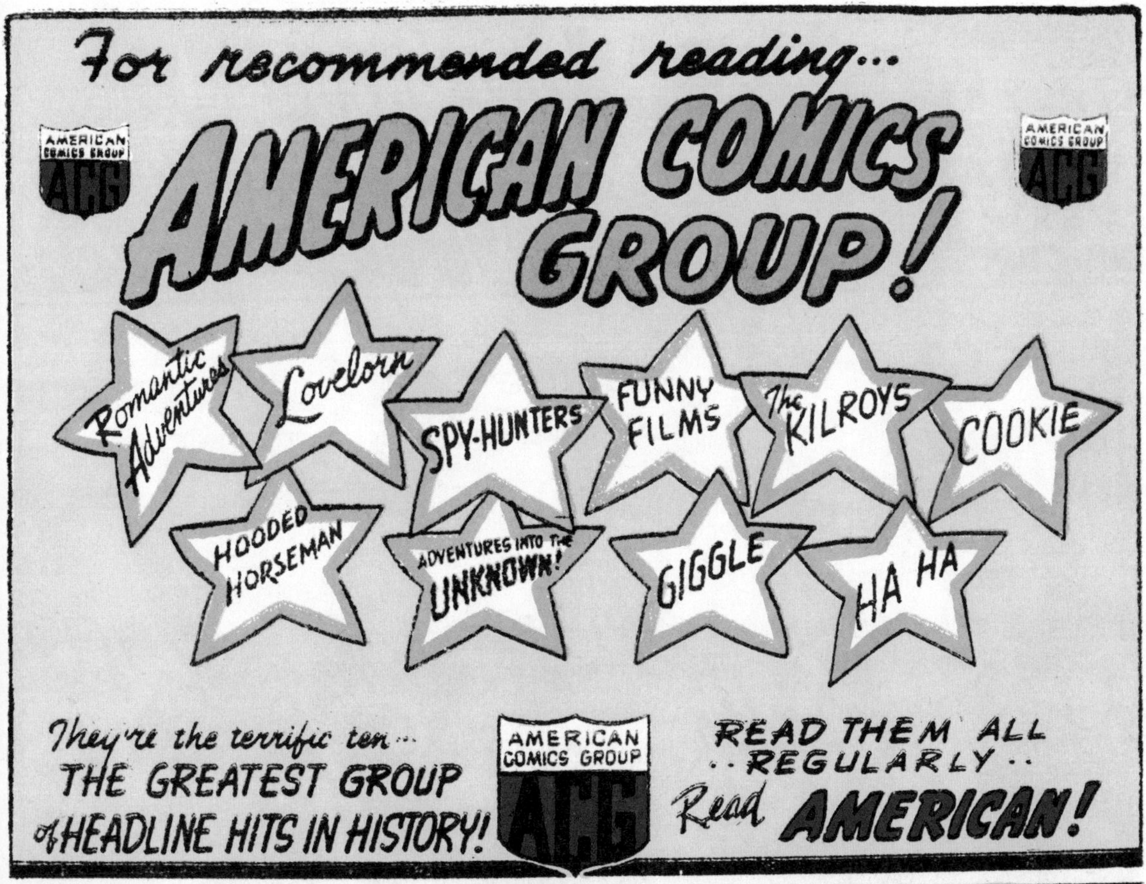

For recommended reading...
AMERICAN COMICS GROUP
ACG
AMERICAN COMICS GROUP!
Romantic Adventures
Lovelorn
SPY-HUNTERS
FUNNY FILMS
The KILROYS
COOKIE
HOODED HORSEMAN
ADVENTURES INTO THE UNKNOWN!
GIGGLE
HA HA
They're the terrific ten...
THE GREATEST GROUP of HEADLINE HITS IN HISTORY!
READ THEM ALL ..REGULARLY..
Read AMERICAN!

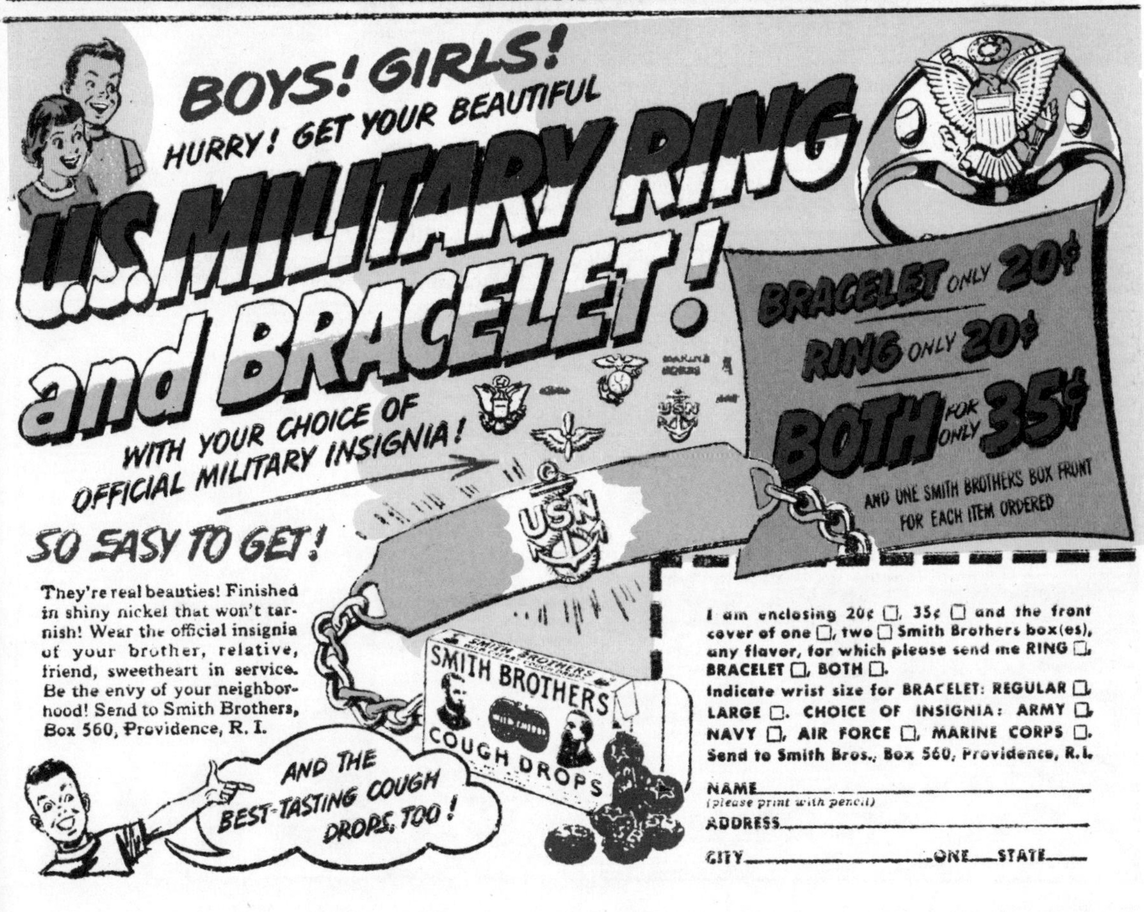

BOYS! GIRLS!
HURRY! GET YOUR BEAUTIFUL
U.S. MILITARY RING and BRACELET!
WITH YOUR CHOICE OF OFFICIAL MILITARY INSIGNIA!
BRACELET ONLY 20¢
RING ONLY 20¢
BOTH FOR ONLY 35¢
AND ONE SMITH BROTHERS BOX FRONT FOR EACH ITEM ORDERED
USN
SO EASY TO GET!
They're real beauties! Finished in shiny nickel that won't tarnish! Wear the official insignia of your brother, relative, friend, sweetheart in service. Be the envy of your neighborhood! Send to Smith Brothers, Box 560, Providence, R. I.
SMITH BROTHERS
COUGH DROPS
AND THE BEST-TASTING COUGH DROPS, TOO!
I am enclosing 20¢ ☐, 35¢ ☐ and the front cover of one ☐, two ☐ Smith Brothers box(es), any flavor, for which please send me RING ☐, BRACELET ☐, BOTH ☐.
Indicate wrist size for BRACELET: REGULAR ☐, LARGE ☐. CHOICE OF INSIGNIA: ARMY ☐, NAVY ☐, AIR FORCE ☐, MARINE CORPS ☐.
Send to Smith Bros., Box 560, Providence, R.I.
NAME
(please print with pencil)
ADDRESS
CITY ONE STATE

THE DOOM OF THE MOONLINGS

How many millions of midnights has the moon floated across the inky sky-- how many forms of horror and evil has it watched skulking through the shadows of the sleeping world? SELENA knows the answer-- SELENA, whose sultry eyes mock the limits of earthbound terror-- whose lips seek release from THE DOOM OF THE MOONLINGS!

Late one night, the full moon looks down with an unblinking stare upon a sandy headland-- a point of land peopled by only a single couple-- a man and a girl fated for a night of unmatched terror!

I SUPPOSE PEOPLE WOULD THINK WE'RE WHACKY, SWEETHEART-- SITTING LIKE THIS HOUR AFTER HOUR!

I DON'T CARE WHAT ANYONE THINKS, BOB! WITH OUR HONEYMOON JUST A FEW DAYS OFF, ALL I WANT IS TO BE ALONE WITH YOU-- MILES FROM NOWHERE-- LIKE THIS!

1

ONLY MIDNIGHT? CUDDLE UP AGAINST MY SHOULDER, HONEY-- AND WE'LL DREAM A LITTLE LONGER!

WONDER WHAT'S HAPPENED TO THE MOON? THE GLOW SEEMED TO FADE DURING THE PAST FEW MINUTES, BUT NOW THE MOON'S GONE COMPLETELY-- AND NOT A CLOUD IN THE SKY!

IT'S AN ECLIPSE, JOYCE! NOTICE HOW THE GROWING DARKNESS MAKES YOUR OTHER SENSES MORE ACUTE?

YES, IT'S ALMOST AS IF I CAN HEAR SOMETHING! IN FACT, NOW I'M SURE OF IT-- A DEEP DRONING NOISE FROM THE DIRECTION OF THE MOON!

IN THE NEXT INSTANT, LIGHT AND SOUND ARE FUSED AS A DAZZLING ROAR SURGES DOWN-- THUDDING AGAINST THE SEA AND THE SAND--

IT'S A BEAM, BOB-- WITH SOMETHING MOVING INSIDE!

TAKE IT EASY-- IT CAN'T BE ANYTHING SUPERNATURAL!

THEN--

CRAK!

GOOD HEAVENS!

THEY DON'T EXIST, JOYCE-- IT'S AN ILLUSION-- OR SOME KIND OF WEIRD TRICK!

HUMANS! SEIZE THEM, MOONLINGS!

AS THE OUTLANDISH CREATURES CLOSE IN--

GREAT GUNS-- THEY ARE REAL! JOYCE-- RUN FOR THE CAR!

POW!

2

199

DO YOU THINK YOU CAN ESCAPE FROM *ME!* I AM MORE THAN HUMAN-- I AM *SELENA*-- QUEEN OF THE *MOONLINGS!*

IT'S NO USE-- I CAN'T SHAKE 'EM OFF! *THEY'VE GOT US!*

WITH ALL RETREAT BLOCKED BY THE UNHOLY THRONG--

I'VE OFTEN HEARD THAT THE MOON IS UNDER AN EVIL SWAY-- BUT WHAT ARE YOU DOING *HERE?*

ON *EARTH*-- THE NIGHT SPIRITS PREY ON HUMANS IN THEIR SEARCH FOR *LIFE!* WE SEEK EXACTLY THE OPPOSITE-- *DEATH!*

ONLY *THEN* WILL WE BECOME TRUE PHANTOMS AND ABLE TO SUBJECT THE EARTH TO THE DARK POWERS OF MY MOONLINGS! WE'VE BIDED OUR TIME FOR CENTURIES FOR A *MIDNIGHT ECLIPSE* -- WHEN MY MOON CHANNEL SWEEPS THE AREA DARKENED BY THE BROODING SATELLITE -- *GIVING US A DAZZLING PATHWAY THROUGH SPACE!*

GOOD GOSH! *THIS* IS THE ONLY PLACE WHERE THE PATH OF THE ECLIPSE TOUCHES LAND -- THE *REST* OF IT CURVES OUT OVER THE OCEAN!

YES-- AND THAT MEANS THAT *YOU* ARE OUR ONLY CAPTIVES! WE WILL CARRY YOU TO THE MOON FOR SACRIFICE -- DEATH WILL ENTER MY SINISTER REALM FOR THE FIRST TIME -- AND *END THE MOONLINGS' CURSE OF HALF LIFE!*

BLACK SPIRIT OF THE COSMOS-- SELENA SPEAKS! LET THE MOON CHANNEL RETURN -- AND SWEEP US THROUGH SPACE!

THEN, BRILLIANT AS THE HIDDEN SUN-- STRONGER THAN A THOUSAND CYCLONES-- THE WEIRD BEAM BORES INTO THE DARKNESS!

BOB! WE'RE BEING CARRIED AWAY FROM THE EARTH!

FASTER THAN THOUGHT ITSELF-- THE SHAFT REACHES THE SCARRED AND PITTED SURFACE OF THE MOON!

CRAK

THERE ARE DOZENS OF OTHER CRATERS BELOW, BOB! LOOK AT THEM-- GLISTENING LIKE JET--- AND ALL OF THEM BLACK, EVIL!

MAKE THE MOST OF THIS FIRST GLIMPSE OF THE MOON-- FOR IT'S THE LAST THING YOUR EYES WILL LOOK UPON!

BOB-- WE'VE GOT TO DO SOMETHING-- ANYTHING THAT WILL LET US LIVE!

WISH WE COULD, HONEY-- BUT THIS LOOKS LIKE THE END! I'M NOT AFRAID TO DIE-- BUT WHEN I DO--

--IT'S GOING TO BE ON MY OWN TERMS!

BOB! NO-- NO-- WHY DID YOU DO IT?

AAAGHHHH!

4

201

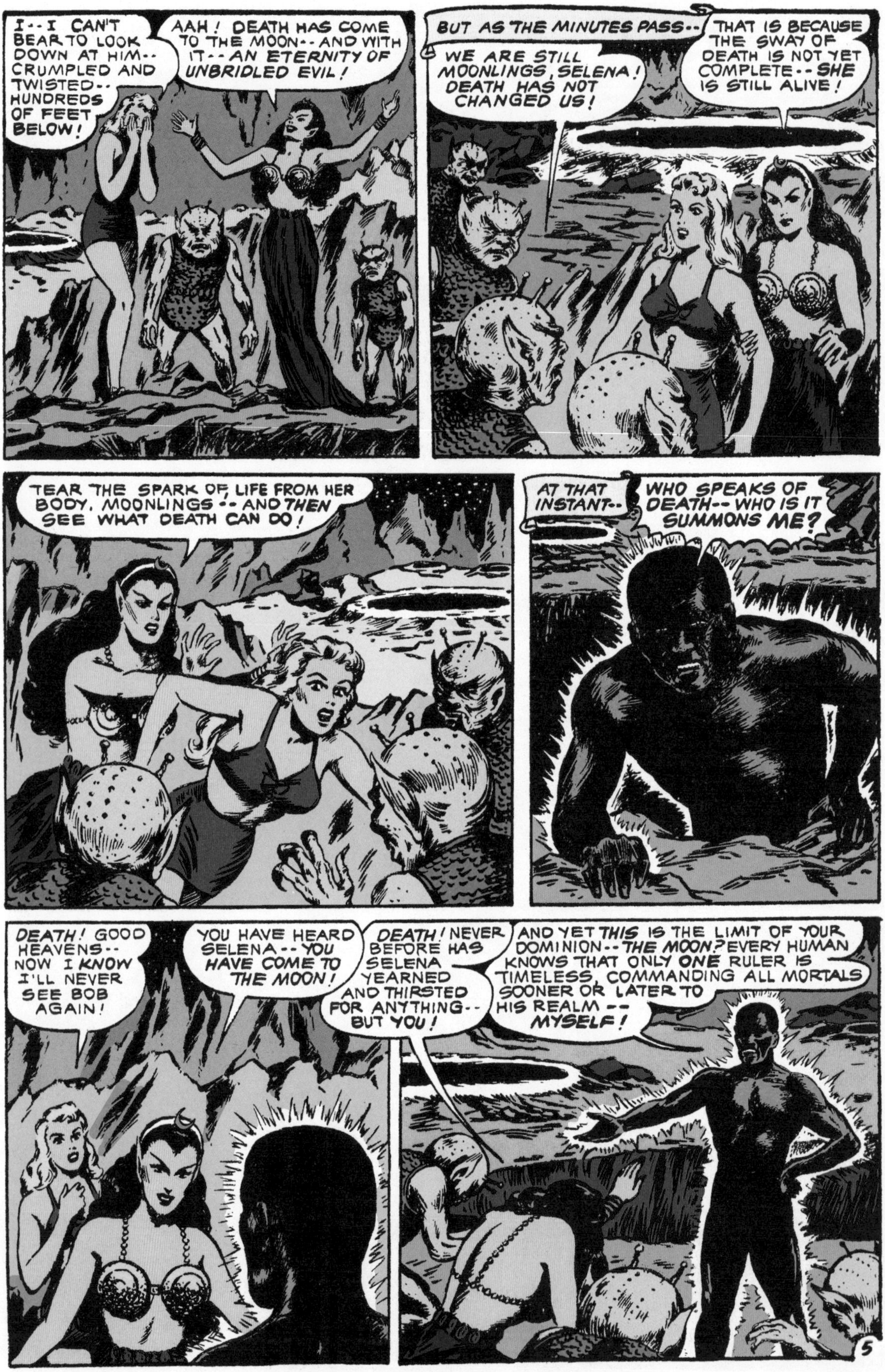
I--I CAN'T BEAR TO LOOK DOWN AT HIM--CRUMPLED AND TWISTED--HUNDREDS OF FEET BELOW!
AAH! DEATH HAS COME TO THE MOON--AND WITH IT--AN ETERNITY OF UNBRIDLED EVIL!
BUT AS THE MINUTES PASS--
WE ARE STILL MOONLINGS, SELENA! DEATH HAS NOT CHANGED US!
THAT IS BECAUSE THE SWAY OF DEATH IS NOT YET COMPLETE--SHE IS STILL ALIVE!
TEAR THE SPARK OF LIFE FROM HER BODY, MOONLINGS--AND THEN SEE WHAT DEATH CAN DO!
AT THAT INSTANT--
WHO SPEAKS OF DEATH--WHO IS IT SUMMONS ME?
DEATH! GOOD HEAVENS--NOW I KNOW I'LL NEVER SEE BOB AGAIN!
YOU HAVE HEARD SELENA--YOU HAVE COME TO THE MOON!
DEATH! NEVER BEFORE HAS SELENA YEARNED AND THIRSTED FOR ANYTHING--BUT YOU!
AND YET THIS IS THE LIMIT OF YOUR DOMINION--THE MOON? EVERY HUMAN KNOWS THAT ONLY ONE RULER IS TIMELESS, COMMANDING ALL MORTALS SOONER OR LATER TO HIS REALM--MYSELF!
5

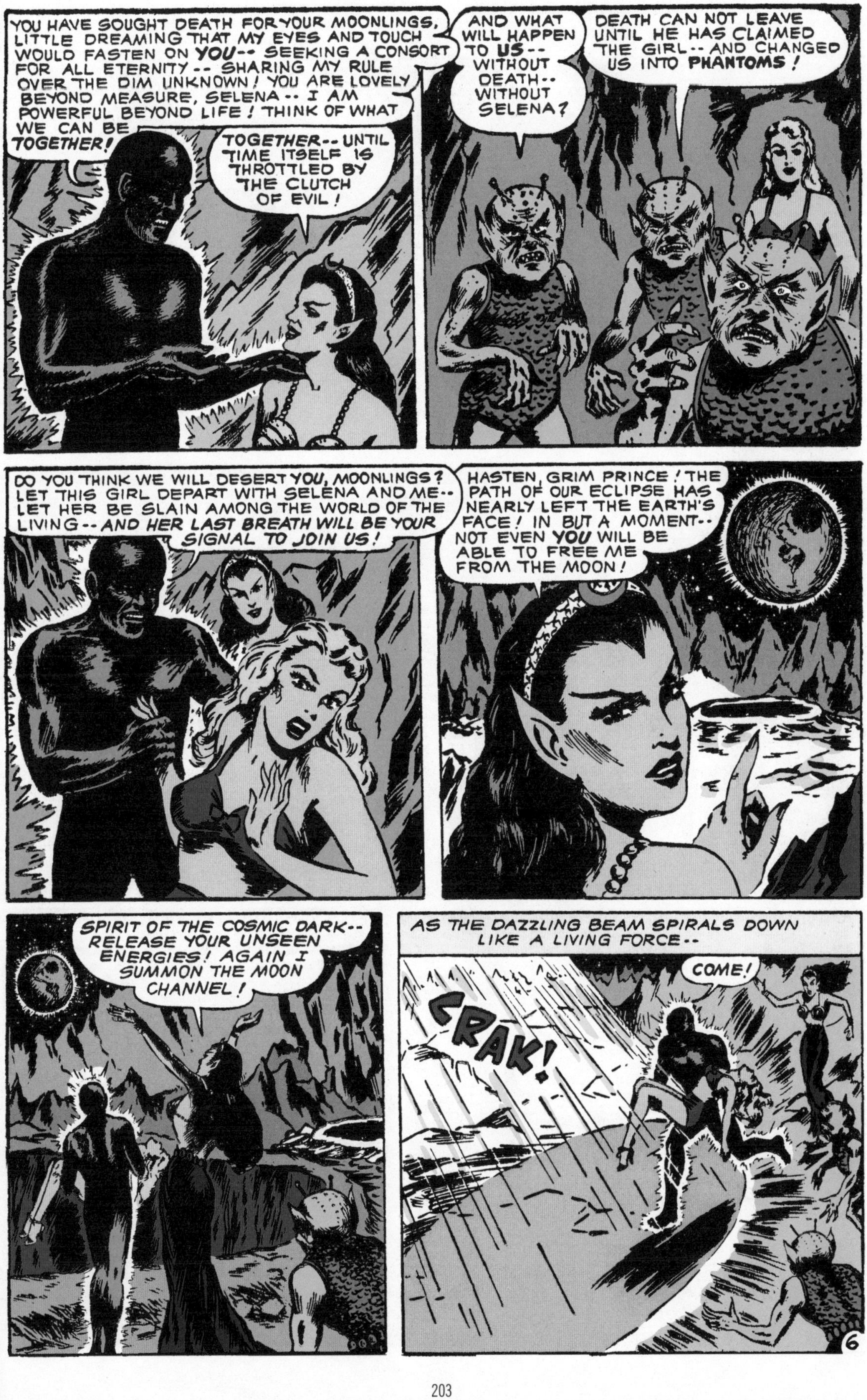
YOU HAVE SOUGHT DEATH FOR YOUR MOONLINGS, LITTLE DREAMING THAT MY EYES AND TOUCH WOULD FASTEN ON YOU-- SEEKING A CONSORT FOR ALL ETERNITY -- SHARING MY RULE OVER THE DIM UNKNOWN! YOU ARE LOVELY BEYOND MEASURE, SELENA -- I AM POWERFUL BEYOND LIFE! THINK OF WHAT WE CAN BE TOGETHER!
TOGETHER-- UNTIL TIME ITSELF IS THROTTLED BY THE CLUTCH OF EVIL!
AND WHAT WILL HAPPEN TO US -- WITHOUT DEATH -- WITHOUT SELENA?
DEATH CAN NOT LEAVE UNTIL HE HAS CLAIMED THE GIRL -- AND CHANGED US INTO PHANTOMS!
DO YOU THINK WE WILL DESERT YOU, MOONLINGS? LET THIS GIRL DEPART WITH SELENA AND ME -- LET HER BE SLAIN AMONG THE WORLD OF THE LIVING -- AND HER LAST BREATH WILL BE YOUR SIGNAL TO JOIN US!
HASTEN, GRIM PRINCE! THE PATH OF OUR ECLIPSE HAS NEARLY LEFT THE EARTH'S FACE! IN BUT A MOMENT -- NOT EVEN YOU WILL BE ABLE TO FREE ME FROM THE MOON!
SPIRIT OF THE COSMIC DARK -- RELEASE YOUR UNSEEN ENERGIES! AGAIN I SUMMON THE MOON CHANNEL!
AS THE DAZZLING BEAM SPIRALS DOWN LIKE A LIVING FORCE --
COME!
CRAK!
6

DEATH--WAIT! THE ECLIPSE HAS RUN ITS COURSE -- I'VE LOST MY CHANCE -- I'M DOOMED TO REMAIN ON THE MOON FOR ANOTHER UNENDING AGE!

THEN-- WITH SELENA'S BESEECHING VOICE TRAILING INTO THE LUNAR NIGHT --

DEATH-- COME BACK! COME BACK!

SECONDS LATER-- AS THE BEAM REACHES THE EARTH--

I'M NOT GOING TO TRY TO ESCAPE! NOW THAT YOU'VE CLAIMED BOB-- LIFE MEANS NOTHING TO ME!

SUDDENLY-- IN A FLOOD OF YELLOW MOONLIGHT--

I WAS HOPING YOU COULD HAVE GUESSED SOONER, HONEY! I KNOW WHAT YOU'VE BEEN THROUGH-- BUT I COULDN'T LET ON IT WAS ME ALL THE WHILE-- DISGUISED!

BOB!

SURE, I TOPPLED HUNDREDS OF FEET-- BUT GRAVITY BEING WHAT IT IS ON THE MOON-- I LANDED LIKE A FEATHER! IT WAS AN EASY MATTER TO COVER MY ENTIRE BODY WITH TAR FROM ONE OF THE SMALL CRATERS-- AND I KNEW I'D LOOK LIKE SOMETHING FROM THE PITS OF HADES! IT WAS A CONVINCING DISGUISE UNTIL WE ENTERED THE MOON CHANNEL-- AND THEN IT WAS SWEPT AWAY BY THE VELOCITY OF OUR FLIGHT!

AS FOR SELENA-- WE WON'T HAVE TO WORRY ABOUT HER UNTIL THE NEXT MIDNIGHT ECLIPSE -- AND THAT'S 3,000 YEARS FROM NOW!

OH, DARLING-- NOW THAT WE'RE TOGETHER-- I WON'T WORRY ABOUT IT UNTIL THEN!

THE END

7

HOUSE of HORROR

THIS MAGAZINE GOES TO GREAT LENGTHS, GREAT EXPENSE TO FERRET OUT THE MOST FASCINATING AND EERIEST STORIES OF ADVENTURES INTO THE FORBIDDEN REALMS OF THE *SUPER-NATURAL!* BUT HERE'S AN ASTOUNDING CASE THAT WAS PRACTICALLY DUMPED INTO OUR LAPS BY TWO OF OUR FAITHFUL READERS, *ALICE CARTER* AND *KEN BAINBRIDGE*---WHO HAD THE GRIT AND COURAGE TO MAKE THEIR *OWN* EXPLORATION OF A FORBIDDING *HOUSE OF HORROR!*

TWO APPLICANTS HERE TO SEE YOU ABOUT JOBS, SIR--- THEY SAY THEY'D LIKE TO WORK FOR *"FORBIDDEN WORLDS"* AS RESEARCHERS OR INVESTI-GATORS!

HMM, THE LAST TWO INVEST-IGATORS I SENT OUT ON THAT REPORTED GHOST CASE SEEM TO HAVE VAN-ISHED INTO THIN AIR, WITHOUT LEAVING A TRACE ---SO I CAN CERTAINLY USE TWO NEW RESEARCHERS! SEND THEM IN, PLEASE!

WE WERE THRILLED BEYOND WORDS BY THE FIRST COUPLE OF ISSUES OF *"FORBID-DEN WORLDS"*, SIR---AND NOTHING WOULD MAKE US HAPPIER THAN TO WORK FOR SUCH A WON-DERFUL MAGAZINE!

WE'RE TAKING UP RESEARCH AND INVESTIGATIVE PROCED-URE IN COLLEGE---AS WELL AS READING EVERY BOOK ON THE SUPERNATURAL AND THE OCCULT THAT WE CAN LAY OUR HANDS ON! WE HOPE *THAT* QUALIFIES US TO WORK FOR YOU!

WELL, YOU'VE APPARENTLY GOT *ONE* IMPORTANT QUALIFICATION FOR WORKING ON *"FORBIDDEN WORLDS"*--A LOVE OF THE WEIRD AND THE SUPERNATURAL! BUT THIS MAGAZINE EMPLOYS ONLY THE BEST AND MOST EXPERIENCED RESEARCHERS--AND INVESTIGATING THE WORLD OF THE SUPERNATURAL REQUIRES *MORE* THAN MERE STUDY! A GOOD RESEARCHER HAS TO HAVE THE ABILITY AND DETERMINATION TO TRACK DOWN LEADS INTO THE FORBIDDEN REALMS OF THE OCCULT AND TO FOLLOW THROUGH NO MATTER *WHERE* THE TRAIL MAY LEAD OR *HOW* DANGEROUS THE PURSUIT MAY BE!

AND I COULDN'T POSSIBLY HIRE YOU UNTIL YOU'VE SHOWN ME EVIDENCE THAT *YOU* HAVE THE NECESSARY ABILITY AND DETERMINATION! I'M SORRY...

NOT HALF AS SORRY AS *WE* ARE, SIR! BUT WE...WE UNDERSTAND!

HE WAS RIGHT, KEN-- WE'RE SO INEXPERIENCED WE WOULDN'T EVEN KNOW WHERE TO *START* AN INVESTIGATION INTO THE OCCULT!

YEAH---AND THERE'S NO SENSE IN EVEN *TRYING* TO LOOK FOR SUPERNATURAL PHENOMENA IN NEW YORK! IT'S SUCH A PROSAIC, MATTER-OF-FACT CITY--*NOTHING* WEIRD OR UNCANNY EVER HAPPENS HERE!

WAIT, KEN--THE OLD DUNSTAN HOUSE--MAYBE *THAT'S* A PLACE WORTH INVESTIGATING!

I REMEMBER READING ABOUT IT! NO ONE HAS SEEN THE OLD DUNSTAN COUPLE FOR 20-ODD YEARS, AND NO ONE HAS ENTERED THE HOUSE IN ALL THAT TIME! A DELIVERY BOY LEAVES GROCERIES EACH MORNING, AND THAT'S THE ONLY CONTACT ANYONE HAS HAD WITH THEM!

WHAT'S SO SUPERNATURAL ABOUT *THAT?* THEY'RE JUST A COUPLE OF HERMITS WHO WANT NOTHING TO DO WITH THE WORLD!

WELL, DR. DUNSTAN WAS ONE OF THE MOST FAMOUS BRAIN SPECIALISTS IN THE COUNTRY---AND HE WAS SUPPOSED TO HAVE BEEN VERY ILL WHEN HE BOARDED HIMSELF UP IN THAT HOUSE AT THE AGE OF 89 WITH HIS WIFE-- *20 YEARS AGO!*

GOSH, ALICE, THAT WOULD MAKE HIM *109*--IF HE'S STILL ALIVE!

EXACTLY! AND IT'S HARD TO BELIEVE A MAN AS ILL AS HE WAS COULD LIVE SO LONG---UNLESS HE FOUND THE *SECRET OF LIFE AFTER DEATH!*

HMM, THAT *IS* A THEORY TO WORK ON--JUST THE KIND OF STUFF THAT *"FORBIDDEN WORLDS"* MIGHT BE INTERESTED IN! BUT--IT MIGHT BE KIND OF RISKY TO GET INTO THE HOUSE AND TRACK THIS DOWN!

AFRAID?

ME--AFRAID? I'LL MEET YOU HERE AT MIDNIGHT, ALICE--- AND THEN WE'LL *SEE!*

IN THE DEAD OF MIDNIGHT...

I...I DON'T LIKE THE IDEA OF BREAKING INTO THE HOUSE, ALICE! AFTER ALL IT'S AGAINST THE LAW!

SHHH! LOOK, KEN!

THAT OUGHTA MAKE A BIG ENOUGH HOLE TA CRAWL THROUGH!

YEAH---AN' WE OUGHTA FIND A *FORTUNE* IN HERE, IF WHAT THE PAPERS SAY IS RIGHT! KEEP YER GAT HANDY IN CASE THE TWO OLD GEEZERS PUT UP A FUSS!

AS THE BURGLARS DISAPPEAR INTO THE HOUSE...

LISTEN--THAT THUD---IT SOUNDS AS IF SOMEONE WAS JUST HIT WITH A BLACKJACK OR GUN! COME ON---IT'S NOT AGAINST THE LAW TO TRY TO STOP A ROBBERY OR MURDER!

I GUESS YOU'RE RIGHT--THAT OLD COUPLE WILL BE *HELPLESS* AGAINST THOSE TWO THUGS! WE'VE *GOT* TO HELP THEM!

THUD!

WHAT AN EERIE PLACE! I DON'T EVEN NEED MY FLASHLIGHT---THAT STRANGE, WEIRD GLOW BACK THERE GIVES US ENOUGH LIGHT!

COME ON---LET'S SEE WHAT'S *CAUSING* THAT GLOW!

KEN---L... LOOK!

3

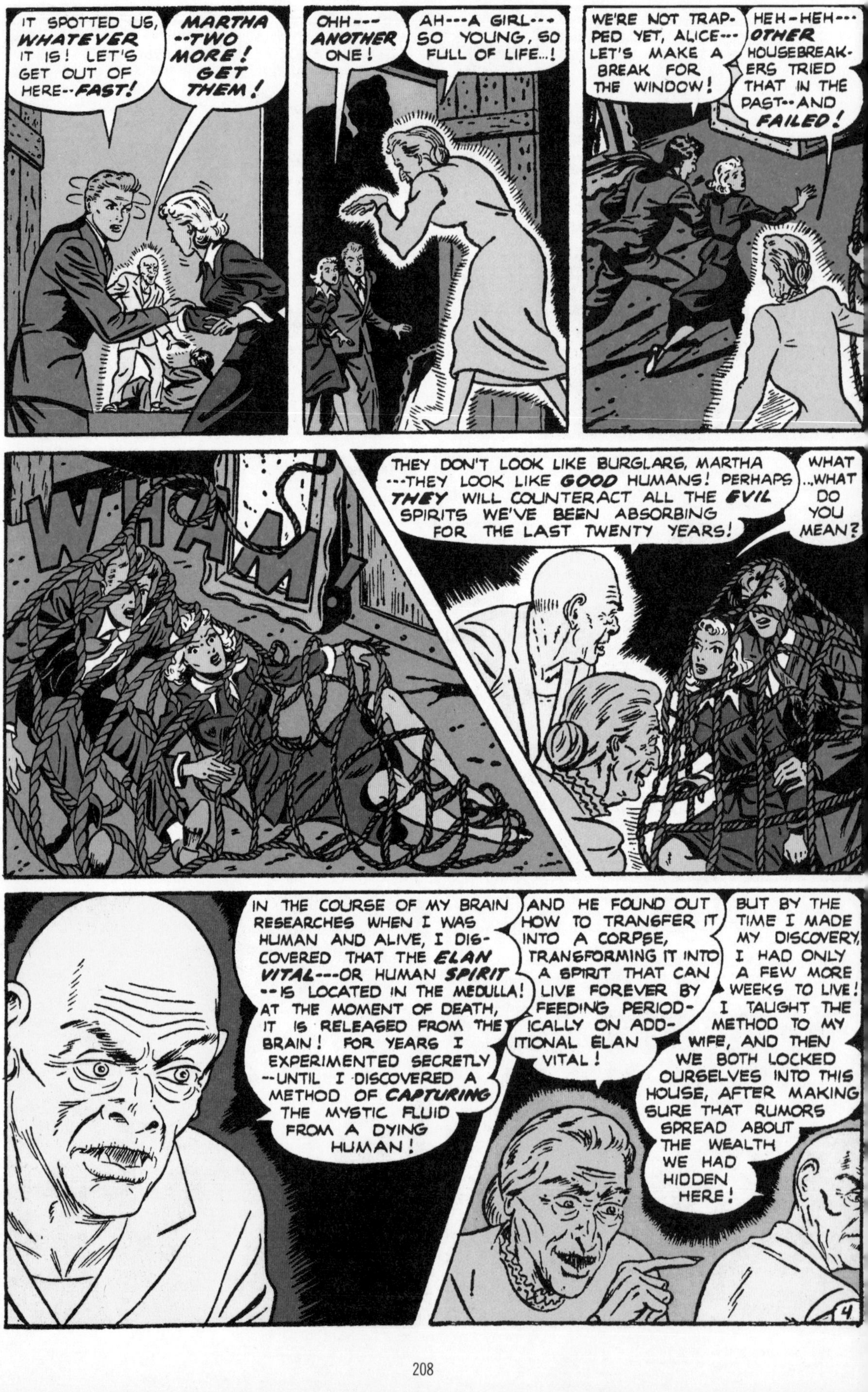
IT SPOTTED US, WHATEVER IT IS! LET'S GET OUT OF HERE--FAST!
MARTHA --TWO MORE! GET THEM!
OHH--- ANOTHER ONE!
AH---A GIRL--- SO YOUNG, SO FULL OF LIFE...!
WE'RE NOT TRAPPED YET, ALICE--- LET'S MAKE A BREAK FOR THE WINDOW!
HEH-HEH--- OTHER HOUSEBREAKERS TRIED THAT IN THE PAST--AND FAILED!
WHAM!
THEY DON'T LOOK LIKE BURGLARS, MARTHA ---THEY LOOK LIKE GOOD HUMANS! PERHAPS THEY WILL COUNTERACT ALL THE EVIL SPIRITS WE'VE BEEN ABSORBING FOR THE LAST TWENTY YEARS!
WHAT ...WHAT DO YOU MEAN?
IN THE COURSE OF MY BRAIN RESEARCHES WHEN I WAS HUMAN AND ALIVE, I DISCOVERED THAT THE ELAN VITAL---OR HUMAN SPIRIT --IS LOCATED IN THE MEDULLA! AT THE MOMENT OF DEATH, IT IS RELEASED FROM THE BRAIN! FOR YEARS I EXPERIMENTED SECRETLY --UNTIL I DISCOVERED A METHOD OF CAPTURING THE MYSTIC FLUID FROM A DYING HUMAN!
AND HE FOUND OUT HOW TO TRANSFER IT INTO A CORPSE, TRANSFORMING IT INTO A SPIRIT THAT CAN LIVE FOREVER BY FEEDING PERIODICALLY ON ADDITIONAL ELAN VITAL!
BUT BY THE TIME I MADE MY DISCOVERY, I HAD ONLY A FEW MORE WEEKS TO LIVE! I TAUGHT THE METHOD TO MY WIFE, AND THEN WE BOTH LOCKED OURSELVES INTO THIS HOUSE, AFTER MAKING SURE THAT RUMORS SPREAD ABOUT THE WEALTH WE HAD HIDDEN HERE!
4

THEN ALL WE HAD TO DO WAS WAIT FOR THIEVES, LURED BY THE RUMORS OF OUR HIDDEN TREASURE! WE OVERCAME THEM BY MEANS OF TRAPS---AND WHEN I DIED, MARTHA TRANSFERRED THEIR ELAN VITAL TO ME, AND GAVE ME LIFE-AFTER-DEATH! WHEN SHE DIED, I DID THE SAME FOR *HER!*

IT... IT'S FANTASTIC ---*IMPOSSIBLE!*

IMPOSSIBLE? PERHAPS YOU'LL THINK DIFFERENTLY WHEN I SHOW YOU THE LIVING HULKS OF THOSE FROM WHOM WE EXTRACTED THE MYSTIC LIFE FLUID!

THERE--- SEE THOSE WHO HAVE GIVEN MARTHA AND ME *PERPETUAL LIFE!*

THEY...THEY LOOK JUST LIKE HORRIBLE *ZOMBIES!*

THAT'S JUST ABOUT WHAT THEY ARE---BECAUSE THEY'RE MORE DEAD THAN ALIVE! WE LEAVE JUST ENOUGH ELAN VITAL IN THEM TO AL-LOW THEM TO EXIST AT THE LOWEST POSSIBLE LEVEL!

THEN, IN CASE THERE'S A SHORTAGE OF HOUSEBREAKERS AT ANY TIME, WE JUST NURSE THEM ALONG UNTIL THEY'RE NORMAL AGAIN--AND WITH-DRAW ANOTHER QUOTA OF LIFE FLUID! AND THAT'S WHAT WE'RE GOING TO DO TO *YOU* TWO!

WAIT---YOU WERE ONCE A GREAT BENEFACTOR OF HUMANITY, DR. DUNSTAN--- AND THE FACT THAT YOU CHOSE TO DO THIS ONLY TO THE *EVIL* MEMBERS OF SOCIETY SHOWS THAT YOU HAD A *CONSCIENCE!* BUT *WE'RE* NOT EVIL--- YOU *CAN'T* DO THIS TO US!

YES, I *DID* HAVE A CONSCIENCE-- *BUT NO LONGER!* REMEMBER, WE'VE BEEN ABSORBING *EVIL* SPIRITS FOR 20 YEARS NOW!

THAT'S WHY EVEN OUR *APPEARANCES* HAVE CHANGED! BUT PERHAPS AB-SORBING THE SPIRITS OF TWO *GOOD* HUMANS WILL COUNT-ERACT THE EVIL IN US!--*THE GIRL FIRST, AMOS!*

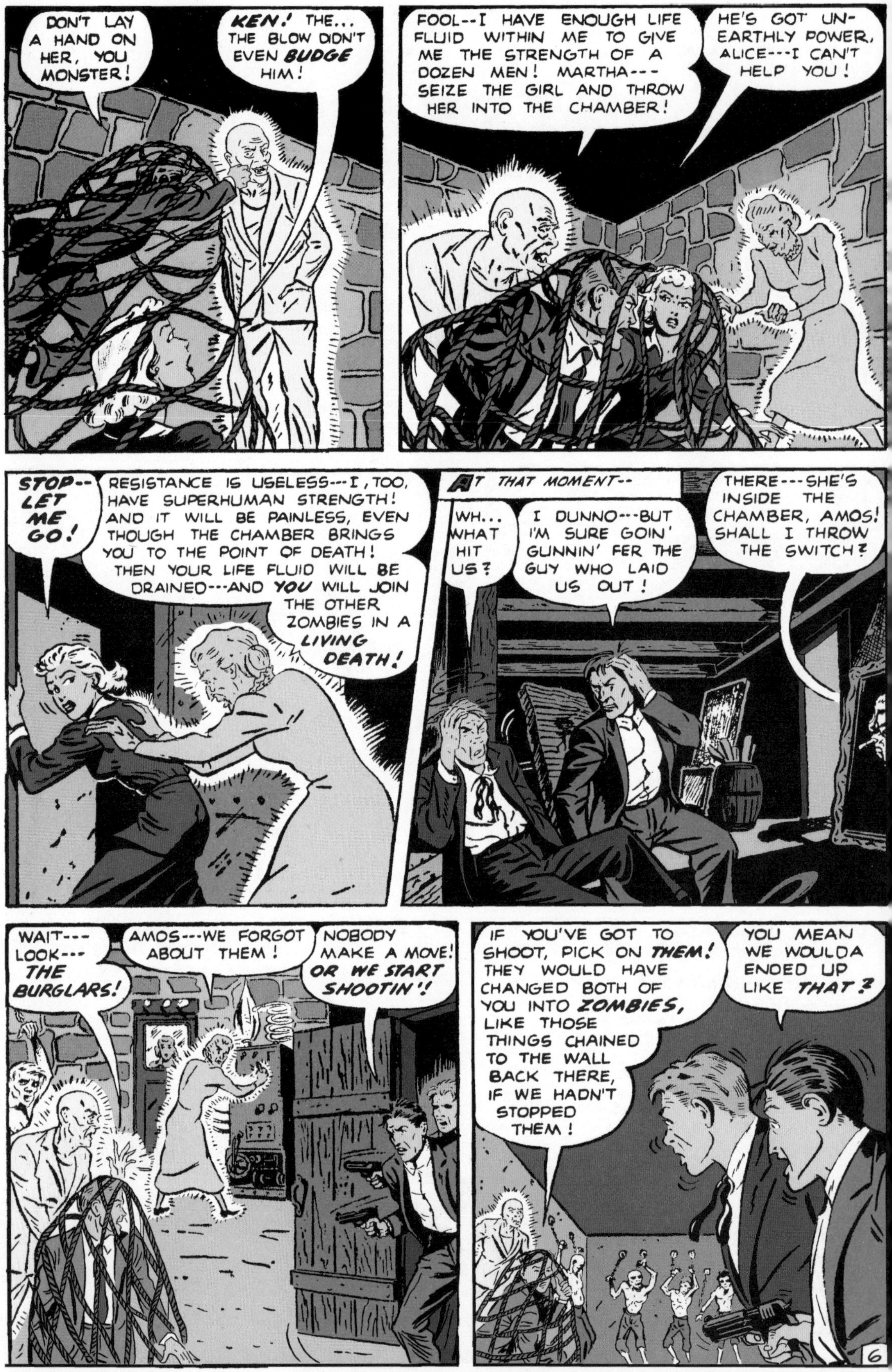
DON'T LAY A HAND ON HER, YOU MONSTER!
KEN! THE... THE BLOW DIDN'T EVEN BUDGE HIM!
FOOL--I HAVE ENOUGH LIFE FLUID WITHIN ME TO GIVE ME THE STRENGTH OF A DOZEN MEN! MARTHA--- SEIZE THE GIRL AND THROW HER INTO THE CHAMBER!
HE'S GOT UN-EARTHLY POWER, ALICE---I CAN'T HELP YOU!
STOP-- LET ME GO!
RESISTANCE IS USELESS---I, TOO, HAVE SUPERHUMAN STRENGTH! AND IT WILL BE PAINLESS, EVEN THOUGH THE CHAMBER BRINGS YOU TO THE POINT OF DEATH! THEN YOUR LIFE FLUID WILL BE DRAINED---AND YOU WILL JOIN THE OTHER ZOMBIES IN A LIVING DEATH!
AT THAT MOMENT--
WH... WHAT HIT US?
I DUNNO---BUT I'M SURE GOIN' GUNNIN' FER THE GUY WHO LAID US OUT!
THERE---SHE'S INSIDE THE CHAMBER, AMOS! SHALL I THROW THE SWITCH?
WAIT--- LOOK--- THE BURGLARS!
AMOS---WE FORGOT ABOUT THEM!
NOBODY MAKE A MOVE! OR WE START SHOOTIN'!
IF YOU'VE GOT TO SHOOT, PICK ON THEM! THEY WOULD HAVE CHANGED BOTH OF YOU INTO ZOMBIES, LIKE THOSE THINGS CHAINED TO THE WALL BACK THERE, IF WE HADN'T STOPPED THEM!
YOU MEAN WE WOULDA ENDED UP LIKE THAT?
6

WHY, WE'LL *MOIDER* THESE TWO FER EVEN THINKIN' OF DOIN' THAT TA US!

FOOL—YOU CAN'T KILL THE *DEAD*! BULLETS CAN'T HURT *SPIRITS*!

NO---BUT THE SOUND OF THE SHOTS MIGHT BRING THE COPS!

THE...THE *POLICE*! D...DON'T SHOOT--- WE'LL DO WHATEVER YOU SAY!

HEY, *WE* DON'T WANT NO COPS IN HERE EITHER!

OH, OH---I CAN SEE I MADE A MISTAKE! BUT MAYBE I CAN STILL RECOUP...

FORGET IT-- YOU'VE GOT 'EM SCARED! MAKE THEM TELL YOU WHERE THEIR MONEY IS HIDDEN---AND THEY'LL LEAD RIGHT TO A *FORTUNE*!

THAT'S JUST WHAT WE CAME HERE FER! TELL US WHERE IT IS, OR WE'LL START BLASTIN' --COPS OR NO!

ALL...ALL RIGHT---COME WITH US! WE'LL GIVE YOU ALL WE HAVE!

HEY-- HOW ABOUT *US*?

WE DON'T TRUST *YOU* EITHER, WISE GUY! MIKE--YOU STAY BEHIND AN' WATCH 'IM!

WHILE WE'RE WAITING FOR THEM TO COME BACK, WHY DON'T YOU LOOK CLOSELY AT THOSE *ZOMBIES*? THEY'RE ALL BURGLARS CAUGHT BY THE TWO OLD CREEPS ---AND SOME OF THEM MIGHT BE LONG-LOST *FRIENDS* OF YOURS!

COULD BE---AN AWFUL LOT OF MY PALS HAVE DISAP- PEARED IN THE LAST FEW YEARS! SAY--- THAT ONE LOOKS LIKE *ONE-EYED FOSTER*!

AN'...AN' THIS ONE MUST BE *SCAR-FACE MIKE*...!

7.

THERE---THIS RABBIT PUNCH OUGHT TO MAKE A TAME RABBIT OUT OF *YOU* FOR A COUPLE OF HOURS!

POW!

THEN...

OH, KEN---I *KNEW* YOU'D GET ME OUT OF HERE IN TIME! NOW LET'S GET OUT OF THIS TERRIBLE HOUSE AS FAST AS WE CAN RUN!

WE'VE STILL GOT A JOB TO FINISH *HERE!* THE POLICE MAY BE ABLE TO DRIVE THE DUNSTANS OUT OF THIS HOUSE--- BUT THEY COULD NEVER *DESTROY* THEM! THE ONLY WAY TO PREVENT THOSE FIENDS FROM SETTING UP SHOP IN ANOTHER LOCALITY IS TO EXTRACT THE *ELAN VITAL* FROM *THEM*---AND ONLY THE *ZOMBIES* COULD DO THAT!

HEAR ME, O MEN OF THE LIVING DEAD! YOU ARE THE ONLY ONES WHO CAN GET BACK YOUR OWN SPIRITS---FROM THOSE WHO SO GHOULISHLY TOOK THEM FROM YOU! TELL ME IF YOU WANT REVENGE---AND I'LL FREE YOU FROM YOUR CHAINS!

FREE US!

REVENGE!

REVENGE!

THEY'RE SOMEPLACE UPSTAIRS! FIND THEM AND TEAR YOUR SPIRITS FROM THEM! KILL THEM--- AND *YOU* WILL LIVE AGAIN!

MEANWHILE, UPSTAIRS...

THAT WAS CLEVER OF YOU TO OPEN THE GAS VALVE, MARTHA---- BY PRETENDING IT WOULD OPEN OUR WALL SAFE! THE GAS MADE HIM UNCONSCIOUS--BUT IT COULDN'T AFFECT *US!*

WE'LL LEAVE IT ON UNTIL IT OVERCOMES THE OTHERS DOWNSTAIRS --AND THEN WE'LL HAVE *FOUR* NEW VICTIMS!

KEN---I...I FEEL SICK AND DIZZY! L...LET'S GET OUT OF HERE--- *PLEASE!*

YES, I,...I'M BEGINNING TO FEEL KIND OF WOBBLY MYSELF! I GUESS I'VE FREED ENOUGH OF THE ZOMBIES--- SO LET'S GO!

.8.

MINUTES LATER, BY THE TIME THE GAS HAS CIRCULATED THROUGHOUT THE HOUSE...

THERE---WE'RE OUT AND NOW I'LL JUST FIRE A SHOT TO SUMMON THE POLICE!

BUT THE MOMENT KEN FIRES INTO THE EXPLOSIVE GAS...

BOOM!

INSIDE, WHERE THE CONFLAGRATION HAS SPREAD INSTANTLY...

THERE THEY ARE! RIP THEM APART--- TEAR OUR SPIRITS FROM THEM!

NO---GET BACK---BACK!

YAAAGHH!

THAT...THAT AWFUL SCREAM SOUNDED AS IF IT CAME FROM THE DUNSTANS, KEN---BUT WHAT ABOUT THE ZOMBIES?

WE'LL NEVER SEE THEM AGAIN! THEY'RE TRAPPED IN THAT INFERNO---BUT AT LEAST THEY HAD THEIR REVENGE! AND NOW WE'D BETTER GET OUR BURNS ATTENDED TO---BEFORE WE WRITE UP A REPORT OF ALL THIS FOR "FORBIDDEN WORLDS"!

THAT'S QUITE A STORY YOU HAVE HERE! THERE'S NOTHING LEFT OF THE DUNSTAN HOUSE TO PROVE IT, BUT I DON'T THINK YOU'D BURN YOURSELVES JUST TO MAKE IT ALL LOOK CONVINCING! I THINK I'LL HAVE THE STORY PRINTED, AND LET THE READERS JUDGE IT FOR THEMSELVES! AND OH, BY THE WAY---YOU'RE BOTH HIRED!

..THE END......

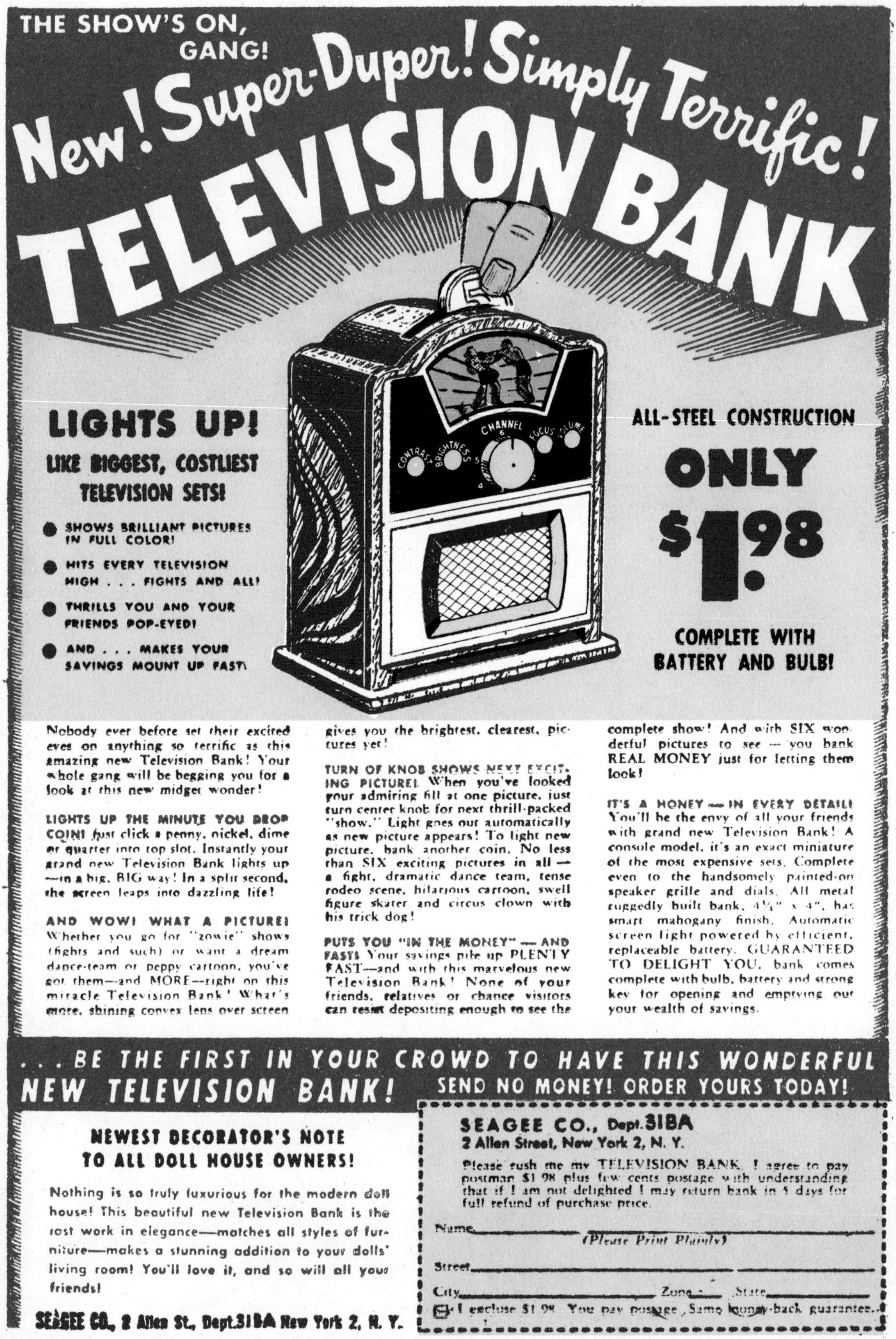

THE SHOW'S ON, GANG!
New! Super-Duper! Simply Terrific!
TELEVISION BANK
CHANNEL
CONTRAST
BRIGHTNESS
FOCUS
VOLUME
LIGHTS UP!
LIKE BIGGEST, COSTLIEST TELEVISION SETS!
SHOWS BRILLIANT PICTURES IN FULL COLOR!
HITS EVERY TELEVISION HIGH . . . FIGHTS AND ALL!
THRILLS YOU AND YOUR FRIENDS POP-EYED!
AND . . . MAKES YOUR SAVINGS MOUNT UP FAST!
ALL-STEEL CONSTRUCTION
ONLY $1.98
COMPLETE WITH BATTERY AND BULB!
Nobody ever before set their excited eyes on anything so terrific as this amazing new Television Bank! Your whole gang will be begging you for a look at this new midget wonder!
LIGHTS UP THE MINUTE YOU DROP COIN! Just click a penny, nickel, dime or quarter into top slot. Instantly your grand new Television Bank lights up—in a big, BIG way! In a split second, the screen leaps into dazzling life!
AND WOW! WHAT A PICTURE! Whether you go for "zowie" shows (fights and such) or want a dream dance-team or peppy cartoon, you've got them—and MORE—right on this miracle Television Bank! What's more, shining convex lens over screen gives you the brightest, clearest, pictures yet!
TURN OF KNOB SHOWS NEXT EXCITING PICTURE! When you've looked your admiring fill at one picture, just turn center knob for next thrill-packed "show." Light goes out automatically as new picture appears! To light new picture, bank another coin. No less than SIX exciting pictures in all — a fight, dramatic dance team, tense rodeo scene, hilarious cartoon, swell figure skater and circus clown with his trick dog!
PUTS YOU "IN THE MONEY" — AND FAST! Your savings pile up PLENTY FAST—and with this marvelous new Television Bank! None of your friends, relatives or chance visitors can resist depositing enough to see the complete show! And with SIX wonderful pictures to see — you bank REAL MONEY just for letting them look!
IT'S A HONEY — IN EVERY DETAIL! You'll be the envy of all your friends with grand new Television Bank! A console model, it's an exact miniature of the most expensive sets. Complete even to the handsomely painted-on speaker grille and dials. All metal ruggedly built bank, 4¼" x 4", has smart mahogany finish. Automatic screen light powered by efficient, replaceable battery. GUARANTEED TO DELIGHT YOU, bank comes complete with bulb, battery and strong key for opening and emptying out your wealth of savings.
. . . BE THE FIRST IN YOUR CROWD TO HAVE THIS WONDERFUL NEW TELEVISION BANK!
SEND NO MONEY! ORDER YOURS TODAY!
NEWEST DECORATOR'S NOTE TO ALL DOLL HOUSE OWNERS!
Nothing is so truly luxurious for the modern doll house! This beautiful new Television Bank is the last word in elegance—matches all styles of furniture—makes a stunning addition to your dolls' living room! You'll love it, and so will all your friends!
SEAGEE CO., 2 Allen St., Dept.31BA New York 2, N. Y.
SEAGEE CO., Dept.31BA
2 Allen Street, New York 2, N. Y.
Please rush me my TELEVISION BANK. I agree to pay postman $1.98 plus few cents postage with understanding that if I am not delighted I may return bank in 5 days for full refund of purchase price.
Name
(Please Print Plainly)
Street
City
Zone
State
I enclose $1.98. You pay postage. Same money-back guarantee.

SILVER STREAK ARCHIVES

Featuring the work of Jack Cole, Jack Binder, Dick Briefer, Bob Wood, and others

In addition to reprinting the original Daredevil's debut episodes and early work by Jack Cole (*Plastic Man*), these essential volumes of comic book treasures will present every story, gag strip, and text piece from the original anthologies!

Volume One
ISBN 978-1-59582-929-0

Volume Two
ISBN 978-1-59582-948-1

$59.99 each

ADVENTURES INTO THE
UNKNOWN!

The first ongoing horror comics anthology, *Adventures into the Unknown!* presents pre–Comics Code weird scares that must be seen to be believed! Contributions from Golden Age greats Fred Guardineer, Al Feldstein, Leonard Starr, Edvard Moritz, and others make these deluxe hardcovers a must for lovers of *The Twilight Zone*, *Creepy*, and classic sci-fi cinema!

VOLUME ONE
ISBN 978-1-59582-930-6

VOLUME TWO
ISBN 978-1-61655-045-5

$49.99 each

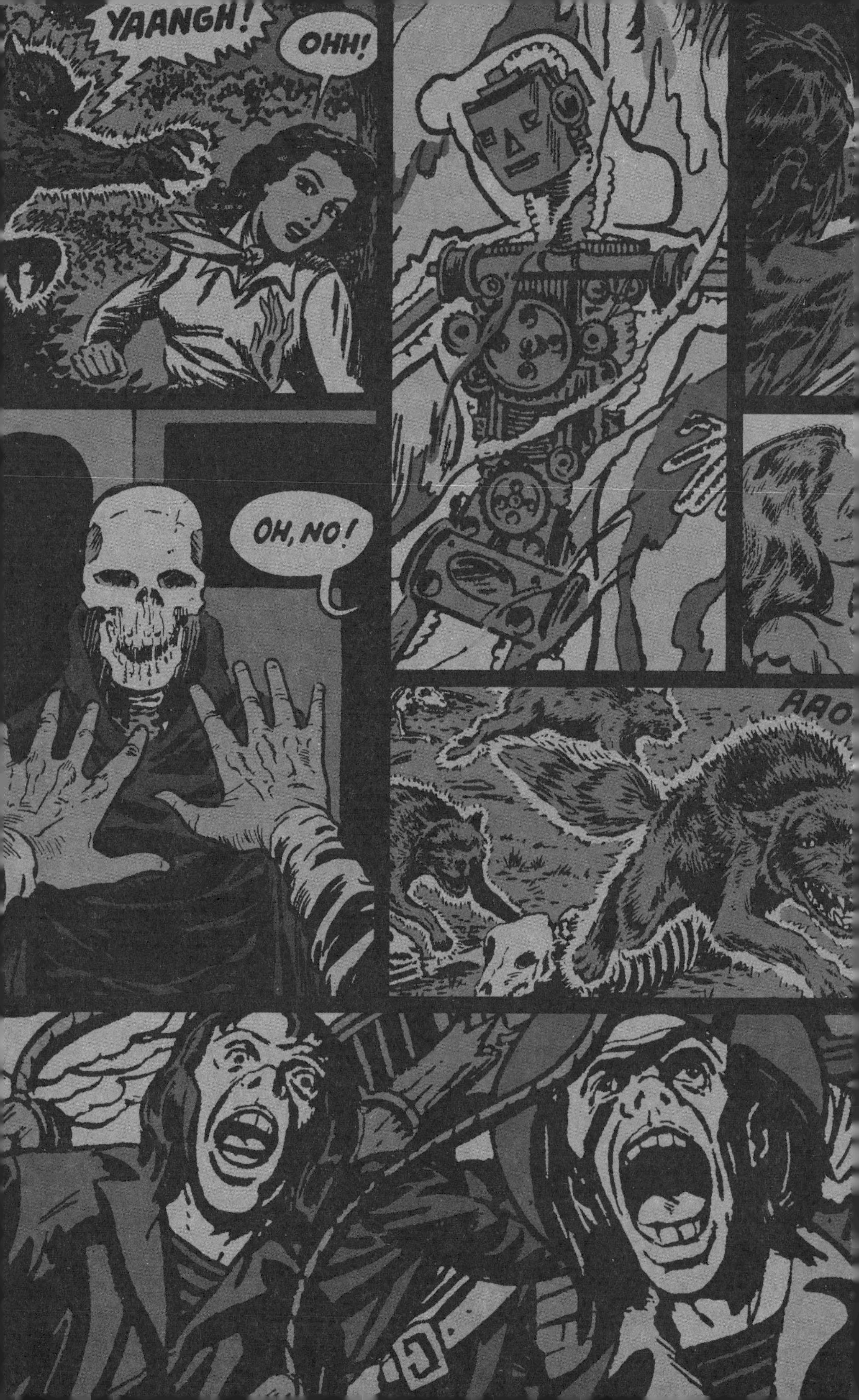
YAANGH!
OHH!
OH, NO!
AAO